Transforming Communication in Leadership and Teamwork

Renate Motschnig · David Ryback

Transforming Communication in Leadership and Teamwork

Person-Centered Innovations

Springer

Renate Motschnig
Faculty of Computer Science, CSLEARN—
Educational Technologies
University of Vienna
Vienna
Austria

David Ryback
EQ Associates International
Atlanta, GA
USA

ISBN 978-3-319-45485-6 ISBN 978-3-319-45486-3 (eBook)
DOI 10.1007/978-3-319-45486-3

Library of Congress Control Number: 2016950741

Printed on acid-free paper

This Springer imprint is published by Springer Nature
The registered company is Springer International Publishing AG
The registered company address is: Gewerbestrasse 11, 6330 Cham, Switzerland

To all those who challenge the conventional state of communication in management, and dare to transform it in ways to gain a deeper level of meaning, agility, collaboration, and success.

Foreword

As a scientist working on cancer research at Emory University, communicating with othcrs is just as important, if not more, than the work involving test tubes, rats, and other paraphernalia that result in the data we need to move forward with a cure for cancer. This book breaks the mold in its interactive approach to leading others in a more humane, authentic, and effective style.

The two-agenda approach, in which the human brain balances focus on task along with focus on human interaction, is a fairly new model which helps understand exactly where the challenge for effective leadership lies. It is not one or the other, as the authors of this book illustrate, but rather the fine-tuning of the two as it applies to individual scenarios and people involved. This is a subtle skill that can be learned by those interested in becoming better leaders and managers. It requires agility and sensitivity as well as focus on the bottom line.

The work of the esteemed Dr. Carl Rogers, one of the most eminent psychologists of the past century, pioneered the work that this book brings to light. It has taken decades for us to appreciate what he had to offer. The fields of psychology, education, and even international politics were more accepting of his work than other organizations and even industry. But the time has finally come to realize the benefits of his person-centered approach. Actually, his work has had a definite impact, but under the guise of other names, primarily emotional intelligence. When Daniel Goleman popularized this in his best-selling book in 1995, leadership took this concept and flew with it. In quick order, research on the topic revealed how successful this approach was. Bottom-line results, including less turnover, higher profits, and more meaningful involvement on the job, were all proven in scientifically based investigations. Even the US General Accounting Office found that recruiters for the US Air Force saved millions using this approach.

Renate Motschnig and David Ryback have taken the work of Carl Rogers and illustrated it with a refreshing warmth and depth of understanding to convey to us how powerful this person-centered approach can be. This is a time of change in all aspects of our culture. The timing of this approach is excellent. We need to pay more attention to the person, at least as much as to the tasks at hand. This book paves the way.

Carrie Qi Sun, M.D.
Emory University, Atlanta, GA, USA

Preface

Finally, there is agreement that one of the most essential elements for survival is the development of a greater sense of cooperation, of community, of ability to work together for the common good, not simply for personal aggrandizement.

Carl Rogers (1980, p. 332)

In this electronic age of information transparency and superfast communication, leadership has taken on new character. It has always been a fierce challenge to define the components of effective leadership, but now it appears that there may be an exciting opportunity for new clarity.

The underlying theme is the ability to communicate effectively. It involves the ability to sense what the other—whether one individual, a small group, or even an audience of hundreds—is feeling and not yet revealing, while keeping in mind the organization's vision as well as the current task at hand. In other words, we need to attend to the "elephant in the room" that everyone else is ignoring, while following both the big picture and the current demand. How these requirements can be reconciled with helpful knowledge inputs and practices are the focal themes of this book.

Communication and leadership, two of the most vital skills in today's workplace, are intricately intertwined: No one can be an effective leader or manager without good communication skills, and clear articulation and good listening skills are the stepping stones. In this context, let us clarify that even though we are aware of the difference between a *leader*, a person who leads, motivates, makes decisions, sets goals, etc., and a *manager* who primarily coordinates and takes care that tasks are accomplished, the two terms will often be used interchangeably. This is because, in modern times, work is frequently organized in the form of projects where the project manager, coordinator, or lead tends to take over, at least in part, leadership functions. Also, we see a strong overlap regarding the communicative and interpersonal capacities any superior would need, be it a leader or a manager. Both hold a clear, climate-setting function and tend to be more in the spotlight regarding the ways they communicate than other team members or employees. However, as will become clear in this book, with transformative communication every single member of a team or organization can have an influence on the larger whole of which he/she is an active part. So, all in all, this book aims to address all who want to make a positive difference in communication in the workplace!

In fact, in recent books and articles, there is an exciting and "newly discovered" focus on the soft skills of personal sharing and transparency in the workplace. We put those words in quotation marks because this focus on more personal sharing and communication has been described years ago by a man who pioneered "active listening" and "well-functioning interpersonal relationships." Revolutionary in its time, this path, referred to as the Person-Centered Approach or PCA, was the work of Dr. Carl Rogers, one of the most influential psychologists in the world. He revolutionized not only the worlds of counseling, psychotherapy, and education by laying the foundations for experiential, lifelong learning. Rogers even initiated a transformation in administration and group leadership. Essentially, he shifted the power balance between superiors and subordinates by listening to them and sharing power with "the other," thereby empowering them and respecting the self-organizing principles at work. This transformative "way of being," when considered in the workplace—as the central theme in this book—gives rise to less hierarchical and more collaborative organizational and project cultures and favors agile management styles, so urgently needed at a time when pivoting with change is the rule rather than the exception.

By considering the whole person with feelings, meanings, talents, and limitations, rather than his/her intellect and IQ only, Rogers laid the groundwork for what we now know as emotional intelligence. Its effects on leadership are outlined in the book, *Putting Emotional Intelligence to Work,* by the second author of this book. Rogers' deep interest in the whole person and his/her interaction with others, however, influenced a wide variety of scientific disciplines and applications, as explored in the twin volumes "*Interdisciplinary Handbook of the Person-Centered Approach*" and "*Interdisciplinary Applications of the Person-Centered Approach,*" co-edited by Renate Motshnig, one of the authors of this book.

Intriguingly, while Rogers is best known as "the quiet revolutionary" in the realm of counseling, psychotherapy, and group work, in his book, *A Way of Being,* he himself discerned the concern of his "life as having been built around the desire of clarity of communication, with all its ramifying results" (p. 66). The theme of *Person-Centered Communication* has been taken up and adopted to the needs of the new century by of Renate and her colleague, Dr. Ladislav Nykl. Thereupon, some of her colleagues working as managers, team leaders and project coordinators, and colleagues holding executive positions, expressed their wish to be provided with a resource that would deal *specifically* with Person-Centered Communication as applied to the *context of their professional lives*, such as to ease the transfer of the theories into practice. So, this current book was written, in part, as a response to their calls and reminders of some shared experiences in communication. The other motivation for writing this book came from both co-authors' desire to share with colleagues, friends, and interested peers what we believe are those concepts, ideas, and experiences that we consider particularly valuable in our professional as well as personal lives.

Despite his significant contribution to science, our culture, and cross-cultural understanding, Carl Rogers is hardly known among the current younger generation. That is not important. What is definitely important is that his contribution be brought to light, along with all the research over the years, to support it. This way, the "newly discovered" material can gain even more meaning by being connected to established theories and practices and be used to enhance success in the world of business, through more effective communication and leadership. That is what this book is all about.

Carl Rogers changed the lives of many people he encountered, both individually and in speaking to large groups. I, for one (David), was transformed by my interactions with him no less than three times in my life.

- The first time, he transformed my personality merely by listening to a question I had for him after hearing him giving a lecture on his approach. I don't recall his answer to my question, but I was transformed by his deep understanding of where my question came from. He made me realize that listening deeply can have a transforming effect. I became a "believer" in active listening, transforming my shy personality to one that opened up to others' perspectives.
- The second occurred when he came as a keynote speaker to a conference I founded. With a bit of free time together, I shared some personal issues with him and his careful listening cut through my considerable defenses to reveal my own need for respect and appreciation from others, something I had carefully denied till then. Now, I could be more genuine and authentic about such needs.
- Thirdly, Carl Rogers affected me by making me more sensitive to the emotional dynamics in my meeting with others, whether at my office, with corporate clients, or with friends. He taught me, just by being himself, about the nature of honesty. There is the inner truth, what you feel. There is outer truth, how others hear what you share. And there is the matter of relevance. How is what you think and feel relevant to those with whom you share in that moment? That is what honesty is all about, I learned from Carl.

I (Renate) would describe my transformation through Carl Rogers and people who live and communicate by his principles (whether consciously or not) more as a gradual and definitely lasting and continuing process toward "seeing" and respecting more of myself and my social environment. This is a development I would never want to turn back from. I will share particular instances of my personal transformation in the third chapter of this book and invite readers to anticipate more on this theme. Just one thing for now: Retrospectively, intensive contact and collaboration with people (colleagues, friends, family) in a person-centered climate and intensive group experiences seem to have had the most precious and formative effect on me. I wish to express my deep gratitude for this to all who had a part in the process!

In a nutshell, clear and transparent communication—based on inner honesty and mutual respect—is becoming even more important for success in the workplace. By the same token, misunderstandings, miscommunication, and defensive hiding tend to be very costly as we cross national borders as well as professional and social networks. This book provides resources that are aimed at facilitating and accelerating the adoption of effective communication in the workplace, addressing the knowledge, skills, and interpersonal attitudes so necessary at every level.

Grounded in the Person-Centered Approach, this book reaches out to integrate wisdom from the neurosciences, management/leadership studies, multicultural teams, numerous case studies, and, last but not least, both authors' experience. In this sense, the book offers a unique combination of features and disciplines while building upon a renowned theory and philosophy of life and work that transcends national cultures and, at the same time, respects them.

Further themes and objectives of this book are as follows:

- To articulate how an appropriate adaptation of the theory of the Person-Centered Approach can serve as a foundation to help managers and leaders master current demands of the workplace. In fact, Carl Rogers had foreshadowed some developments, including an increase in transparency, flexibility, and the need for a constructive climate for increased long-term success. In particular, this book aims to facilitate the transfer of the theory into practical situations such as business meetings, hiring process, decision-making, agile management, negotiation, and multinational teams.
- To respond to international calls for practices that facilitate dialogue and cooperation to stimulate new ideas and innovation and address twenty-first-century challenges, such as globalization, dealing with change, and cross-cultural understanding.
- To represent the Person-Centered Approach as a persistently developing, yet altogether modern, direction with widespread scientific support, integrative structure, and influential practices for more successful management and leadership.
- To authentically integrate the perspectives of an experienced international consultant in the field of leadership and a professor with extensive experience in leading and managing international information technology projects. At several points in the book, we share our viewpoints through personal dialogue, inviting you, the reader, to reflect on your own experience that we consider pivotal.
- To introduce the concept of two intertwined agendas—a task-oriented agenda and an experiential, people-oriented one—in order to allow us to see a bit more clearly where the challenges lie, not only behaviorally but also in the realm of how our brains and bodies work together. We want and need to get the job done as efficiently as possible, but alternately, there is a part in us that can take into consideration others' feelings, needs, and ideas. When the two integrate and

build over time, then we are bringing in more of ourselves and learning to win. That is a core message of the book: *We're afraid of listening closely (to others' emotions) for fear of losing sight of our own agenda (the project).* Around that message, numerous practices, examples, and applications are integrated to optimally support the book's message and increase the opportunity for demonstrated, constructive change in the workplace.

This book is organized into five parts. Part I introduces the subject matter by taking you on a tour through the eminent challenges and opportunities of the modern workplace and indicating how the book is going to address them. Moreover, the basic concepts of the book, such as the two-agenda approach, the people-oriented "agenda" (actually more a mind-set that an agenda), and the concept of transformative communication are introduced. Furthermore, a test is provided for self-assessing one's attitudinal conditions for following the people-oriented agenda at work.

In order to connect theoretical concepts with the readers' authentic, practical challenges, Part II provides case examples of transforming leadership, written by prominent representatives from the person-centered tradition working in leadership positions. We thank them most sincerely for enriching the book by providing their unprecedented experience! Each case example is reflected on by the authors of this book, and we are also inviting you to reflect on key issues so as to sharpen awareness of your own leadership values, preferences, and paths.

Part III deepens the basic concepts by offering further resources and practical application scenarios for key leadership/management and teamwork situations, such as decision-making, working in/with agile teams, responding to conflict, and communicating in/with culturally diverse teams. In addition, dialoging practices, the intensive group experience, communication workshops, and the novel "open case" setting are introduced as safe "spaces" for practicing and developing transformative communication.

In Part IV, you will find the scientific, research-based grounding of selected aspects of the transformative communication framework put forth in this book. As in all parts, the authors use language that is meant to be as accessible and comprehensible to its practice-oriented audience, who may be interested in the scientific facts that underlie the approach.

Finally, Part V concludes by suggesting the social and value ramifications we aspire to in the book.

The authors trust you will find a way that best fits you in your exploration of the book. Moving through sequentially, or starting with the case examples in Part II, or jumping from chapter to chapter, according to your interests, would all be appropriate. Also, you can accept the invitations to reflect immediately at the places you find them, or choose to continue reading the main text and postpone reflection at your leisure or when sharing with colleagues. Readers new to person-centered thought, however, may want to read Chaps. 1 and 2 first.

Before beginning to read, we would like to call your attention to the fact that this book may change the way you communicate with the world around you, whether at home or at the office. It may even make you become more aware of who you are and what you stand for. This may make your job more fulfilling for you. In any case, transforming communication requires energy, time, and courage: It is for those who are ready for transformation and change—to more personal power, expressiveness, and "response-ability" at work.

Vienna, Austria
Atlanta, USA
May 2016

Renate Motschnig
David Ryback

Contents

Part IV What Are the Facts?

About the Authors

Authors

Dr. Renate Motschnig is a professor of computer science and the head of the Research Group CSLEARN—Educational Technologies at the University of Vienna, Austria. Since her studies in the 1980s, she has been conducting research on the multiple ways in which understanding and significant learning happen, both in education and through life experience. Renate Motschnig has held positions at the University of Technology, Vienna; the RWTH Aachen in Germany; the University of Toronto, Canada; the Masaryk University in Brno, the Czech Republic; and the Higher School of Economics, Moscow, Russia. Renate is an author/co-author of more than 150 peer-reviewed, scientific articles; three books on person-centered communication; and a co-editor of two recent books with Springer on Interdisciplinary Aspects of the Person-Centered Approach. She participated in numerous international events based on the Person-Centered Approach and is applying the resulting insights in proposing and leading major international research projects in the field of constructive communication, teamwork, and Web technology. Currently, she is determined to foster a style in management and higher education that is based on person-centered attitudes, our co-actualizing potential, and thoughtful support by Web-based technology. She appreciates synergies between presence and distance, cognition and feeling/meaning, and a multitude of disciplines and cultures.

https://cs.univie.ac.at//cslearn/team/worker/infpers/Renate_Motschnig

David Ryback, Ph.D., ABPP is an adviser to corporate presidents and trains executives and managers on the advantages of using emotional intelligence to create better and more successful companies. His programs and books have been seen and read throughout the world. He is the author of *Putting Emotional Intelligence to Work: Successful Leadership is More Than IQ* and author of six other books. He is an internationally recognized authority on emotional and social intelligence in schools and workplace and remains at the forefront of the latest research on applications of emotional awareness and related aspects of effective communication. A former consultant with Rohrer, Hibler and Replogle in Montreal, Canada, he has also done research and published on such topics as perception affected by mind-set, emotional intelligence, interpersonal communication, scholastic achievement, and enlightened management. After publishing his book on emotional intelligence, Dr. Ryback founded his consulting and speaking business, EQ Associates International. In response to the demand for his speaking and consulting services, he has traveled across the country, to Canada, Europe, the Middle East, and Far East where he speaks and consults. He made a presentation to the National Speakers Association national convention in San Diego and presented a seminar for McGill University in Montreal, Canada, on integrating emotional intelligence into the classroom. Dr. David Ryback is a unique speaker with a unique message. Using concepts from his book, *Putting Emotional Intelligence to Work,* he shows his audiences how to face what is authentic in themselves and others and develop their deeper self, with the help of clearly understood takeaway points. As a former teacher, college professor, and international consultant, he has the depth of experience for that message.

http://eqassociates.com

Case Study Authors

Jeffrey H.D. Cornelius-White, PsyD, LPC is a professor of counseling at Missouri State University and doctoral faculty at the University of Missouri—Columbia. He is a former editor of The Person-Centered Journal and current co-editor of Person-Centered and Experiential Psychotherapies. He has published more than 75 works, including Learner-Centered Instruction (Sage, 2010) and Carl Rogers: China Diary (PCCS, 2012), and two large works with Renate Motschnig and Michael Lux, the Interdisciplinary Handbook of the Person-Centered Approach and Interdisciplinary Applications of the Person-Centered Approach (Springer, 2013).

Jef studied at the Chicago Counseling Center, the Pre-Therapy Institute, Roosevelt University, and Argosy University, Chicago. He enjoys cycling, volleyball, friends, and family.

Dipl.-Ing., Dipl.-Journ. Klaus Haasis Hypno-systemic coach—Person-centered organizational developer, born 1955, is a coach, trainer, mentor, and business angel. He delivers a unique blend of decade-long leadership experience, person-centered consulting excellence, and hypno-systemic coaching expertise, packaged within management know-how of technology sectors, creative industries, and politics. Klaus holds degrees in engineering and journalism, he is a certified effectuation expert and scrum master, and he was 5 times founding CEO and has over 30 years of experience in innovation management. He has successfully built companies, agencies, and clusters like Baden-Württemberg: Connected and the Open Source Business Alliance. He is a director of TCI—network for clusters, competitiveness, and innovation in Barcelona and since 2013 founding board member of the German Initiative on Future Leadership, izf. Klaus held a number of key leadership positions, such as one at the private television network SAT.1 and another a tHoechst, one of the biggest chemical and pharmaceutical companies in the world. For many years now, he is advising and supporting seasoned executives, emerging talents, fledgling entrepreneurs, and teams and organizations within a business, science, political, and cultural environment. He lives in Stuttgart and Rome.

Maureen O'Hara, Ph.D. is a professor in the Psychology Department at National University, La Jolla, CA, and president emerita of Saybrook University, California. Working with American psychologist Dr. Carl R. Rogers, she helped develop the Person-Centered Approach to psychotherapy and large group process. More recently, her work has examined the relationship between the "big picture" changes underway and psychological adaptation to help us take effective and humane action in a world we can no longer understand or control. Combining her background as psychotherapist, organizational consultant, and futurist, she is a frequent keynote speaker nationally and internationally on the evolution of new ways of being in a changing world.

Eva Sollárová, Ph.D. is a professor of psychology and former dean of the Faculty of Social Sciences and Health Care at Constantine the Philosopher University in Nitra, Slovakia. She graduated with trainings in client-centered psychotherapy and PCA applications for organizations. For the past two decades, she has been intensively engaged with establishing the PCA within university study programs for helping professionals as well as lifelong education and trainings for helping professionals and managers on national level within the Ministry of Work and the Ministry of Education. She has published books, research articles, and book chapters on applications of the PCA beyond therapy, the PCA coaching model, the effects of trainings facilitating PCA competence for various professional roles, and facilitating the psychological integration in persons.

Part I
Leadership, Management, and Communication in a Time of Rapid Change

Chapter 1
Contemporary Challenges and Opportunities at Work

In a person who is open to experience, each stimulus is freely relayed through the nervous system, without being distorted by any process of defensiveness. […] It means lack of rigidity and […] a tolerance of ambiguity where ambiguity exists. It means the ability to receive much conflicting information without forcing closure upon the situation.

Carl Rogers (1961, p. 353)

This chapter focuses on the following:

- A brief historical overview of leadership to lay the ground for exploring a number of contemporary challenges to responsible ("response-able") management
- Identifying challenges and opportunities at work
- Discussing the limitations of pure science in dealing with the challenges
- Introducing Carl Rogers' Person-Centered Approach (PCA) as an underlying thread leading to opportunities to meeting such challenges
- A road map for exploring particular challenges and opportunities such as speed of decision-making, employees' scope of goals, flexibility, empathy for individuals and groups, and more.

1.1 Introduction

The basics of leadership as well as communication go way back beyond recorded history. Dominance hierarchies among animals preexisted human awareness. Among many species, the alpha male ruled his group without knowledge of any theories of leadership or communication. Only in the past century have we begun scientific analysis of the dynamics of communication in leadership—how to lead more effectively than ever before.

R. Motschnig and D. Ryback, *Transforming Communication in Leadership and Teamwork*, DOI 10.1007/978-3-319-45486-3_1

1.1.1 Silverbacks, Kings and Other Alpha Males

Among gorillas, silverbacks are the leaders of their groups, by dint of their strength, audacity, and ripeness of age (Goodall and van Lawick 1967). Should any of these three fail, then another individual takes over and, with that, all the perks of first choice of food, sex, and territorial imperative. Our cavemen (and cavewomen) ancestors may have ruled in similar fashion until, as history progressed, the leaders began to wear bejeweled crowns to signify their powerful status as kings and queens. Political competition, always the companion of rulers, became more sophisticated as governments became more key to the power of the ruler.

Political evolution progressed. Athens was the first laboratory of democracy. In Europe, it took a bit longer. By the end of the seventeenth century, democratic revolution was in the air. Royalty and imperial powers were no longer as self-assured. The American and French revolutions crossed the tipping point and, Napoleon notwithstanding, democracy began replacing monarchies.

1.1.2 The Evil Power of Fascism

When the Industrial Revolution took over in the British Isles, kings (and queens) were no longer sacrosanct. Soon after, the Communist Revolution in Russia marked the beginning of the end of the status quo. The relatively new concept of democracy began to take hold. But, at the same time, there was the opposition—fascism. Here was a form of leadership that hearkened back to the silverbacks, based on strength, audacity, and timing. Adolf Hitler was such a leader. With his single-minded persistence and mind-numbing chauvinism, he led a confused and broken country to the heights of military grandeur by his combination of strident nationalism and victimizing minorities with his aggressive blitzkrieg maneuvers against weaker neighbors. His glorious, banner-waving rallies held in the historically cloaked city of Nuremberg convinced tens of thousands of Germans that he was the savior come to right the wrongs of the punishing Versailles Treaty. Hitler was, for the moment, a leader without equal. For the moment!

When England and the USA entered the war, that moment began to falter. It was not only a war of politics and territory, it was also a war of ideas, a war about what kind of leadership would prevail. Fascism, particularly National Socialism and divinely inspired empires such as Japan, would no longer prevail. The USA, stirred to action by Japan's sneak attack on Pearl Harbor, was now a strong power, founded on the basis of rejection of British royalty and instead committing to the process of democratic institutions. This relatively new country prevailed and established the groundwork for democracy throughout Europe, supporting it with the Marshall Plan to help Germany find its financial footing once again, as well as establishing an overriding democratic influence through the United Nations.

1.1.3 From Ford to Iaccocca

Certainly, the earliest and possibly the most successful entrepreneur to take advantage of this new virgin market of a large nation of consumers with money to spend was Henry Ford, who sold his cars to all comers, in any color so long as it was black. Ford did not have to worry much about the subtleties of leadership. He could do as he liked, pretty much, and get away with it for the most part. He had too much going for him with his monopoly of car sales. But, as the century went on, such arrogance of industrial leadership was no longer tolerable. The demands of board members and shareholders, not to mention the power of emerging print and radio media, grew so that, by the time more contemporary leaders such as Lee Iaccocca came to prominence, leadership became a topic of great interest. It could now be taught, finely honed, and studied under the microscopes of business professors and their myriad MBA students.

1.1.4 A Turning Point

A significant milestone of change came about the middle of the last century when the concept of *active listening* was first brought to light by the American psychologist Carl Rogers (1902–1987). In books such as *Carl Rogers on Personal Power* (1977) and *A Way of Being* (1980), Dr. Rogers fleshed out the process of listening carefully and, with that, the overarching principle of democratic respect for each individual's voice. This was what the Lee Iaccoccas of contemporary leadership had to learn too, if they were to maintain the respect and loyalty of their boards and shareholders.

In this chapter, following the brief historical perspective above, a number of contemporary challenges to responsible management are explored. Examples of such challenges are the speed of decision-making, Internet time, globalization and diversity, and rapid technological shifts. For each of these, opportunities for meeting these challenges are identified. Table 1.1 illustrates for each challenge a corresponding number of opportunities that this book is going to address.

While identifying opportunities is a highly complex activity, nevertheless it is possible to provide a thread of responses contributing to successfully meeting the challenges. One common feature of the majority of responses is their connection to the Person-Centered Approach and the respective way of being (Rogers 1980). Hence, this approach is briefly introduced and referred to as the theoretical baseline for leading interacting and collaborating successfully in these powerful times. Table 1.1 illustrates for each challenge a corresponding number of opportunities that this book is going to address.

Table 1.1 Challenges and opportunities for the contemporary workplace

Challenges	Opportunities
Tough competition	Collaboration, even across distance and culture
Fear of emotions in the workplace	Cultivation of empathy
Speed in decision-making	Access to rich information sources and feelings, valuing the whole person—even organization—as a dynamic, organic entity
Internet time	Communication and sharing faster via Internet
Rapid change, making planning more challenging	Agile methods, flexible people and systems, clear communication paths
Feeling lost when working alone, encountering unexpected obstacles	Teamwork, networking, trustful interpersonal relationships, social media
Globalization and diversity—trying to work across cultures, languages, and disciplines	Flexibility, sensitivity, inclusion, know-how in personal and organizational development, and systems dynamics
Ambiguity, multiple realities, decline in traditional values	Emerging new values from mindful valuing processes including experience, rich knowledge sources, theories, communication paths, and technologies
Complexity	Interdependence, empowerment, shared responsibility, motivation, self-organization

1.2 Encountering and Meeting Challenges: A Personal Perspective

1.2.1 The Limits of Pure Science

Solutions to current workplace challenges likely include precognitive elements and require involving the whole person, including aspects that potentially do not reside in consciousness at a given point in time but nevertheless make up the human potential of a person or team. Just as science is critical in finding solutions, it is also valuable to consider inner experience, intuition, feelings, art, and more of what the inner self makes available. Some prominent voices on this issue can be found in Resource Box 1.1.

Carl Rogers, David Bohm, Otto Scharmer, Peter Senge, Maureen O'Hara, to name just a few have made the point that, in order to meet the challenges of our society and economy, we need to cultivate our consciousness to reach beyond its traditional role. This includes the development of advanced (inter-)personal capacities, as much as the invention and use of technological tools that have succeeded in extending what is already known by our senses and what can be done manually. Moreover, technologies like the Internet are helping us to connect across the globe virtually independent of time and distance. Yet, phenomena such as climate change, overpopulation, exploitation, to name just a few, challenge us to seek paths beyond the traditional ones.

Resource Box 1.1 Excerpts calling for transcending the limits of the scientific method

Identified need for reaching beyond the scientific method:

- A central thought will emerge from building three integrated capacities: A new capacity for observing that no longer separates the observer from what is observed, a new capacity for stillness that no longer fragments who we really are from what's emerging, and a new capacity for creating alternative realities that no longer fragments the wisdom of the head, heart, and hand. [...] "What's emerging is a new synthesis of science, spirituality, and leadership as different facets of a single way of being." Otto Scharmer in Senge et al. (2005, pp. 211–212).
- If science is an unfinished project, the next stage will be about reconnecting and integrating the rigor of scientific method with the richness of direct experience to produce a science that will serve to connect us to one another, ourselves, and the world (Senge et al. 2005, p. 212).
- The best way to address such messy and complex problems is not to reduce them to fit our existing competencies but rather to expand ourselves to encompass more of the complexity of the situation; not to work on solving a set of abstractions derived from the situation but to immerse ourselves in the experience of the situation itself—to see what it evokes and what can be learned when we bring out full range of intelligences to bear (O'Hara and Leicester 2012, pp. 127–128).

It is our experience (not only) at work that gives us the courage to walk this new path, integrating human capacities with advances in science and technology, to create this book.

David's transformed perspective I know, deep in my heart, that pure scientific research does not reach the deeper dimensions of human interaction at work. I sometimes marvel at the inabilities of logic and reason to explain what we all experience on an ongoing basis—the sense of connection between some of us that defies theoretical explanation. Why can I connect so much more deeply on an emotional basis with some more than others? Why is it so difficult—almost impossible—to say in words what accounts for such depth of interaction? I have tried my best to do so. Here's what I've determined so far. I enjoy a deep emotional connection more with some than with others. As I try to put words and logic to this, the best I can come up with, so far, is that, with these individuals, I can share two things more easily: (1) a broad spectrum of focus, from concrete to highly abstract, that is, from a focus on our own personal experience all the way to broad generalizations and (2) a sense of trust between us that allows for sharing some degree of vulnerability as we play along this spectrum of concrete to abstract. I suspect there's more to it, but that's my working explanation so far.

Regardless of the accounting for this, what if we could communicate at work in such a way that solutions to challenges are more forthcoming? What if a group of managers or executives could open up about their thoughts and feelings so that the solutions come much more readily and much more quickly than they do in the meetings we go to on a daily basis and find so boring if not irritating, while one egotistical type dominates the meeting with irrelevant opinions? What if a supervisor and her direct reports could communicate openly and clearly, unconcerned about being judged by their peers for whatever reason? If we can somehow come to an understanding of what allows for such effective, meaningful communication, then we will have achieved our objectives. That is precisely what this book is about.

Renate's transformed view and goals I was deeply influenced—one can call it transformed—by Carl Rogers' work on experiential learning and interpersonal relationships. Immediately, I was convinced that this work was relevant far beyond its psychological and therapeutic origins and had the potential to influence our daily life and work in a direction that felt intensively worthwhile to follow. It felt and still feels simply right, period.

While reading Rogers' books, I became more aware of my own experience and direction that perfectly resonated with Rogers' writing. I was fascinated in particular by the high value of granting freedom to those with whom we relate and accepting them the way they are while permitting our genuine reactions. All this was strengthened by intensive group experience that had several transformative effects on me and, in particular, opened my eyes toward the self-organizing potential in such groups and the intrinsic motivation that can be set free by accepting a person or group the way they are.

Boosted by Rogers' writing that I saw as definitely supported by my own management- and team-/group-work experience as well as more recent work on dialogue (Bohm 1996) and on "Presence" by MIT, Massachusetts Institute of Technology Professors (Senge et al. 2006), I co-edited two volumes on the interdisciplinary impact of the Person-Centered Approach (PCA) (Cornelius-White et al. 2013a, b), including authors from 6 continents. This experience convinced me to put forth the PCA as an overarching paradigm, acknowledging the known as well as precognitive, spiritual, (yet) unknown of people and their relationships. Since the "application" of this "wisdom" to projects and my work environment proved enriching and, in fact, indispensable for moving forward, I long to pass it on to all who are receptive to such ideas, practices, and the implied way of being.

While the Person-Centered Approach (PCA) provides a rich "knowledge-, experience-, and value base" with a neuroscientific grounding (Cornelius-White et al. 2013a), it needs to be adapted and opened up to practical workplace application, and this is what this current book aims to accomplish. In other words, we are reaching to transform the PCA to the current, urgent need to communicate constructively and effectively in the workplace. If received well, the potential influence is enormous: More effective communication habits can initiate a "catalytic" reaction, extend like a spiral and spark over from one team, department, or organization to another.

1.3 The Person-Centered Approach and Its Current Scope in a Nutshell

For those readers who are new to the Person-Centered Approach, the Resource Box 1.2 briefly captures a few facts while a more thorough characterization follows in the subsequent chapter and Chaps. 9 and 11.

Resource Box 1.2 Carl Rogers' Person-Centered Approach (PCA)
Sparks of the Person-Centered Approach:
Primacy of experience. "First there is experiencing, then there is a theory." (Rogers and Wood 1974, p. 274).

Actualizing capacity and facilitative climate. A deep trust in people's inherent capacity for personal becoming and constructive action, paired with capacities for genuineness, respect, and empathic understanding tend to bring about transformative effects in people and their interactions. "This simple hypothesis was tested and validated in virtually every situation where one human being meets another—counseling, psychotherapy, education, business, conflict resolution, community development, family process, and medicine for the purposes of growth and healing." (O'Hara 2003, p. 65).

Rogers describes the direction of development in a person-centered atmosphere as follows: If I can create a relationship characterized on my part:

- by a genuineness and transparency, in which I am my real feelings;
- by a warm acceptance of and prizing of the other person as a separate individual;
- by a sensitive ability to see his world and himself as he sees them.

Then, the other individual in the relationship:

- will experience and understand aspects of himself which previously he has repressed;
- will find himself becoming better integrated, more able to function effectively;
- will become more similar to the person he would like to be;
- will be more self-directing and self-confident;
- will become more of a person, more unique, and more self-expressive;

- will be more understanding, more acceptant of others;
- will be able to cope with the problems of life more adequately and more comfortably (Rogers 1961, p. 37, bullets added).

Rogers' theoretical model of the person who has experienced optimal psychological growth:

- A person functioning freely in all the fullness of his organismic potentialities;
- A person who is dependable in being realistic, self-enhancing, socialized, and appropriate in his behavior;
- A creative person who is ever-changing, ever-developing, always discovering himself in each succeeding moment of time (Rogers 1983, p. 295).

> We are, in my view, faced with an entirely new situation in education where the goal of education [...] is the facilitation of change and learning. The only man who is educated is the man who has learned how to learn [...] how to adapt and change [...]. Changingness, a reliance on process rather than upon static knowledge, is the only thing that makes any sense as a goal for education in the modern world. (Rogers 1983, p. 120)

> Finally, there is agreement that one of the most essential elements for survival is the development of a greater sense of cooperation, of community, of ability to work together for the common good, not simply for personal aggrandizement. (Rogers 1980, p. 332).

1.3.1 The Person-Centered Approach as Emergent Paradigm

As summarized in Fig. 1.1, the PCA forms an emergent paradigm, consistent with interdisciplinary systems theory (Motschnig-Pitrik et al. 2013). It uses research to link theory with experience, posits a unitary inherent motivational construct, and focuses on the quality of interpersonal interaction and a whole-person approach. The PCA nurtures a way of being and relating that is respectful of cultures yet transcends them by offering a meta-culture that is more universal, based on values that actualize human being and relating regardless of any particular culture, depending only on a specified but unspecific interpersonal climate (Rogers 1980). All these characteristics make the PCA a most promising, well-founded generic framework that lends itself to be adapted as one of the pillars of effective leadership, management, and teamwork in our quickly changing world of work.

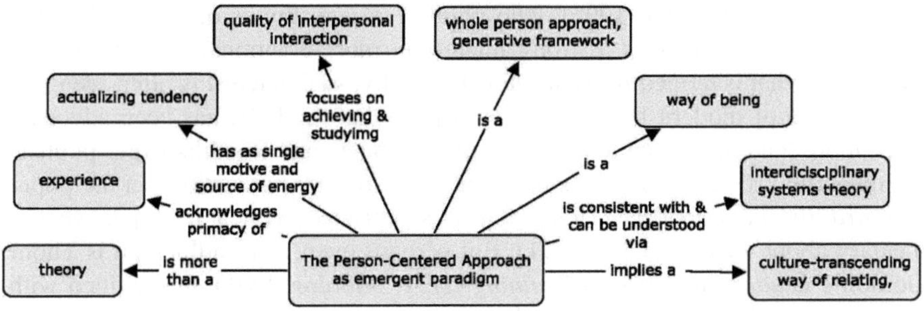

Fig. 1.1 Overview of the PCA as an emergent paradigm (Motschnig-Pitrik et al. 2013, p. 250), used with permission by the publisher.

1.3.2 The Person-Centered Approach in the Workplace from a Historical Perspective

Being more facilitative and open to new information coming both from the working environment and from members of the organization—from bottom to top—is what appears to be characteristic of the modern day of organizations. They have to operate at the speed of trust, that is to say at the rate of more effective communication, because the people involved are more open and receptive to new ideas and information (Senge et al. 2000), as well as being more transparent themselves (Bennis 2009). There are few secrets in this age of electronic communication. One leader cannot hope to have a monopoly on the important facts or on the shifting dynamics of interpersonal influence. So s/he has to be open to others' thoughts and even feelings if the best decisions are to prevail.

Our sense is that the persistent huge number of project failures, for example, about two out of three IT projects, according to ongoing research of the Standish group (2015), along with bruised interpersonal relationships, point to the need for better communication at work. For example, Carl Rogers described the benefits of focusing on the speaker wholeheartedly while putting one's own ego, ideas, and counterpoints aside, at least temporarily. As simple as this practice—known as active listening—is to state, it is quite rare in conversations (see Chap. 17). Most people are so busy anticipating their responses to what they are hearing that this inner talk interferes with the empathic listening that Rogers advocated. But how can we understand the other if we do not actually listen to them?

Apparently, the PCA is offering a practical theory and value-base; however, it needs to be discovered and adapted to better match the mental model of a manager, leader, or team member, whoever has the courage to start this exciting journey. This is what we seek to initiate with this book and the seminars, workshops, and courses we are conducting.

Historically, active listening remained the colloquial reference to what Rogers was describing until the advent of the popularization of the concept of emotional intelligence by Goleman (1995), who pointed to empathy as one of its four basic components. Now there is a strong interest in more emotionally open communication and what is termed *transparency*. Ironically, such interest is often seen as the cutting edge of modern leadership, yet is just what the PCA has been advocating since more than half a century. For example, Rogers and Roethlisberger published an impactful article on "Barriers and Gateways to Communication" in the popular *Harvard Business Review* (1952) that was reprinted with a retrospective commentary about 40 years later (1991). But perhaps even more influential is Thomas Gordon's *Leader Effectiveness Training L.E.T.* (Gordon 2001). It is written with a person-centered mindset while clearly keeping its core audience—management—in mind.

Finally, the two of us have been active in advocating the PCA in the context of leadership, management, and teamwork (Ryback and Motsching-Pitrik 2013). Ryback (1998) published a book on *Putting Emotional Intelligence to Work* which includes several dialogues with Carl Rogers on the issue of the PCA in leadership, and even though it uses the terminology of emotional intelligence, its person-centered value base is clearly evident. Finally, Renate and her team (iCom Team 2014) recently published an "experiential guide" to "Constructive communication in international teams" that includes several cases that all draw upon the PCA and its application in business, research, and teamwork. In the following, we shed some more light on particular opportunities we have identified above in order to give a first idea on how this book may contribute to meeting contemporary challenges at work.

1.4 The Nature of Contemporary Challenges and Opportunities

1.4.1 Feelings in the Workplace

Rogers (1961, 1980) pointed to the importance of feelings as a basis for interacting with the world. In our time, this is more important than ever. For example, decisions have to be made quickly with little room for error. And the best decisions are based on feelings rather than thinking, though both are, of course, part of the parcel. Current brain research points to the non-conscious components of decision-making that is most accurate most of the time. The part of the brain that is central to this process (both functionally as well as anatomically) is known as the insular cortex, where, according to recent research, our brain is "focused enough to make a split-second decision … when to execute a stock trade, when to make a putt on the 18th green." (Cloud 2011). What has evolved over eons is now becoming essential in the twenty-first century. We may no longer be threatened by saber-toothed tigers to determine the fight-or-flight response, but we are dealing with the need to make very quick decisions in a time when the Internet is merciless in its demand for go/no-go decisions in quick time mode. The demands for instant communication among international organizations, and their reliance on the PCA-resonant mode for decision-making based on feelings, are undeniable (Mount 2005).

1.4.2 *Speed of Decision-Making*

One of the greatest challenges in present-day leadership is the speed at which the decision-making process must take place. Computers work on the basis of fractions of a seconds rather than the few seconds (at least) that the human mind needs. In complex matters, it might take 24 h to make the best decision possible. So how do we match up to the contemporary challenge of thinking and deciding more quickly?

One solution that Steve Balmer, CEO of Microsoft, brought to the table to match up to the challenge of thinking and deciding more quickly is to get information prior to a meeting. He would rather be prepared for the subject matter prior to the meeting, rather than wasting time getting up to the par when everyone is sitting at the table. Why waste the time of all participants sitting at the table learning the subject matter of the meeting at the meeting when this information could be dispensed on a prior basis and then the decision-making process can move forward swiftly and more effectively (Bryant 2009).

To us, it makes a lot of sense to come prepared to a meeting. From a person-centered perspective, our meeting partners were provided with useful information beforehand signals caring and mindfulness. And reading the information beforehand signals the reciprocal mindful and caring response—all the more reason to devote further space on exploring effective meetings in a subsequent chapter on key situations for transformative communication. Unfortunately, in practice, we often come unprepared to meetings, due to too many responsibilities we tend to take on.

1.4.3 *A Fluid Communication Process*

According the PCA, being congruent or transparent and attuned to the feelings of others is what's needed for effective leadership and management. Brain research has revealed that the amygdala, a core part of the feeling brain, sometimes referred to as the "detector of threat" as it alerts the cerebral cortex and hormonal system when danger seems apparent, registers emotional danger even when our intellectual contributions are not appreciated or accepted by our peers. We only show an accepting attitude when that happens, not to make waves, but within our minds and bodies, there is stress and withdrawal and a sense of vulnerability as a result of not being recognized for what we have to offer. Being a good leader used to mean dominating those being managed, but current thought has emerged into the realization that the PCA lies at the core of what's needed—a fluid communication process, based on integrity and respect, between the leaders and managers and those reporting to them. It is not about domination; it is to "Be the change you want to see in people," as Gandhi once said. In *ConnectAbility*, I (David) point out the need to "Hang up your ego long enough to listen," a defining component of the PCA (Ryback 2010, p. 21). No matter how widespread or global the organization, there is still the need to be a careful and compassionate listener, even more so in order to span the distance that electronic communication can cover. This theme will turn out to be central in the case studies provided in Part 2 of this book.

Those in a position of leadership can often blame others without recourse, not daring to be transparent. It is so easy to criticize others when we are in leadership positions. We do not have to think about the effect of our criticism—just react and then move on to the next challenge, leaving behind hurt and resentment. But research at the School of Business at UCLA (Weisinger 1989) has revealed that it is essential that leaders bring a PCA approach to their communication styles. The worst way to motivate someone, according to a study of 108 managers and their reports (Baron 1990), was through such inept criticism when a mistake is made. That is so easy, though thoughtless.

Why not interact in a person-centered way—share your perceptions openly while respecting the other person? Together, seek the steps that need to be taken to improve the situation objectively and with a sense of personal support. These days, with such pressure to get things done more and more quickly because of Internet and intranet demands, it is so easy to forget about the need to respect others' feelings and sensibilities. But this makes it all the more important to leave a trail of camaraderie and appreciation. We are, after all, highly social creatures, not robotic mechanisms to just get the job done.

Invitation to reflect:

Are there situations at work in which you feel you cannot be as transparent as you would like?
Think of two or three such situations and imagine what would happen, in the worst and best case, if you were more transparent. Could the situations be transformed somehow to allow for more transparency?
Do you wish others to be more transparent in their contact with you? Who, in particular? Are you yourself open or do you need to protect yourself in the relationship with that person?
If you hide something from another person, how does that feel to you?

1.4.4 Effective Use of Virtual Space

In this age of the dominance of electronic communication, one group (the International Constructive Communication Project, or iCom, www.icomproject.eu, with Renate as the scientific lead) has experimented with transparency over the Internet by collectively sharing among themselves as they completed their project, to see how much openness they could muster and to what appropriate measures (iCom Team 2014). They focused on a sense of inclusion and consensus in decision-making. As they emerged into a powerful team, they found that they could overcome their initial fears of openness and eventually begin to trust one another to risk greater transparency. The group even included potential consumers of their project as equal partners, both in face-to-face meetings as well as online, resulting in a high degree of transparency. They discovered the dynamic of complementary skills, where one individual could pick up where another left off, where one skill could make up for limits in another's repertoire. Another experience of the iCom team was the benefit of pairing electronic communication with face-to-face interaction, when time allowed, to ensure the ongoing deep sense of trust. When individuals were not in the same area, phone interaction or videoconferencing could be used to complement the e-mail.

1.4.5 Integrating Uniquely Personal Qualities

Ultimately, one or more individuals might be recognized for his/her or their sensitivity to these issues, and the group then might look to such individual(s) for ongoing guidance. Carl Rogers had an exceptional ability for these dynamics and that is what earned him so much respect when he appeared in group interactions. He shared a strong sense of respect for all voices, but also a subtle drive to get things done as needed, all with extraordinary transparency on his own part. How to work with others with compassion, yet reach the collective goal developed through a shared process is a talent that characterizes what this book's main focus is. The core of the process appears to require three components:

- Expressing primarily what you feel deeply
- When it is relevant to the process at hand
- With an awareness of how what you share will be received.

So, besides integrity, two key capacities for the present-day leader and manager are flexibility and interpersonal sensibility.

1.4.6 Rapid Change

"Innovation" is a buzzword that permeates our culture. Everything is susceptible to modification to make it more appealing to the consumer. It may be that the consumer has become addicted to such change. Newly adapted iPhones bring about crowds of young consumers lining up to purchase the first release of such products. Modifications in the next generation of iPhones crowd the headlines of the business section of our newspapers. Research in Motion, the Canadian makers of the BlackBerry, had to be sufficiently flexible to shift their priorities from exclusive network to a more open one which could integrate with emerging technology (Marlow 2012). Security had to give way to touch screen technology in order for this product to continue to have a place in the ever-growing marketplace. Staying in touch with consumer needs with an ongoing sensitivity can be seen as a technologically based application of the PCA ("listening" to the consumer). Contemporary organizations demand a broader application of PCA values. Without an ongoing sensitivity to rapidly changing demand for rapidly changing products, businesses will be left to linger in wonder as the world moves rapidly on. Apple, Microsoft, Nintendo, and Sony, all have to be extremely sensitive to such changes if they are to stay viable entities (O'Reilly and Tushman 2004).

1.4.7 Empathy and Beyond

Just as feelings are important in rapid decision-making, so is empathy important to contemporary success in leadership. One CEO is quoted as saying, "if you really want to get the best out of people, you have to really hear them and they have to feel like they have been really heard." Rogers could not have said it any more clearly. Not only must modern leaders listen, they also have to ensure that the speakers feel heard.

But empathy alone does not a leader make, as Rogers said (Ryback 1998). When I (David) asked him what advice he would give a novice leader, he replied, "I'd say honesty is most important … about the basic aspects of each individual's performance … no judgment, no blame, just objective feedback on how something is lacking or could be improved upon, and with a warm smile, with a reassuring demeanor" (Ibid, p. 31). The PCA to empathy is important, but so is a fair-minded approach to supporting others in their growth and development, holding them accountable, but in a highly supportive mode.

Research is revealing that the "empathy" that is needed by the successful leader is not just for individuals, but also for group dynamics. How does a group respond to a particular speaker promoting a particular program or project? What can the empathic leader learn as her/his associates vote for a project or veto it merely by the direction of their gazes or the expressions on their faces? The successful leader with empathy is in a much better situation than the non-empathic counterpart. This ability to read group feelings is referred to by some as "aperture," referring to the broad and narrow focus, just as a camera can focus on the close-at-hand or the distant object (Sanchez-Burke and Huy 2009). This sensitive reading can save loads of time and money by detecting the group reaction earlier rather than later. The underlying dynamics are revealed, in particular, in Chap. 15 on the neuroscience of emotions and empathy.

One other aspect of the PCA that Rogers described and demonstrated in his personal interaction with groups is the need for a sense of security for taking the risk of personal openness in groups (Rogers 1970, p. 53). This principle of a safe harbor for openness has just recently been recognized in the second decade of this twenty-first century era. We mention this just as one of several instances where a "recent" finding in fact has been foreshadowed by Carl Rogers. Thus, his original work is very worthwhile to be read even though it stems from the previous century!

Creating a safe place for risking vulnerability is one way to get a group to become more productive and effective (Druskat and Wolf 2001). Readers wanting to try an exercise on simply being oneself in a group will find instructions in the Resource Box 1.3. Subsequently, a case example illustrates Rogers' openness in group and its effects.

Resource Box 1.3 Exercise on simply being oneself (summarized from Lencioni 2014, p. 7)

In a novel approach to group dynamics, titled, *The Five Behaviors of a Cohesive Team,* Lencioni (2014) advocates the facilitation of an exercise he calls "Personal Histories," in which individuals can share their reasons for choosing the actions they do. The basis of his approach is the establishment of trust. "At the heart of vulnerability," he writes, "lies the willingness of people to abandon their pride and their fear and simply be themselves. While this can be a little threatening and uncomfortable at first, ultimately it becomes liberating for people who are tired of overthinking their actions and managing interpersonal politics at work" (p. 7).

Case example of Carl Rogers' openness in groups.

At one conference experience, an exercise referred to as the "fishbowl" involved having a group of 6–8 people sitting on the floor at the center of the room, sharing their most personal feelings, while the remaining participants observed silently, but could occasionally switch places with someone in the inner group. I (David) was amazed to see, over time, that whenever Rogers was in the fishbowl group, his openness resulted in all the others in the small group to risk greater openness. However, when he left the small group, replaced by one of the observers, the overall level of risk-taking plunged dramatically. Then, sure enough, when Rogers reentered the small group some time later, the level of trust and risk-taking rose dramatically, and the whole enterprise took on a much greater sense of emotional sharing. Of course, this is merely an example of modeling, but the effect of Rogers' personality in this dynamic was substantial, fairly surprising to me at the time and even over time.

Finally, it should be mentioned that even though the PCA encourages emotional openness and creates a "safe harbor" for such openness, there is also the need for accountability, and holding others accountable for the aspects of honesty that are unpopular, especially when they must disagree wholly with those they otherwise respect. As Rogers told me, "I'd rather have someone really stoutly opposed [to me] say, 'I don't like your ideas—I'm 100 % against them,' than to have someone say, 'Oh, I'm for your ideas.' Then, when I watch them at work, I find that he's really making a pseudo-something out of it that's very false and phony" (Ryback 1989).

1.4.8 Collaboration in Teams and Groups

There is currently a lot of curiosity, among researchers on team effectiveness, as to what makes for the best results. In a comprehensive essay on this matter (Duhigg 2016a), the question arises, what makes for the most effective teams? In 2012, Google made it a point of interest and started a study on this issue. They called it Project Aristotle and applied much man—and womanpower to find some solutions. But they came up with more confusion than certainty. "We looked at 180 teams from all over the company," remarked Abeer Dubey, a manager in Google's People Analytics division. There were lots of data, but no definitive answers as to what kinds of people made for the best groups. "After looking at over a hundred groups for more than a year," the essay explains, "the data did not offer clear verdicts. In fact, the data sometimes pointed in opposite directions. The only thing worse than not finding a pattern is finding too many of them. Which norms, [they] wondered, were the ones that successful teams shared?" (p. 24).

Eventually, two patterns began to emerge: The first was that, in successful teams, the members all spoke about equal amount; the second was that the members of such teams "all had high 'average social sensitivity'—a fancy way of saying they were skilled at intuiting how others felt based on their tone of voice, their expressions, and other nonverbal cues" (p. 24). Furthermore, in addition to these qualities of emotional sensitivity and "conversational turn-taking," there was, according to Harvard Business School professor Amy Edmonson, a "shared belief held by members of a team that the team is safe for interpersonal risk-taking." Such a team, she goes on, has a climate "characterized by interpersonal trust and mutual respect in which people are comfortable being themselves" (p. 26).

Almost incredibly, these results mirror closely what Carl Rogers articulated some decades ago. The new research adds over a hundred studies on this topic that validate and confirm what Rogers and his associates were promulgating decades ago. When Google spends so much time, money, and person power to uncover what works best for effective teamwork, as do others (see Duhigg, *Smarter Faster Better* 2016b), and the ultimate findings are in tune with what Rogers revealed some time ago, it is intriguing to uncover, in this book, what Rogers had to say, and what, amazingly, is possibly more relevant in our time than it was before (Ryback and Motschnig-Pitrik 2013; Motschnig-Pitrik 2015)!

1.5 Conclusions

Thus, to be well adapted to managing/leading and communicating in today's and tomorrow's new world of work, traits including the following are particularly vital. For resonant and complementary thought, see also O'Hara and Leicester (2012):

- Flexibility, adaptability
- Dealing with new situations constructively, creatively, and effectively
- Being a lifelong learner with interest and curiosity about the new
- Communicating effectively and keeping up or establishing flow in interaction
- Attention economy (Davenport and Beck 2001)
- Empathy for individuals and groups
- Appropriate openness and a skilled and creative use of social media
- Being able to establish and cultivate constructive, well-functioning interpersonal relationships, teams, networks, and communities (Barrett-Lennard 2013).

Now we may pose the question: Does the Person-Centered Approach bring to the table everything that the modern manager/leader needs to be successful? As will be argued in the remainder of the book, we are convinced that it offers the foundations, the basis of being human in responsible positions. However, to claim that it would offer everything a modern leader or manager needs would be presumptuous. This is why, in this book, we are going to use a multifaceted approach proposing to put various theories within a reliable basis: the PCA. This approach focuses on the quality and impact of interpersonal relationships, and acknowledges the primacy of nothing less than our first-person experience and capacity to reflect upon it, embedded in the world of work that often calls for tangible outcomes. Thus, we see the major challenge and opportunity of this book to help transforming communication at the *interface between the task-oriented and the people-oriented level*, aiming for a *synergy* as we move forward in either of these directions.

References

Barrett-Lennard, G. T. (2013). *The Relationship Paradigm. Human Being Beyond Individualism*. Houndmills, UK: Palgrave Macmillan.

Baron, B. (1990). Countering the effects of destructive criticism. *Journal of Applied Psychology, 75*(3).

Bennis, W. (2009). *On becoming a leader*. New York: Basic Book.

Bohm, D. (1996). *On dialogue*. London: Routledge.

Bryant, A. (2009). Meetings, version 2.0, at Microsoft, *New York Times, May 16.*

Cloud, J. (2011). Thought control. *Time, 178*(19), 52–54.

Cornelius-White, J. H. D., Motschnig-Pitrik, R., & Lux, M. (2013a). *Interdisciplinary handbook of the person-centered approach: Research and theory*. New York: Springer.

Cornelius-White, J. H. D., Motschnig-Pitrik, R., & Lux, M. (2013b). *Interdisciplinary applications of the person-centered approach*. New York: Springer.

Davenport, T. H., & Beck, J. C. (2001). *The attention economy: Understanding the new currency of business*. Harvard Business School Press.

Druskat, V. U., & Wolff, S. B. (2001). Building the emotional intelligence of groups. *Harvard Business Review* (March), pp. 80–90.

Duhigg, C. (2016a). Group study. *The New York Times Magazine (February), 28*, 20–75.

Duhigg, C. (2016b). *Smarter faster better*. New York, NY: Random House.

Goleman, D. (1995). *Emotional intelligence*. New York, NY: Bantam Books Inc.

Goodall, J., & van Lawick, H. (1967). *My friends, the wild chimpanzees*. Washington, DC: National Geographic Society.

Gordon, T. (2001). *Leader effectiveness training L.E.T.* New York: Penguin. (first published in 1976).

iCom Team. (2014). *Constructive communication in international teams*. Münster: Waxmann.

Lencioni, P. (2014). *The five behaviors of a cohesive team*. NY: Wiley.

Marlow, I. (2012). Lunch with RIM CEO Thorsten Heins. *Globe and Mail, August 24.*

Motschnig-Pitrik, R. (2015). Developing personal flexibility as a key to agile management practice. In G. Chroust & Sushil (Eds.), *Systemic flexibility and business agility* (pp. 131–141). India: Springer.

Motschnig-Pitrik, R., Lux, M., & Cornelius-White, J. H. (2013). The person-centered approach, an emergent paradigm. In J. H. D. Cornelius-White, R. Motschnig-Pitrik, & M. Lux (Eds.), *Interdisciplinary applications of the person-centered approach* (pp. 235–252). New York: Springer.

Mount, G. (2005). The role of emotional intelligence in developing international business capability. In V. Druskat, et al. (Eds.), *Linking emotional intelligence and performance at work*. Mahwah, NJ: Lawrence Erlbaum.

O'Hara, M. (2003). Cultivating consciousness; Carl R. Rogers's person-centered group process as transformative androgogy. *Journal of Transformative Education, 1*(1), 64–79.

O'Hara, M., & Leicester, G. (2012). *Dancing at the edge competence, culture and organization in the 21st century*. Devon, UK: Triarchy Press.

O'Reilly, C., & Tushman, M. (2004). The ambidextrous organization, *Harvard Business Review* (April), pp. 74–81.

Rogers, C. R. (1961). *On becoming a person. A therapist's view of psychotherapy*. London: Constable.

Rogers, C. R. (1970). *Carl Rogers on encounter groups*. New York, USA: Harper and Row.

Rogers, C. R. (1980). *A way of being*. Boston: Houghton Mifflin.

Rogers, C. R., & Roethlisberger, F. J. (1951, 1991). Barriers and gateways to communication. *Harvard Business Review* (*HBR*). November–December 1991, pp. 105–111 (first published in 1952, with retrospective commentary republished in 1991).

Rogers, C. R., & Wood, J. K. (1974). Client-centered theory: Carl Rogers. In A. Burton (Ed.), *Operational theories of personality* (pp. 211–258). New York: Brunner/Mazel.

Rogers, C. R. (1983). *Freedom to Learn for the 80's*. Columbus, OH: Charles E. Merrill.
Ryback, D. (1989). An interview with Carl Rogers. *Person-Centered Review, 4*(1), 108.
Ryback, D. (1998). *Putting emotional intelligence to work* (p. 136). Woburn, MA: Butterworth-Heinemann.
Ryback, D. (2010). *ConnectAbility* (p. 20). NY: McGraw-Hill.
Ryback, D., & Motschnig-Pitrik, R. (2013). successful management with the person-centered approach: Building the bridge to business. In J. H. D. Cornelius-White, R. Motschnig-Pitrik, & M. Lux (Eds.), *Interdisciplinary applications of the person-centered approach*. New York: Springer.
Sanchez-Burke, J., & Huy, Q. N. (2009). Emotional aperture and strategic change: The accurate recognition of collective emotions. *Organizational Science, 20*(1), 22–34.
Senge, P., Cambron-McCabe, N., Lucas, T., Smith, B., Dutton, J., & Kleiner, A. (2000). *Schools that learn. A fifth discipline fieldbook for educators, parents, and everyone who cares about education*. New York: Doubleday/Currency.
Senge, P., Scharmer, C. O., Jaworski, J., & Flowers, B. S. (2005). *Presence exploring profound change in people, organizations, and society*. New York: Currency.
Standish Group, (2015). The Chaos report. http://www.standishgroup.com/. Retrieved September 1, 2015.
Weisinger, H. (1989). *The critical edge*. Boston: Little, Brown.

Chapter 2
As a Manager—Can I Be Human?—The Two-Agenda Approach

> *Being genuine also involves the willingness to be and to express, in my words and my behavior, the various feelings and attitudes, which exist in me. [...] It is only by providing the genuine reality which is in me, that the other person can successfully seek for the reality in him.*
>
> Carl Rogers (1961, p. 33)

This chapter focuses on:

- Characterizing the two-agenda approach,
- The features of each of the two agendas,
- The preconditions for following the people-oriented agenda,
- Describing and illustrating the synergy between the two agendas by case examples,
- Characterizing the leadership style emanating from the intertwined task and people orientation as symbolized by the two-agenda approach.

2.1 Introduction

This chapter puts forth a central idea of this book: the ubiquitous two-agenda approach, briefly denoted as the 2agendas@work. The basic idea is simple: To best meet the challenges of the contemporary workplace, a mature "rapport" between task-oriented and people-oriented activities and skills is needed. The objective of this chapter is to put forth a conceptually simple approach—the 2agendas@work. In this approach, the concept of a "people-oriented agenda" is introduced and paired with the more familiar concept of a task-oriented agenda. The use of the term "agenda" for both task- and people-oriented issues helps to explicate features of a people-oriented mind-set in the people-oriented agenda. This "agenda" is aimed at raising awareness of the need of "items" such as transparency or desire for understanding, as much as the usual task-oriented agenda has become an acknowledged part of any meeting. In particular, the people-oriented agenda is

R. Motschnig and D. Ryback, *Transforming Communication in Leadership and Teamwork*, DOI 10.1007/978-3-319-45486-3_2

Table 2.1 Characteristics of the two-agenda approach (2agendas@work)

Task-oriented agenda	People-oriented agenda
Focuses on some specific task, goal, or plan	Focuses on providing evidence-based, socio-environmental conditions
Follows a business or impact plan	Respects self-organizing principles, shared responsibility, and subjective experience and awareness
Is specified, explicit, and tends to be in the foreground during meetings	Often resides in the background, becomes known as attitudes and feelings, and tends to be explicated on occasion
Is rather short term, can be composed, and changed quickly as strategies and goals change	Needs experiential learning and social contact to be acquired; is being assimilated; and can mature through experience
Is planned, strategic, and follows lockstep logic	Can be simple or complex, interwoven, dynamic, seeking integration, revealing the "big picture"
Has specified end goal	Is an ongoing process, sustainable, fluent rather than rigid Aspects of it are best explicated as part of the mission statement

explicated and specified in terms of its items and the preconditions necessary for following them, since this agenda often seems to be forgotten in Western cultures. Examples of transforming communication in the workplace by achieving a synergy between the two agendas will serve to illustrate a good rapport between them and between people who can access and follow each of the agendas as appropriate.

Table 2.1 describes each of the two agendas by listing their characteristic features.

2.2 The Two-Agenda Approach

As a manager, leader, or team member, we can imagine to always follow not only one but two agendas, a task-oriented agenda and a basic people-oriented "agenda":

- *Task-oriented agenda*: Transparently specifies whatever needs to be accomplished to reach some goal and result, or to follow a plan. It tends to be quite short-lived, having the lifetime of a meeting, a project, or working toward a specified outcome. Valuable previous work provides guidelines on how to design and follow task-oriented agendas (Doyle and Straus 1982) and online resources, such as making meetings work (KnowHow NonProfit 2016)
- *People-oriented agenda*: Implicitly holds and, at appropriate occasions, calls to life socio-environmental conditions and consequent behaviors that promote personal growth of all involved and the forming of constructive interpersonal relationships at the workplace. In brief, the people-oriented agenda stands for

putting forth person- and relationship-centered ways of being, acknowledging that we are human beings, above all (Rogers 1980; Barrett-Lennard 2013). The people-oriented agenda draws upon millions of years leading to human evolution, yet not in a naïve way, but seamlessly integrated with state-of-the-art evidence- and research-based interpersonal knowledge, skills, and attitudes (Cornelius-White et al. 2013a, b). Note that the term "agenda" in this context is used symbolically, aimed to call people aspects to mind explicitly, comparable to the well-known and practical notion of an agenda.

As Kurt Lewin remarked: "There is nothing more practical than a good theory" (1951, p. 169). However, its practice can become challenging, indeed, in our competitive and rapidly changing world of work. For example, a project is at risk, or production goes down and we can be left with employees but without resources to pay for their contracts. Moreover, the time pressure can work against our intention to find solutions that are acceptable to all. Or we may need our people to meet deadlines or acquire new projects and, at the same time, know that their families need them as well. We are left with ambiguity and conflicts and need all our capacities to find a solution or ways to cope with the situation.

2.2.1 Creative Tension

Again and again, I (Renate) am freshly experiencing the two simultaneous agendas generating creative tension—an evocative term I first encountered while reading Senge (2006). Typically, creative tension arises when we aim to bridge the gap between our vision and "reality," or when we aim to head toward two directions at once, such as to achieve some goal, task, or outcome ("productivity") on the one hand and to improve our human and social capacity on the other hand ("self-actualization," "social capital," "multidimensional intelligences") as in Gardner (Gardner 2006), Goleman (1995, 2011), Motschnig and Nykl (2014), Rogers (1961), and Ryback (1998). For example, consider an organization that wants to build and market a state-of-the-art mobile phone and, at the same time, improve the social relationships within the design team such that they look forward to collaborating on this and the next project (Motschnig-Pitrik 2015).

Below, I (David) recall a situation in which there is a conflict between what others consider the right, "standard" decision and one more specific, "exception-to-the-rule," "just-this-time" decision.

Example from experience:

For example, right now, I (David) am terminating a long-distance consulting relationship with an executive for which I am being paid by a large firm. The executive asked me whether I would consider continuing the consulting relationship with him on a self-pay basis, since the existing contract is coming to an agreed-upon term limit which does not allow for extending the time period. My first impulses are twofold: (1) There is a boundary issue here that might be violated if I continued the consulting, leading to a conflict of interest between me and the large firm; hence, I should not consider this offer. (2) I really enjoy working with this executive, and our interaction has evolved into a very meaningful exploration of his life issues. So currently, I'm exploring my inner impulses on how to deal with this new situation in a way that would be beneficial to all parties or at least not harm any of them.

The task-oriented agenda is to respect the needs of the large firm in terms of not compromising its contract with its client, i.e., making sure I don't solicit the client's business while I am working with the client on behalf of the firm. The people-oriented agenda is to be able to work with that client as my own, but making sure that this new relationship is created only after the first relationship is clearly terminated.

So when the client asked if I could take him on as my own client after the contract with the large firm ended, I responded by saying, "Let's not consider that until the first contract is clearly terminated. I don't want to be in a position of considering such business with you until the time is appropriate. And that time will be only after the first contract is clearly over." When the contract was over, I waited for the client to approach me with his request, which he did. Before we began the new contract, I checked with the large firm, and they agreed that this process was definitely acceptable to them according to their policy.

Before exploring how leaders and managers with a person-centered mind-set integrate the two agendas in Part II of the book, we compare and contrast the two-agenda approach with classical leadership terminology, such as Blake and Mouton (1964, 1985) or Bennis (2009).

2.3 Excursion to Leadership Styles

Traditionally, leadership styles have been characterized, among others, on two essential dimensions: task-oriented versus relationship-oriented, often drawn as the x- and y-axes of the Cartesian coordinate system (Fig. 2.1). This induces the image that the dimensions are independent and each leader personality would be posited in some range on the space spanned by the two axes, as in the famous grid suggested by Blake and Mouton (1964).

But this image does not depict what we feel when leading a team. What we do aim for is a tight interaction between the task and person/relationship aspects,

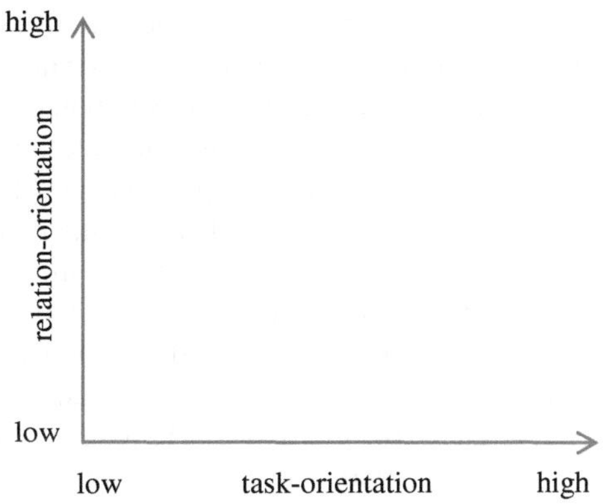

Fig. 2.1 Task-oriented and relationship-oriented leadership styles as leadership dimensions in the classical perspective

resulting in a movement iterating between the two, as depicted in Fig. 2.2. The intention is to find—for each task, goal, or issue—a way to accomplish it in a way that would both

(i) accomplish the task, goal, or issue as effectively as possible *and*
(ii) be coherent with person- and relationship-centered principles/values as much as possible.

For brevity—and risking some oversimplification—let us refer to (i) as the task orientation and to (ii) as the people orientation. The term *orientation* has been chosen intentionally over the term *dimension* because the notion of a dimension (like horizontal, vertical) tends to signal independence. Typically, dimensions are independent, whereas orientations can have a common projection and head to close or to distant end points over time (Fig. 2.2).

Typically, the degree to which the people orientation can be followed will depend (among others) on the task orientation and vice versa, but the people orientation would inevitably always be there to influence us in the choice of

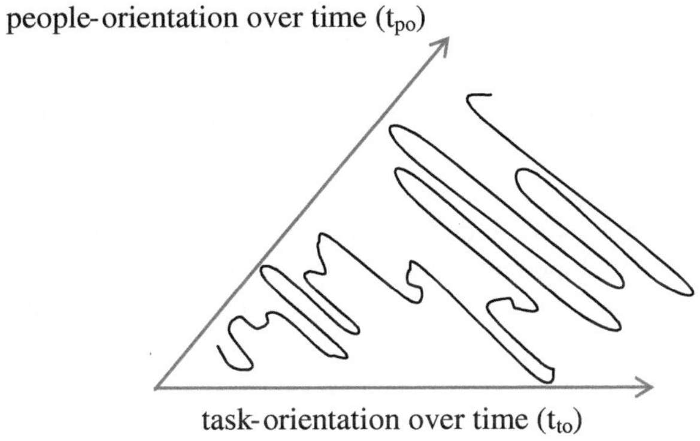

Fig. 2.2 The task and people orientation over time in transformative communication

task/goal, given we have a choice at all. So, for example, the human factor would make a difference in which project or task we engage in and how we choose to go about accomplishing the project, potentially calling for unorthodox approaches. However, in the longer term, this intertwined task *and* people orientation tends to result in credibility and cooperative, constructive relationships while accomplishing tasks satisfactorily. This is because the people component of the overall direction is consistent with who we are or, in more scientific terms, with the principles of self-organization (Goldstein 1939; Kriz 2008; Rogers 1951) and interpersonal development (Barrett-Lennard 2013). This dynamic has been confirmed in education and to some degree in organizations and management (Cornelius-White and Harbaugh 2010; Gordon 2001; Rogers 1975, 1978; Ryback 1989, 2010; Ryback and Sanders 1980; Ryback and Motschnig-Pitrik 2013).

What needs to be expressed is the interdependence of the two aspects. We need to reach some goal, accomplish something, *and* thereby be as person/relationship-centered, mature, resourceful, and cooperative as possible. We need to be authentic in a humanistic sense, not in the void or "per se," but in *some context*, we perceive as relevant—so to speak, to crystallize our personalities and relationships according to some challenge that would help us move forward in a particular *task* or goal as *social human beings*. We would bring our cultural and personal predispositions, but equally be aware that people issues and tasks are intricately intertwined (Böhm 2016).

To find an image for this new idea/insight that speaks to people at work, we created the two-agenda approach. Our communication and behavior would ideally be expressive of both agendas, although with varying focus on the one or the other. The way our brain supports us in following the two agendas and the competitive relationship between associated brain networks is discussed in Part 4 of this book.

To make the concept of the 2agendas@work more accessible, let us illustrate the interplay between them by an example from David's experience.

Example from experience:

Some time ago, in my younger years, while doing a training with a group of federal employees, I (David) was conflicted between the explicit task of "getting the job done," i.e., making sure every participant completed every task without fail, on the one hand, and allowing some slack so that the participants also enjoyed the process according to their whims, on the other hand. There was one woman, in particular, who just did not want to participate in one of the exercises. I confronted her from the head of the class and more or less forced her into participating at least at some level. This behavior on my part was a leftover from my more traditional teaching experience at the high school and college levels, where the level of maturity was not as developed and where an occasional student saw his role as defying authority (me) as part of his personality. In such situations, a contest between a student's negative attitude and my skills of maintaining control over defiance justified my coming across with all the strength I could muster.

After receiving feedback on my rigid demands, I realized how foolish I was to try and get this woman to do something which she found uncomfortable, for whatever reason. I was overwhelmed by my explicit demand to "get the job done" at the expense of listening to the needs of one individual for autonomy and self-direction. I learned, though it was a painful lesson. What I learned was to allow more of the basic agenda to enter the scene and to put into a less rigid context my need for control. The integration of explicit goals and basic attitudes could now spiral upward for a more successful approach to training.

Over time, I'm becoming more aware that the PCA is not always easy to manifest in our complex human interactions, particularly as trainers or leaders. The two-agenda approach allows us to see a bit more clearly where the challenges lie: I want and need to get the job done as efficiently as possible, but there is a part of me, if I nurture it and allow it, that can take into consideration others' feelings, needs, and sentiments. When the two integrate and spiral upward over time, then we are all winning. That creative inclusion is the beauty of the PCA at work, as we allow the two agendas to become integrated.

2.4 The People-Oriented Agenda

The people-oriented agenda is so basic that it underlies any meeting or activity that aims to move forward:

- its participants,
- the subject matter,
- the relationships among participants,
- the relationship between participants, subject matter, and the environment.

2.4.1 The Core Principle

The basic, people-oriented agenda is followed because it expresses part of who we are. It is not followed in order to achieve something except for meeting the other and, as a consequence, to ultimately meet oneself. It serves essentially to keep the flow of thoughts, feelings, meanings, ideas, words, and actions in and between us going. The flow is meant as the contrary to getting stuck, unable to move from some position.

2.4.2 Origin

The people-oriented agenda has been constructed from principles and ongoing research in person-centered psychology and related fields, as well as the authors' practical experience at the workplace in multiple contexts such as business, leadership, project management, educational settings, intercultural teams, workshops, etc.

2.4.3 Agenda Items

While having a logical sequence, the "items" in the "agenda" are connected and relevant all the time. They can be imagined as the instruments in an orchestra, all contributing to the masterpiece being performed. In particular, none of the items should be ignored completely at any time. They include the highest—under given circumstances *appropriate*—levels of the following capacities:

- Contact,
- Transparency of goals, vision, and participants,
- Respect toward the other, oneself, and the environment,
- Trying to understand and to be understood comprehensively and thoroughly,
- Collaboration and genuine sharing.

There are many ways to express and enact the "agenda." Resource Box 2.1 captures some of them in a concise form, while subsequent examples and experiences provide more lively information and thought.

Resource Box 2.1 Some ways of expressing and enacting the people-oriented agenda

- Contact
  - Establishing and maintaining contact by the means available and appropriate,
  - Greeting, shaking hands, making a bow, nodding, eye contact (in some cultures),
  - Taking time, presence, responding, responding to e-mail, calling, etc.
- Transparency of goals, vision, and participants whenever appropriate
  - Stating and elaborating goals,
  - Honesty, candor, open dialogue whenever appropriate,
  - Avoiding hidden agendas as much as possible,
  - Articulating with clarity,
  - Showing oneself and opening up appropriately.

- Respect toward the other, oneself, and the environment
  - Expressed through language (verbal and body), behavior, etc.,
  - Respecting the other's and one's autonomy and supporting it,
  - Including the other in meetings, decisions, information flows, social events, etc.,
  - Positive expectation, trust as attitude from which to start encountering the other and oneself,
  - Meeting at eye level of personhood, trying to be fair,
  - Feeling and showing respect toward nature and systems.
- Trying to understand and to be understood comprehensively and thoroughly
  - Active listening,
  - Empathic understanding of the other and the whole context,
  - Rich, encompassing understanding of the other in the context of the subject matter at hand and rich understanding of the project and its context,
  - Clarifying,
  - Simplifying appropriately,
  - Expressing oneself at multiple levels, facilitating understanding,
  - Using language in a way the other can understand.
- Collaboration and sharing
  - Being a resourceful person,
  - Removing blocks and aiming at flow within and between persons,
  - Constructive, appreciative as well as critical feedback,
  - Co-sensing, co-reflecting, co-actualizing (Motschnig-Pitrik and Barrett-Lennard 2010) and fostering a sense of inclusion and belonging,
  - Collaborative attitude, seeking for solutions cooperatively and co-owning them,
  - Avoiding harmful rivalry,
  - Facilitating self-organization and acknowledging systems dynamics.

2.4.3.1 Contact

Just as bird's-eye one another, dogs sniff one another and ants touch antennae, so do we humans approach one another with invisible "feelers." In our culture, we are most likely to shake hands or hug. The Japanese traditionally bow, how low depending on the difference in status. The traditional Inuit rubbed noses. Mandarins assessed one another by the nature of the gifts they exchanged. Most likely, when I (David) first meet you, our eyes make contact, and our hands reach out for the traditional handshake. Whatever the rituals are, contact—initial and ongoing—is crucial before we get down to the business of our interaction.

2.4.3.2 Transparency of goals, vision, and participants whenever appropriate

Most of us value our time very highly. We believe that most would agree that our time will be spent most efficaciously if we are honest at the outset. Can we state the point of our meeting early and clearly? Can we face the differences we bring to the table without rancor or ill feeling? Can we respect and appreciate that our differences, once clarified and resolved, only add to the mix of resources that harbor success? There is no power stronger than transparency among team members to get the job done quickly and effectively. And the better we know one another, according to Professor John Mayer of the University of New Hampshire, the better we will know how to interact with them (2014).

2.4.3.3 Respect toward the other and yourself

As a tyro consultant, I (David) was taught that everybody puts his pants on one leg at a time. I took from this that each person, even the most esteemed CEO, was, at the end of the day, just another human being, an individual independent of status. Years ago, this came home to me when I was hosting Carl Rogers who had come to my college to deliver a keynote address. Everyone was awed by him, hoping to be in his presence for a moment or two. One morning, as I had some responsibilities to take care of, I left Carl alone to relax at an outdoor table near the central building. When I returned, I found Carl in a deep conversation with an outlier student, who just happened to be passing by in his more-than-casual style of dress. I was surprised, but should not have been, that Carl did not give a flip for status. He treated everyone, and I mean everyone, with the same respect, appreciation, and even caring, as he did with his closest friends or distinguished colleagues.

2.4.3.4 Trying to understand and to be understood comprehensively and richly

Working with an intercultural team with members coming from industry and academia, we (Renate's team) tried to understand and respond to the business needs of our business partners rather than considering them "greedy" and ignorant of the scientific aspects of the project. With the feeling of being understood, they opened up and supported us academics as well as they could by incorporating the results from a study among end users into the software they were constructing. Taking the effort to understand members' different backgrounds definitely paid off, since finally the project was concluded successfully, even though, at times, it looked as if misunderstanding and conflict would make collaboration impossible.

2.4.3.5 Collaboration and sharing

After befriending Carl while hosting him for his keynote address at the college where I (David) taught, we got in the habit of exchanging letters and I subsequently wrote him about my desire to work on some projects with him. He consistently rebuffed my invitations by insisting how much he preferred to work alone. But a number of months later, he called me and invited me to come down to La Jolla to be considered by his colleagues to take on the task of helping to develop his group along new dimensions, such as business and education. In addition to that, I was able to co-author a significant paper with him when he was open to my doing some research on using the PCA for international peace negotiations. What this taught me was that by being open with him about my desire to work with him and allowing him to be honest about his desire not to do so and co-reflecting on our different styles, we were able, ultimately, to collaborate in ways that were comfortable to both of us. Appreciating the "co-construction" of a relationship with our different styles eventually led to constructive projects that benefitted from both our skill sets.

2.4.4 Features of the People-Oriented Agenda

The people-oriented agenda is characterized by the following features. It:

- *Is independent* of a particular national culture, field of work, or scientific discipline.
- This does not imply that the expression of the agenda items would be the same for all cultures; it just means that the agenda items as such are valid for all cultures, even though the manner and intensity of expression may vary considerably.
- Is *shared* by all, which means that all participants can follow it collaboratively.
- Is applicable to any kind of meeting directed toward some gain or value for each person or party involved as well as the interpersonal relationships among all involved. *It excludes a purely autocratic leadership* style and favors democratic, situational, inclusive, and transformational leadership styles.
- *Blurs* the "classical" *distinction* between task-oriented and relationship-oriented leadership as it challenges participants to follow both ends through time. This does not imply that both ends are in the forefront at each instant, but it means that overall, both ends are considered at least to some degree.
- Does not stand alone. It is typically, but not necessarily, *intertwined* with some task-oriented agenda in the particular work context. The items on that agenda

can be imagined as instruments in the orchestra that take turns in delivering aspects of the melody.
- Can be very simple to follow or pose a major challenge, depending on the situation, and in how far participants have internalized *interpersonal capacities* and skills.
- *Is directed* toward moving forward in the relational context and toward constructive transformative learning and knowledge.
- Tends to be *transformative*. The end results it delivers are open yet specifiable. It is expected, though, that due to the evidence-based, self-organized forward movement of persons in a constructive atmosphere, the results of following the people-oriented agenda are favorable, whatsoever "favorable" means in any particular situation. For example, see Part II of this book.

A remarkable *paradox* arises around the people-oriented agenda:

The more convincingly and naturally we implement the basic, people-oriented agenda, the less it will actually serve as an agenda until it ceases to be an agenda. It can be imagined to transform itself into unfolding deep and significant learning in the participants. One can see it as contagious and residing in the participants, waiting to be released again and again. In other words, it can be seen as a natural tendency in people, to want to know more about others, appreciate them, and feel known and appreciated in turn. This satisfies deeply ingrained needs to feel connected with one another. The safer the environment feels, the more this natural tendency will prevail. A sense of threat can destroy this tendency very quickly. The challenge lies in circumventing this sense of threat by dealing with the inevitability of conflict with openness and transparency.

In the absence of threat, people can be very good at understanding others. "In five seconds," according to Randall Colvin at Northwestern University, people "can easily pick up on extraversion and conscientiousness as well as intelligence and any negative affect. It takes only several seconds longer for judges to accurately home in on openness, agreeableness, and neuroticism, as well as positive affect" (Weintraub 2015, p. 49).

Another useful feature of the people-oriented agenda is its capacity to serve as an *analytic tool* (see also the questionnaire in Table 2.1). We hypothesize that every interpersonal conflict can be traced back to not adequately addressing at least one (often several) of the "items" of the people-oriented agenda.

2.5 Preconditions for Following the People-Oriented Agenda

Following the people-oriented agenda can be either very simple or difficult, depending on our and the others' interpersonal capacities and the situation. Here are some preconditions that need to be met in order to be "fit" to follow this "agenda." On a personal level, they include:

- Having access to our feelings and being able to express them appropriately,
- Being sufficiently open toward the new, the unfamiliar, the ambiguous, people's multiple realities, the unorganized and, in general, the self-organizing principles and systems dynamics at work in the universe,
- Feeling respect toward yourself and others and being able to express it such that the other can experience it,
- Being able and desiring to listen actively and wanting to understand others from their perspective,
- Knowing about the principles of systems dynamics and self-organization capabilities,
- Having experience in working with groups, definitely it is a considerable advantage.

From an organization's or project's perspective, following the people-oriented agenda is facilitated by a number of environmental factors such as:

- Cultivating a style of communication where the expression of feelings is considered acceptable and even desirable,
- Empowerment by *including* employees in forming project goals and making decisions,
- Making employees *co-responsible* for reaching project success,
- Providing employees with opportunities for developing a comprehensive *understanding* of the project or organization, including its interfaces with customers and the surrounding system(s),
- Acting to support a feeling of community and *forming of bonds* among employees that reach beyond pure business matters,
- Granting and supporting of each employee's response ability and autonomy in areas in which it does not hinder project success, while living a leadership style that offers guidance where needed and dedicated personal support.

In particular, the factor of "autonomy support" has been confirmed to play a profound role in people's perceived well-being (Lync et al. 2009). In the context of researching self-determination theory (SDT), the authors found that people would experience less stress (be more congruent) when being with partners who are not imposing or controlling but rather accepting them as they are and even supporting their autonomy. Interestingly, the positive effect of autonomy support could be confirmed for populations from China, Russia, and the USA, i.e., for all three nations studied.

Interestingly, research by Bernier et al. (2010) at the University of Montreal found that those youngsters who were encouraged by their mothers to make their own decisions, rather than being told what to do, were more likely to have more impulse control and concern for others than those whose overcontrolling mothers told them how to respond. This held true even when the mothers' education and cognitive abilities were taken into consideration (Hane and Fox 2006).

Our strategy for deriving the preconditions was to integrate information from various sources such as Senge's 5 disciplines of the learning organization (Senge

2006), Rogers' theories of personality and interpersonal relationships (Rogers 1951, 1959, 1961), Barrett–Lennard relationship paradigm (Barrett-Lennard 2013), and Damasio's contributions to social neuroscience and phrase the conditions to suit the work context. We decided to put them forth as an assumption and leave further empirical testing to follow-up research. From our perspective, there may be other preconditions for following the people-oriented agenda that might be added to this list.

Table 2.1 is intended as a resource to self-assess yourself or your colleagues on the items of the people-oriented agenda by responding to 5 key questions. The last, sixth question serves to assess your or your colleagues' competence in the task-oriented agenda in order to be able to relate people- and task-oriented aspects.

A. **Contact**
The manager/associate

1. avoids contact as far as possible and tends to keep the door closed (both literally and figuratively),
2. has minimal contact with others and it is difficult to really communicate with,
3. keeps in touch on demand and approaches others when contact is indispensable,
4. is interested in keeping in touch, sometimes initiates contact, and communicates openly,
5. is genuinely interested in others and initiates and nourishes contact.

B. **Transparency and openness**
The manager/associate

1. avoids questions, is not accessible, and refuses open conversation,
2. hides behind his/her position and it is difficult to communicate with him/her with any degree of transparency,
3. responds with some degree of openness,
4. tends to communicate openly and transparently,
5. communicates totally transparently, gives honest feedback, and is perceived as genuine.

C. **Respect**
The manager/associate

1. meets associates without any respect and does not consider their requests,
2. hardly respects the associates' requests and demands,
3. respects the associates' needs and requests to some minor degree,
4. is generally respectful toward associates and encourages them,
5. is full of trust in associates, encourages them, and lets them experience his/her acceptance.

D. **Trying to understand**
The manager/associate

1. completely ignores the associates' needs,
2. hardly responds to the associates' needs and interests,
3. to a minor degree reacts to what the associates share,
4. usually reacts appropriately to what the associates share so that they feel understood,
5. completely understands the associates' needs and interests and is supportive of them.

E. **Collaborative attitude**
The manager/associate

1. meets others in a demotivating way, ignores their ideas, and does not invite cooperation,
2. tends not to be interested in any collaboration and avoids it as far as possible,
3. collaborates with selected partners if benefits are clearly perceivable,
4. is generally supportive of making progress together,
5. meets others with encouragement and support and acts proactively in promoting collaboration.

F. **Competence in subject area: Bridge to the task-oriented agenda**
The manager/associate

1. appears to be lost in wide areas of the meeting's or project's subject area,
2. seems to be quite incompetent in the respective subject area,
3. is moderately competent in the subject area and reasonably capable of expressing it,
4. leaves a competent impression and is skilled in expressing key issues of the subject area,
5. proves expertise in the subject area and can raise enthusiasm in associates.

Table 2.1: Questionnaire assessing attitudinal conditions to follow the people-oriented agenda in work situations. The questionnaire is extended by the feature "competence in subject area" to establish a connection to the task-oriented agenda and thus assess the competence to follow both agendas in some particular subject area. The questionnaire loosely follows Aspy's (1972) questionnaire, basically sharing the five-point scale where three serves as a threshold for person-centered communication [*Version 1.0 by Renate Motschnig, 01/09/2014*].

In a research study among students of computer science, instructors who were rated high on their interpersonal capacities were those who could motivate students most to participate in class (Motschnig-Pitrik 2005). Interestingly, low or intermediate ratings in the interpersonal aspects came with somewhat lower ratings on the subject-related competencies, suggesting that instructors who do not interact very well with students are perceived as less competent in the subject matter.

In the questionnaire above, level 3 means a threshold. Being below that level on any of the attitudes designated by "A" to "E" indicates that the people-oriented agenda tends to be dropped at some situations. It is difficult for the respective person to follow it consistently. On the other hand, being above (including) level 3 means that the testee fulfills the preconditions of following the "people-oriented agenda." In any case, we conjecture that we can always move upward. The case example below is intended to illustrate two variants of a whole interaction sequence between a manager and a team member with a varying sensitivity to people issues (iCom Team 2014, pp. 185–186).

Case example

Both of the following two conversations aim at setting up a plan on how to resolve a delivery problem [MG stands for manager; TM stands for team member].

Situation 1:

MG (*with a critical tone*): Did you deliver the system to our client, McDuck?

TM Not quite. They brought some old data sets that our database didn't upload

MG How could this happen?

TM (*defensively*): It was not specified precisely. Who could know that they wanted to import from ancient database versions!

MG (*upset*): Why was this not included in the specification? You know that omissions and errors in the specification can be very costly!

TM (*explaining*): We had specified data imports from the client's database and tested their samples all the way back to version 5. The representative from McDuck was given still older data to be uploaded and they hold the position that these datasets must be handled as well

MG So either you can deliver this extension within the next three days or we need to argue that these very old versions are not part of the contract! Why the hell is there always something not working properly!

TM (*submissively*): I'll work on it as soon as possible. Clients can be nasty, for sure.

Situation 2:

MG (*with an interested voice*): Hi, how are you today? Did you deliver the system to client McDuck?

TM Not quite. They brought some old data sets that our database didn't upload. So you can imagine I'm not really happy about that

MG I see. (*pause*) They brought some old formats that they wanted to have uploaded, hmm, and I assume this was not explicitly specified beforehand? (*looks up to TM, TM nods his head for approval, pause, then with a voice expressing curiosity and openness*) Well, what is your sense of this situation?

TM (*thoughtfully, kind of thinking aloud*): Well, as far as I know, they really need those datasets for their business statistics, so I'd sure like to extend the code to cover the old data formats. (*pause*) I guess I need to take a look at how much effort this would mean. I assume it's not a big issue and I can resolve this soon or ask them for a time extension. (*genuinely after a short pause*) My sense indeed is, that the way we deal with them and provide our services, this time will be decisive for any future contacts!

MG (*frankly*): Makes a lot of sense to me. Just go ahead and let me know whenever you need me and how things are going. Good luck, great to have you "on board"!

Invitation to reflect:

How does each scenario resonate with you? How would you describe/label each of them?
How far does each of them implement or ignore each of the two agendas?
In which situation does the manager have two agendas on his/her mind?
How does the team member react in each case?
In the first situation, which items of the "people-oriented agenda" are neglected? How is the second situation different regarding these items?
As a manager, how would *you* react? As the team member, what would you say?

While further ideas and inspiration on integrating the people-oriented agenda follow throughout the book, below we share what we have found useful to improve our people-oriented "fitness":

1. *Openness*. Be open to the questions that others ask. Sympathize with the perspective that leads to their question, as this may be much more relevant than the answer you might offer. Rather than giving a complete response to the question, allow it to be a bridge to mutual understanding.
   Example: "What should I do, A or B?" Response: "Seems like a tough decision you have to take. Tell me, what brings you into the situation of needing to choose between A and B?"
2. *Being a mediator*. Facilitate others to explore their options while accompanying them in taking the risk of considering what feels right to them rather than just what others expect of them.
   Example: "If I understand you correctly, the coordinator wants you as expert to make design decision regarding the web-portal, while you are convinced that you need to include end-users to produce a usable solution. Well, what feels appropriate to you to move on in this situation?"

3. *Stepwise approach.* Realize that using the people-oriented agenda of transformative communication with others—as opposed to the conventional style of appearing as if you are in control of every detail—is not at all easy. It comes with a considerable portion of risk and needs empathy to result in tactful interaction. Be aware that the freedom once granted to others is extremely difficult to reclaim and introducing control later on in all likelihood may cause lots of trouble. So, rather than radically switching from being in control to granting total freedom to others, you may want to be "diplomatic": Establish good communication first and then move in deliberate steps such that all can learn to deal with the newly acquired responsibilities.
4. *Nonjudgmental stance.* Don't look down at those insisting on convention and predictability and the traditional, competitive approach. Be open to a world that has room for both. Otherwise, we risk becoming authoritative on behalf of a democratic approach.
   Example: "Oh, you're missing the detailed plan for the activities of the transition phase? I see. What if you were to go ahead and propose such a plan from your perspective, then we'll see how much it will help us once we come as far as installing the software at our customer's site?"
5. *Lifelong learning.* Whatever skills or techniques you acquire to use with others, always consider that you can improve on them and become a better facilitator for others and yourself. Stay open to experiential learning and transformation in each situation as these tend to lead to becoming spontaneously tactful and acquiring a quality that resembles diplomacy but is much more genuinely owned.
6. *Conflict and support network.* Don't be surprised when your non-traditional approach leads to conflict with those who do not understand it. In such cases, just accept the difference and continue to be open and tactful. Professor Mischel (2014) of Columbia University maintains that such self-control is an important factor in ultimate success. Having others around you, who understand the challenge and occasional loneliness and vulnerability of being so open-minded, can be an ongoing support in this highly meaningful process. Just as you support others in their quest for authenticity, so do you benefit by having a safe community of others who value the process.
7. *Reflection and making sense.* Any experience can be considered as a source of learning that can be vastly multiplied if the experience is reflected upon, by oneself and in particular with others.
   For example, trying to reflect from multiple perspectives what it was that let a small project fail can be an enormous resource for the next large project in order not to repeat the same mistakes.
8. *Creative tension.* Usually, there is a gap between the given "realities" and our vision, plan, solution, etc. That gap can be perceived as causing tension. It is up to us to potentially use this tension to let something new, creative, desirable evolve by sensitively listening to others rather than rushing into "fix things" the way we think they need to be resolved.

9. *Physical fitness*. Being fully present at the moment, resourceful, flexible, showing one's genuine interest, surviving conflict, etc., all consume energy. In research with teachers, it was found that "physical fitness is necessary to sustain constructive interpersonal relationships across long periods of time" (Rogers 1983, p. 214). Also, "student teachers with higher levels of physical fitness accepted their students' ideas more often and criticized their students less often than did student teachers with lower levels of physical fitness" (Rogers 1983, p. 214). We assume that being as physically fit as possible would also be an advantage for sustaining constructive interpersonal relationships in workplaces other than classrooms.
10. *Self-acceptance as a bridge to power*. Allow your openness—to yourself and others—be a bridge to power, a sense of your own self-acceptance and self-respect. Your individual growth, and sharing and supporting others' growth, is the transformation to a "new diplomacy," the bliss to be followed and enjoyed. That direction is always your choice—forever.

Invitation to reflect:

Identify one or two items above that speak to you and imagine how you could implement them in your project or organization.
If you know another item that you think should be added to the list please contact the authors at the contact given in the foreword—thank you in advance!

2.6 Conclusions

This chapter argues that long-term, effective work is tightly intertwined with the complex, evolutionary, social, and human basis of our interpersonal nature, enriched by lifelong learning, experience, and knowledge. To illustrate the interdependence between the task and people orientation at work, we introduced the two-agenda approach. It allows one to explicitly distinguish between the task requirements on the one hand and the human demands, the imagined people-oriented agenda, on the other hand. At the same time, however, the notion of two complementary agendas implies that both have to be kept in mind and followed by taking turns as to which one is called to the foreground, while the other is left to rest in the background awaiting its turn. While this chapter has focused on introducing the two-agenda approach and illuminating the "items" of the people-oriented agenda, Chap. 12 will explore integrating the people-oriented agenda in key situations such as negotiation, conflict management, and decision-making.

So how does all this contribute to the transformation of interpersonal dynamics in the workplace? The two-agenda approach sets the basis for transforming how we communicate in all aspects of our work. By being more candid and transparent from the beginning, we get to the basis of what our meeting or project is all about. We listen to the other more carefully and with the intent to understand more deeply the relevant issues at hand. We are more honest about our own reactions to the extent that they are relevant and authentic. When all this happens, the transformation takes place. What has changed is that the honesty of all this contributes to a form of communication that is not only more enriching and fulfilling but also much more highly effective in reaching solutions that work more effectively. If this sounds revolutionary, it is merely making sense of what works and has worked. Interacting with genuine openness to others' perspectives *is* the challenge. And to be honest about a reality that objectively rings with clarity, this trumps the customary, traditional modes that have not worked so well in the past.

Thus, managing to integrate the two agendas—to hold the creative tension and to realize the potential that accrues from it—tends to have transformative effects. Depending on where we start from and how others come along, the transformation can be tremendous or subtle; in any case, however, it tends to have a constructive direction and feel right, reducing stress.

References

Aspy, D. N. (1972). *Toward a technology for humanizing education.* Champaign, IL: Research Press Company.

Barrett-Lennard, G. T. (2013). *The Relationship paradigm. Human being beyond individualism.* Houndmills, UK: Palgrave Macmillan.

Bennis, W. (2009). *On becoming a leader.* New York: Basic Book.

Bernier, A., Carlson, S. M., & Whipple, N. (2010). From external regulation to self-regulation. *Child Development, 81*(1), 326–339.

Blake, R., & Mouton, J. (1964). *The managerial grid: The key to leadership excellence.* Houston: Gulf Publishing Co.

Blake, R., & Mouton, J. (1985). *The managerial grid III: The key to leadership excellence.* Houston: Gulf Publishing Co.

Böhm, Ch. (2016). A framework for managing diversity in ICT projects—Processes and Techniques for explicating soft facts and dealing with behavioral differences. *Dissertation.* University of Vienna, Faculty of Computer Science, Research Group CSLEARN—Educational Technologies.

Cornelius-White, J.H.D., Harbaugh, A.P. (2010) *Learner-Centered Instruction: Building Relationships for Student Success.* Thousand Oaks, CA: Sage Publications.

Cornelius-White, J. H. D., Motschnig-Pitrik, R., & Lux, M. (2013a). *Interdisciplinary handbook of the person-centered approach: Research and theory.* New York: Springer.

Cornelius-White, J. H. D., Motschnig-Pitrik, R., & Lux, M. (2013b). *Interdisciplinary applications of the person-centered approach.* New York: Springer.

Doyle, M., & Straus, D. (1982). *How to make meetings work.* New York, USA: The Berkley Publishing Group.

Gardner, H. (2006). *Multiple intelligences: new horizons in theory and practice*. Basic Books. ISBN 978-0465047680.
Goldstein, K. (1939). *The organism*. New York: American Book.
Goleman, D. (1995). *Emotional intelligence*. New York: Bantam Books Inc.
Goleman, D. (2011). *Leadership: The power of emotional intelligence*. Northhampton, MA: More Than Sound LLC.
Gordon, T. (2001). *leader effectiveness training: L.E.T.* New York: The Berkley Publishing Group.
Hane, A. A., & Fox, N. A. (2006). Ordinary variations in maternal caregiving influence human infants' stress reactivity. *Psychological Science, 17*(6), 550–556.
iCom Team, (2014). *Constructive communication in international teams—An experience-based guide*. Münster: Waxmann. www.waxmann.com/buch3025
KnowHow NonProfit, (2016). Making meetings work. https://knowhownonprofit.org/people/your-development/working-with-people/copy_of_meetings. Last retrieved on June 1, 2016.
Kriz, J. (2008). *Self-actualization: Person-centred approach and systems theory*. Ross-on-Wye, UK : PCCS-books. ISBN 978 1 906254 03 2.
Lewin, K. (1951). *Field theory in social science: Selected theoretical papers*. New York: Harper & Row.
Lynch, M., La Guardia, J. G., & Ryan, R. M. (2009). On being yourself in different cultures: ideal and actual self-concept, autonomy support, and well-being in China, Russia, and the United States. *The Journal of Positive Psychology, 4*(4), 290–304.
Mayer, J. D. (2014). *Personal intelligence*. New York: Farrar Straus Giroux.
Mischel, W. (2014). *The marshmallow test: Mastering self-control*. New York: Little, Brown.
Motschnig-Pitrik, R. and Barrett-Lennard, G.T. (2010) Co-actualization: A new construct for understanding well-functioning relationships, *Journal of Humanistic Psychology* 50(3): 374–398. New York, USA: SAGE.
Motschnig, R., & Nykl, L. (2014). *Person-centred communication: Theory, skills, and practice*. UK: Open University Press, McGraw Hill.
Motschnig-Pitrik, R. (2005). Person-centered e-learning in action: Can technology help to manifest person-centered values in academic environments? *Journal of Humanistic Psychology, 45*(4), 503–530.
Motschnig-Pitrik, R. (2015). Developing personal flexibility as a key to agile management practice. In G. Chroust & Sushil (Eds.), *Systemic flexibility and business agility* (pp. 131–141). India: Springer.
Rogers, C. R. (1951/1983). *Client-centered therapy*. Boston: Houghton Mifflin.
Rogers, C. R. (1959). A theory of therapy, personality, and interpersonal relationships, as developed in the client-centered framework. In S. Koch (Ed.), *Psychology: A study of a science* (Vol. 3). New York, Toronto, London: McGraw-Hill Inc.
Rogers, C. R. (1961). *On becoming a person. A psychotherapist's view of psychotherapy*. London: Constable.
Rogers, C. R. (1975). The politics of education. In *Keynote at the Second National Conference on Humanistic Education*, West Georgia State University, Carrollton, GA.
Rogers, C.R. (1978) *On Personal Power*. London, UK: Constable.
Rogers, C.R. (1980). *A Way of Being*. Boston: Houghton Mifflin.
Rogers, C. R. (1983). *Freedom to learn for the 80's*. Columbus, OH: Charles E. Merrill Publishing Company, A Bell & Howell Company.
Ryback, D. (1989). An interview with Carl Rogers. *Person-Centered Review, 4(1),* 99–112.
Ryback, D. (1998). *Putting emotional intelligence to work*. Boston: Butterworth-Heinemann.
Ryback, D. (2010). *ConnectAbility* (p. 20). NY: McGraw-Hill.
Ryback, D., & Motschnig-Pitrik, R. (2013). Successful management with the person-centered approach: Building the bridge to business. In J. H. D. Cornelius-White, R. Motschnig-Pitrik, &

M. Lux (Eds.), *Interdisciplinary applications of the person-centered approach* (pp. 151–176). New York: Springer.

Ryback, D., & Sanders, J. A. (1980). Humanistic versus traditional teaching styles and student satisfaction. *Journal of Humanistic Psychology, 20*(1), 87–90.

Senge, P. M. (2006). *The fifth discipline. The art & practice of the learning organization*. New York: Doubleday.

Weintraub, P. (2015). The 10-second take. *Psychology Today, 48*(6), 46–88.

Chapter 3
On Transformation

> *"... because in order to shift the culture we must challenge it: we must do something countercultural. And it is creative rather than merely disruptive because it appeals to the culture's deeper values ..."*
>
> O'Hara and Leicester (2012, p. 129).

This chapter focuses on:

- The notion of transformation, including the features of an atmosphere that facilitates it.
- Reflecting why transformation is needed to succeed in the workplace.
- Illustrating transformative communication by a case example.
- The authors' personal experiences of being transformed.
- The effects and benefits in taking the risk of being transformed.

3.1 Introduction

Since the turn of the millennium when change has become "all there is" (Allee 1997, p. 5), numerous authors have explored the nature, conditions, and effects of transformation, or more precisely, transformative learning. Much of what they expressed applies equally to transformative communication. This is why we first turn to their process characterizations and cognitions and note that, in all cases, these cognitions are based on first-person experiences as the sources of knowing, and reflections as a way of capturing the transformative experience. Subsequently, we explore our personal transformations and characterize the effects of engaging in transformative communication and learning. Some of the changes initiated by a transformative experience include a richer repertoire of responses to any situation, a better capability of dealing with change, and an increased flow of information when interacting with others. This chapter is aimed at providing information deemed essential for understanding the phenomenon and process of transforming communication,

R. Motschnig and D. Ryback, *Transforming Communication in Leadership and Teamwork*, DOI 10.1007/978-3-319-45486-3_3

3.2 The Experiential Basis of Transformation

Bernie Neville recognized that taking the risk to be transformed needs, first of all, the absence of threat and, second, an accepting, nonjudgmental environment. While he describes transformation in an educational environment, we suggest that—in the quote below—readers substitute the term "student" with "team-member" and "teacher" with "manager" without even the slightest loss in the validity of the quote and with more relevance to their field.

> Transformation rarely takes place in situations of threat. People under threat learn (if they learn at all) in order to survive, not in order to change. You need to acknowledge that resisting your teaching about (say) violence or racism is perfectly reasonable behavior on the part of students whose violent or racist values and assumptions (and sense of who they are) are being threatened (or who think their values and assumptions are going to be threatened). If the content of your teaching is indeed threatening to particular students, you need to make the context of your teaching as supportive as possible—giving serious attention to building good teacher–student and student–student relationships, accepting your students as they are without judging them, listening with real attention to what they say and taking it seriously. I believe that personal change almost always takes place in the context of a relationship, and the better the quality of the relationships in your class (including the quality of your relationship with each student) the more open your students will be to changing the quality of their knowing, and not just the quantity of their information (2011, pp. 48–49).

Neville points us to another core dynamic of transformation, namely that we cannot exert any influence if we are not susceptible to influence. He writes:

> … if we want to talk seriously about transformative education, we need […] to be prepared to let go of what we 'know' and of our fixed notions of who we are if we are to have any chance of witnessing significant change in the assumptions and attitudes of our students (2011, p. 49).

Maureen O'Hara witnessed far-reaching transformation in intensive groups. Since we believe that teams working intensively together share some (though not all) characteristics of the intensive group experience, let us listen to Maureen's experience and her observation that the support of a caring other can turn most adverse situations to a measure of transformative learning:

> Through intimate meetings with people struggling to find their way, we encounter … but actually come through them transformed, better adjusted, closer to their lived sense of who they are, more in touch with the deeper meaning of their being, and more generous and open-hearted to their fellows. We have all experienced that when given the right kind of support from some caring other, even the most bewildering or anxiety-provoking of situations can lead to psychological growth and new orders of consciousness (O'Hara 2003, p. 67).

On an even more general level, O'Hara observed that "When old patterns unfreeze and reconfigure, new learning can occur at deep, transformational levels" (O'Hara 2003, p. 74). Together with Keith Wood, an experienced group facilitator, they reflected that letting go required a kind of faith and that it was *not* important whether it resided in God, nature, selfish genes, evolution, immutable laws of physical or biological reality, self-organizing systems, human creativity, implicate order, or all of the above. The point is that it is faith that the universe is not random and meaningless that enables human beings to transform themselves and move toward more complete ordered wholes (O'Hara and Wood 1984).

On a more practical level, O'Hara and Leicester (2012, p. 28) suggested the following characteristics for actions likely to initiate some kind of transformation. It should be:

- Inspiring.
- Capable of inspiring others.
- Desirable but out of reach (and therefore requiring transformational competence to deliver).

Intriguingly, the action can start at any level and scale, its impact being determined not by its scale but its quality.

David Ryback and Renate Motschnig describe the process of transforming communication as involving a totally different way of communicating with others. Instead of hiding behind a persona of being strong and right, once the transformation takes place, the individual has the option to communicate as a transparent, vulnerable—in the sense of less guarded, less defensive, or more open–human being who can accept others' vulnerability and maintain an attitude of support for such individuals. In a nutshell, there is a richer repertoire of options how to interact, something that was not readily available before. This can be imagined as a kind of growth of the emotional, cognitive, and behavioral repertoire. Less inner resources are needed to hide, disguise, or suppress aspects of ourselves.

As a consequence, in each transaction, once an individual has accepted the transformation we describe in this book, s/he can choose to be more open, vulnerable, authentic, and transparent with others. We believe that would involve decisions to choose with whom to be transparent because treating everyone that way without relevance to the matter at hand would be somewhat self-centered, i.e., ignoring the real situation and context with which the other(s) may be concerned. The transformation involves a choice or option to share the transformed self with others. Hopefully, that group of individuals would grow over time such that transformed communication would become more comfortable and familiar. Others would come to expect it, as it becomes assimilated into our personality.

Invitation to reflect:

You may want to recall a transformative experience. How would you describe its effects on you?

Here are some aspects that the authors feel to come along with transformed communication. Do they resonate with you?

- Not more of the same but something fundamentally different appears;

- Something that was hidden becomes visible and is associated with a strong sense of revelation, like "puzzle stones" falling together and allowing a picture to form;
- A tendency to feel a desire to use the new revelation, not let go of it, move on with it, engage it, making one feel more motivated;
- There is a sense of deeper meaning and relevance to our focus in what we share with others;
- It is as if there is a greater clarity of vision that helps explain complex ideas more easily and with greater mutual understanding. There may be a sense of shifting values that make the shared enterprise more meaningful and powerful.

To make our description more lively, we looked for examples from the business context that illustrate the difference between communicating out of a formal manager/leader role versus communicating as a real human being who happens also to be a manager. Here is one that my (Renate's) former student, Markus Schett—now a successful project manager at 42virtual—came up with from his experience.

3.3 Case Example—Manager–Team Interaction

3.3.1 Formal Versus "Eye-Level" Leadership

Situation: the project team is facing a delivery milestone. There are still some bugs in the software and it is very likely that a high-quality delivery will require the team to work on a Saturday, given the team's motivation is sufficiently high. The pressure and stress in the team are quite high but everybody gives their best. A side constraint is that all employees have all-inclusive salaries and extra hours are paid in exceptional situations only. In the given project, extra payment is not possible due to budgetary limitations. As a consequence, the project manager depends on the good will of the team members to work on the coming Saturday.

The question is, how a project manager would reveal to his or her team that he would like them to work on a Saturday instead of enjoying the leisure time they expected? Below you will find two possible scenarios, a formal, traditional one and an experiential, transformative one:

PM: Project Manager; Peter, Eva, Susan, and Felix: Team Members

(i) **Formal procedure**:

PM	"I looked at the list of open bugs. There are quite a few that we need to fix before delivery. And I talked to the director. He said that we need to keep the date as the customer expects this. This means that we'll need to work this coming Saturday. Please take this into account. Unfortunately, there will be no extra money for that but I think that we all know how important it is to deliver the project on time."
Peter	"Why should I come? If the company doesn't care to make extra money available, then I don't care to sacrifice my Saturday. And, by the way, I'm going to be done with my tasks by Friday!"
Susan	"Oh, great! I've got the majority of the tasks. Just because I've more expertise in the field than others I should come in on Saturday? I'm definitely not coming."

Felix and Eva show a sour face.

Comment: from this position, it is practically impossible to motivate people to do unpaid extra-work during the weekend.

(ii) **Experiential "eye-level" procedure**:

PM	"During the last few days we've been quite successful with bug-fixing. It looks as if we could manage to meet Monday's delivery milestone. What is your estimate?"
Peter	"I'll finalize my issues by Friday, no problem!"
Susan	"This will be extremely tight. I still have some issues regarding the topic XY and I don't think that I'll manage to finish by Friday."
PM	"Hmm, can we help you with some things? Why not distribute them among the team? Felix and Eva, do you have some free resources?"
Felix	"Absolutely not. I'm not going to finish till Friday. Peter already gave me two bugs because I can handle them more quickly."
Eva	"I need to do the quality assurance—so even if the others finish on Friday, I certainly won't be done."
PM	(Pause, looks around): "I can't postpone Monday's milestone. Furthermore, it would benefit us to manage the delivery so that we'd finally have some time to start the next steps with less stress. I realize that currently we're working up to our limit. The sooner this is over, the better. What do you think?"
Eva	"Actually, you're right. I can't look at the test cases any more …"
PM (smiling)	"Yeah. I don't like it either. And the same holds true for quality assurance. (To Eva) I'm going to help you with it. I'd be willing to come here on Saturday as well. Would that be an option for you?"
Eva	"Definitely not an option that I would enjoy."

PM "So at least we'd be two who wouldn't enjoy it. Are there any other volunteers who'd be willing to sacrifice enjoying their Saturday? You'd gain my appreciation and eternal gratitude and I'd supply you with pizza."

Peter "If you find a bug in my module, then I should come to fix it. I hope you can afford more salami for our pizzas."

Comment: the project team managed to deliver a high-quality milestone. The Saturday was quite fun and not too long.

☕ Invitation to reflect:

What is it that makes the project manager in the PCA case example succeed?

Do you think that the eye-level situation as described above could be learned in some way? If yes, try to explain how, if not, argue why it cannot be learned.

Does the following statement hold true for you as well? Can you recall an example that supports your view? In successful situations as well as cases of failure, taking some time to reflect on the experience may help to learn the benefit of being more mindful: What went wrong? What felt o.k.? How do you feel about individual players, strategies, behaviors, actions? What do you want to do differently next time?

Only if you let yourself truly be touched by a problem can you then be part of the solution. Do you agree?

In order to capture some characteristics of the complex process of transformation, let us first identify features that would facilitate rather than hinder the process of transformation.

3.3.2 *Examples of Features Facilitating Transformation*

- Feeling sufficiently secure in oneself and offering a safe ambience for others.
- Having faith that constructive changes are possible and building supportive interpersonal relationships.
- Living a new openness to others' ideas, approaches to dealing with challenges, and opinions. Approaching differences with a new dynamic: holding one's agenda flexibly so as to embrace those of others.
- Letting oneself be touched by the problem or challenge so as to feel it in one's body and be part of the solution. Not distancing oneself from the problem and fragmenting the system.

- Initiating dialogue or action that inspires some initial transformation to get started and take off.
- Anticipating results as a team commitment to shared perceptions of the bottom-line goals.

These features address the actual process of initiating transformation. Nevertheless, they head in the same direction and draw on the same value base as the preconditions for following the people-oriented agenda, listed in the previous chapter.

3.4 What Changes Are Likely to Result from Transformation?

What you might notice is:

- More transparency and openness when appropriate; the interactions becoming more real yet maintaining a sufficient level of respect.
- A more supportive and less distanced demeanor among all team members.
- A sharper awareness of and respect for others' ways of being and acting at work.
- A richer variety of choices and pathways, including unorthodox and innovative ones.
- Acknowledging ambiguity and disordered states as temporary steps in mastering change.
- Team members' or co-workers' increased sense of a community with all of them feeling included and responsible as part of the project or enterprise that they understand to a satisfactory degree.
- Expecting more successful results as team members take as much pride in the collective effort as they do in their individual contributions.
- Feeling more thankful for any experience and complaining less about what happened, based on more insight and less helplessness throughout the process. As a consequence, we may enjoy our work more and make it more meaningful and thus become more engaged while gradually improving the results as well.

Invitation to reflect:

Based on our experience, being transformed in one's work environment exerts its influence also on the private lives of employees. This is because by feeling intricate parts of a project or organizations, employees tend to invest remarkable amounts of time and energy into their jobs and get intensive rewards through being successful and cherished. This may cause tension with one's family that might not be able to keep up with the flow of the positive work environment. If not dealt with consciously and wisely, there is the danger that families and in particular children might be neglected, with unfavorable consequences for society.

Do you perceive the above as a challenge? If so, what, in your view, can be done to extend the transformation to family life?

Speaking personally, I (Renate) am sure I need to be transformed over and over again to be able to transform others. What I want to say is that "to be transformed" isn't some "all or nothing" quality so that it happens to you once and then you are done. I rather sense it needs to be recreated, reenacted over and over so that you can stay in the transformed state and not slip back. The environment does not always promote the transformed qualities; rather, the opposite is true. For example in the media, you hear people showing how great they are and what they have achieved and hardly ever sharing their weaknesses. So, in my view, at deliberately chosen times, you need to risk swimming against the current and, first of all, trust yourself that you are heading in the right direction. In other words, create and then cultivate your opportunities for transformation.

Transformation is a life-long, nonlinear process with peaks and stable phases, happening as people interact and adapt to their environment or reflect on such interactions. The transformation typically brings about some significant change in a person that can be perceived by others. It tends to give rise to an extended repertoire of a person's responses and make us better adapted to a constantly dynamic environment. And it is the communication style that is being transformed, as much as the individual.

Since each situation is different—some are more easily dealt with in terms of open-hearted communication and some may be quite resistant—the resistant ones are the challenge. How can we infuse emotional awareness and sensitivity when the other party keeps insisting that emotions should play no role in the discussion? So it is not hard to imagine a situation in which the "transformed" party is hitting a wall if the other is closed to hearing the more open-hearted dynamics. Here is where the rubber hits the road. This is where I (David), myself, fall back on looking at Rogers for a model that is sustainable in such resistant circumstances.

With the spirit of Carl behind me, I can more easily reveal my own awareness of the "elephant in the room," i.e., important, but unspoken and unidentified dynamics that are totally relevant to the issues at hand, and own my own awareness of them. I strongly believe that it is precisely owning my own awareness and not trying to foist it on to the other party that makes it so powerful and undeniable. I am not trying to convince the other, but rather "confessing" my own awareness of something that has not yet been seen by others. Yet, if I am authentic and honest about my awareness, there is a very good chance that the other will not deny it.

But that does not mean that I'll always be successful in getting the other to open up at a more implicit emotional level. We are all different and some people just do not open up about their feelings. Then, the challenge is to deal with that person or party with my own authentic feelings yet not insisting that the other do likewise.

I can try my best to accept that party on terms that are not my preference and do so without undue judgment.

Renate: David, you expressed exactly what I experienced too. Sometimes I feel really humiliated at not getting to the other the way I'd so much wish to and this has made me simply accept this experience and believe the other will have his or her good reasons to behave like they do, as I have my reasons to be the way I am. And sometimes, after a while, some meta-communication comes up where these differences are explored, with fascinating revelations, but not always. At other times, each moves a step to become more like the other and this may change the dynamics too. To me, the least helpful thing that can happen is when I get frustrated, but again there is no rule since this was exactly the course that changed an unproductive communication pattern recently. So again I agree that dealing with one's authentic feelings appropriately is the true challenge.

In order to make the notion of transformation more accessible for readers who appreciate "stories" to inspire their assimilation of ideas, below we are going to provide three examples experiences that appeared transformative to us.

Example from experience: When Carl Rogers felt transformed. Excerpt from David Ryback interviewing Carl Rogers (Ryback 1989, pp. 102–103):

I had a workshop some years ago and had the pleasure of working with my daughter on the staff … I personally thought of myself as being quite open as to what was going on and being quite facilitative and someone made the remark that some of the things that were going on in that large morning discussion could easily be topics for special subgroups. I said, "Yeah, that's so. Some of the things that *he* said, and that *he* said, and that *he* said, would all make very good topics." And my daughter just flew up in a rage. She said, "Where are the women? Why don't you mention any of the women who spoke up?" And that really hit me where I live. I thought for a while and then said, "Well, I guess my awareness hasn't extended to that point yet." … So, I'm quite convinced that it's a lifelong process of trying to learn from each experience to be a little more open than we were before.

Example from experience: Renate being transformed:

Recently, I saw a photograph of a musician in the newspaper with the headline that she would represent Austria at the renowned European Song Contest. The photograph showed a very thin, bearded woman with long, black hair and some tattoos on her arms. I thought: "What's that? Doesn't Austria have anything more aesthetic to offer than this? No chance Austria is going to get a good placement." Time passed and I didn't think much about the song contest, up to the time that I heard on the news that Austria's representative, Conchita Wurst, won the contest! I couldn't believe what I heard and became curious. How could that happen? There must be something to it that I had overlooked. I found Conchita's song "Rise Like a Phoenix" on "YouTube" and, while listening, a profound change must have taken place in me. Once I had stopped judging if the bearded lady in fact was a woman or rather a man, I found the person in her golden dress wonderful and so expressive in posture, body language and gesture. The person seemed so authentic and feeling herself in her skin and beautiful voice. The words of the ballad appeared to match the reality for Conchita; everything was a perfect match and a musical masterpiece. Immediately, I felt quite ashamed of my initial judgment, how could I hold such prejudices, where I had thought that I was quite open-minded? But simultaneously I was also content about having checked my own experience and not just hung on to my prejudice. This was a profound learning—and it had profound follow-up effects. One of them is that Conchita and the refrain of her song: "From the fading light I fly, rise like a phoenix, out of the ashes seeking rather than vengeance, ..." validates me in following my way, always seeking and not so much worrying about possible negative reactions of others. As Conchita said in a later interview (rephrased from my memory): "I always tried to see how I can fit in the game. Then I realized: I'd rather make the game." So here you have another amazing transformation that Conchita shared and that potentially could be so vitalizing for many who suffer from the domination of others and feel a chance to change something.

Example from experience: David being transformed:

My interaction with Carl Rogers was highly transformative, but it took time for me to recognize the change. I first met Carl when he came to a graduate class in psychology when I was a student at San Diego State University. He talked about unconditional positive regard in terms of caring for others without expecting anything in return. That was definitely a novel approach to people as far as I was concerned. I was puzzled about this one-way caring relationship.

I recall walking with him to his car at a brisk pace under a gray sky. I finally was able to utter my concern. How could he be recommending a one-way caring relationship when it was clear in our culture that this just wasn't something people did?

I don't recall Carl's answer to my existential question, but what did impress me was his openness to considering it as a meaningful question and not to be placed aside because of its challenge to his philosophy. So I was in that moment a convert to his way of thinking. My new approach to people, to be open to their needs and to respond to them without expecting anything in return, changed my life, transforming me from a shy, terribly reserved individual to one who could break through that shyness and now reach out to people wherever I went, meeting them at a juncture where their needs could be something that I might attend to, creating open relationships that might last over time. I was transformed, open to other people, allowing me to feel the fulfillment of being of significance to others as I paid greater attention to how I might be supportive of them.

As well, Carl taught me that my own openness was something I could demonstrate to encourage others to similar transparency, giving me a substantial sense of confidence in helping others, whether in pairs or in groups, to be more authentic themselves.

3.5 Conclusions

In this chapter, we have researched the phenomenon of transformation from sources found in the literature as well as from our own experience. As a result, we described the sort of organizational or team climate that facilitates transformative learning and investigated some of its effects. Summarizing, we pose the following question:

What are the benefits of taking the risk to engage in transformative learning and being transformed? In our view, the following changes are likely to result:

- Better capability of dealing with radical change and new situations.
- Better capability of adapting to change in a way that is most beneficial under the given and often absolutely unprecedented circumstances.
- Higher repertoire of responses to any situation; more creativity.
- Higher repertoire of choices in general.
- More engagement, interest, responsibility, loyalty, and more reasonable results, allowing for greater consensus.
- More flow in the interaction with others due to having greater access to all our inner resources as well as those of our colleagues.

In any case, a transformative learning experience typically reveals something that already exists, but has been concealed or ignored by some subconscious mutual consent (like the proverbial elephant in the room). It now makes its way to conscious awareness, to be noticed and finally also expressed. Each time that happens, it can be compared to the opening of a new awareness, like the seeds that lead to the growing of a new plant.

References

Allee, V. (1997). *The knowledge evolution: Expanding organizational intelligence*. Newton, MA: Butterworth-Heinemann.

Neville, B. (2011). Teaching and transformation. *The Person-Centered Journal, 18*(1–2), 35–52.

O'Hara, M. (2003). Cultivating consciousness: Carl Rogers's Person-centered group process as transformational andragogy. *Journal of Transformative Education, 1*(1), 64–79.

O'Hara, M., & Leicester, G. (2012). *Dancing at the edge: Competence, culture and organization in the 21st century*. Devon, UK: Triarchy Press.

O'Hara, M., & Wood, J. K. (1984). Patterns of awareness: Consciousness and the group mind. *Gestalt Journal, 6*(2), 103–116.

Rogers, C. R. (1970). *Carl Rogers on encounter groups*. New York, NY: Harper and Row.

Ryback, D. (1989). An interview with Carl Rogers. *Person-Centered Review, 4*(1), 99–112.

Part II
Case-Studies on Transforming Communication in Management

Chapter 4
Carl Rogers' Counseling Center in Chicago—A Case Study

Renate Motschnig and David Ryback

> *"There has been one other input to my learning [...] that my thinking and action seemed to be something of a bridge between Eastern and Western thought."*
>
> Rogers (1980, p. 40).

4.1 Introduction

As Rogers founded the Counseling Center of the University of Chicago in 1945, he gradually became aware of the revolution in administrative procedure that a Person-centered approach might bring about. Rogers asked himself—and this happened gradually: "If I trust my clients"—and he felt this was a very constructive way of dealing with people—"could I trust a staff in that same way? Could we all share the power?" (Rogers and Russell 2002, p. 146) Rogers implemented that more fully at the Counseling Center than he had at any other time in his life. This case is aimed at capturing the essence of Rogers' leadership experience—as far as experience can be mediated by words.

4.2 Insights on Participative Management from Carl Rogers' Leadership Practice

4.2.1 Context

During the twelve years Rogers had been leading the Counseling Center of the University of Chicago, it grew to a staff group of approximately 50. Rogers acquired prestigious research grants to pay the staffs' salaries. The Center was incredibly productive in fulfilling its major mission: providing high-quality counseling services and conducting as well as publishing research. Rogers wrote that he never had seen "such dedicated group loyalty, such productive and creative effort" (Rogers 1978, p. 93) as he saw during his Chicago years. Working hours meant

R. Motschnig and D. Ryback, *Transforming Communication in Leadership and Teamwork*, DOI 10.1007/978-3-319-45486-3_4

nothing and staff members were working because they wanted to. Nevertheless, Rogers shared that it had been dismaying to him that the staff never seemed to be able to find the *right* way of operating the Center. When all decisions had been made by consensus, this had been too burdensome. When they had delegated decision-making to a small group, that procedure proved too slow. Then, they chose a coordinator and agreed to abide by her decisions though she could be given a vote of no confidence. Only gradually Rogers had realized that there was no right way and that the vitality and growing capacity of the Center had gone hand in hand with its lack of rigidity and with its surprising capacity to change its collective mind and to utilize new modes of operation (Rogers 1978, p. 94).

4.2.2 Participative Management

The administration of the Center was done in a truly democratic way, in which all the power was in the hands of the total group. The organization was truly Person-centered —a real example of participatory management. Rogers felt that he really wanted to try out if and to what extent his person-centered principles work in a real organization. How can they be implemented and what did that mean for hiring people, firing people, or promoting them, about salaries, etc. For example, there were no assigned caseloads —people were regarded as self-responsible and self-disciplined. They were responsible for their work, and it was assumed that they would handle as many cases as they were able to handle. If you needed time for research, that was your decision.

Rogers found that when power was distributed, it had not been a big thing to be the coordinator or chairman or whatever. So, for example, an intern might chair the budget committee and thereby become acquainted with the workings of the operation.

A distinguishing characteristic of the Center was its egalitarian nature. All were equal and that never had been faked by Rogers. Rogers used to approach people as equals—and that was because he was convinced that he had learned so much from people. For Rogers, this egalitarian attitude was not a pose, and he really expected that he could learn something exciting from that person. If Rogers could tap into what really was going on in a person, that always had been exciting and full of learning for him.

4.2.3 Dealing with Conflict

Rogers had experienced an enormous importance in personal feelings in administrative matters. Often, people spent hours in arguing some triviality, until a perceptive staff member sensed and stated the feelings, such as an animosity, competition, or insecurity, underlying the issue. Once the feelings were expressed and a person was really heard, the issue became resolved fast. Each time when the staff was in open communication, even heavy issues such as the budget allocation or the adoption of a new policy were resolved in a few minutes.

The staff developed effective ways in dealing with crises. When the threat or attack came from outside—such as from another department—the group tended to coalesce and to delegate full authority to members or a member to deal with the crises. When the crises was internal—a conflict between staff members or questions about the ethics of a member's actions—the tendency was to call special meetings of the whole staff to facilitate some sort of acceptable interpersonal solution.

4.2.4 Meetings

A staff meeting was a place where anything could occur and any issue might be brought up by even the newest member. They could ask, for example: "Why do we do things this way?" The staff meeting always was exciting because one never knew what might come up. It was a very unstructured process and a very profitable one. The process was very much of the reverse of what happens in a hierarchical organization and that was experienced as very exciting. It meant a degree of commitment that is just unbelievable. For example, once Rogers forgot something in his office and came to pick it during Thanksgiving. When he went over to the Center to get it, everyone was at work.

4.2.5 Growth-Promoting Atmosphere

An indicative feature of the Center was that people could grow beyond what they were initially trained to do. For example, a person who started as a coordinating secretary and initially did a lot of typing but also handled intake and was a general factotum got interested in play therapy. While doing her secretarial job, she spent part of her time in play therapy and gradually realized that she could not advance professionally unless she had more degrees. She went ahead and (after Rogers had left) even finished her PhD. For Rogers, this story was indicative of the growth people went through in the person-centered atmosphere that he and his staff had created and cultivated at the Center.

4.2.6 Clearly Specified Interface to the Rest of the Organization

Rogers realized that it was very rare for the impact of a Person-centered approach to move upward in the organization. The working of the Counseling Center did *not* change the administrative practices of the dean under whose supervision the Center was operated and it did not change the hierarchical organization at the University. Rogers came to the conclusion that an individual with a person-centered philosophy could carve out an area of freedom, as Rogers did in his interpersonal relationship with the dean, and then implemented this philosophy to the full in his or her organizational unit with those reporting to him/her. It is, however, unlikely that the Person-centered approach will seep upward the hierarchy unless those on the top are highly receptive and innovative.

Thus, the Center's staff had sufficient sense to recognize that the world did not operate the way the Center did, so staff members tried to meet that situation. For example, someone was chosen to formally present the budget to the dean in order to meet external demands with a clear face. This was necessary to get the acceptance and recognition from the overall organization that was hierarchically organized.

4.2.7 *Further Insights*

Some further learnings by Carl Rogers in the context of participative management are as follows:

- The wish to vest authority in the group must be genuine. If there is some resentment to share authority or power, feeling some need to retain control, then there needs to be openness about this.
- It is perfectly possible for an organization or group to function with some freedom and some control if it is made clear unequivocally what will be controlled by the one in power and what are the areas in which the individual or group is free to choose. However, to grant a group pseudo-control that is taken away from them in a crisis is a devastating experience for all concerned.
- First good communication among all needs to be established, then power can be shared. Failing to establish good communication first cannot be made up later. Rogers (1980, p. 40) shared that during his time at Wisconsin, he violated one of his learning he had acquired in Chicago: In a large research project with schizophrenics, he gave over the authority and responsibility to the group, but he did not go far enough in establishing the climate of close, open, interpersonal communication which is fundamental for carrying such responsibility. Then, as serious crises developed, he made the even more fatal mistake of trying to draw back into his own hands the authority he had given to the group. Rebellion and chaos were the very understandable results. To Rogers, this was one of the most painful lessons he had even learned—a lesson in how not to carry on participative management of an enterprise.
- Rogers felt that his influence has always increased when he had shared power or authority. By having freed people to "do their thing," he had enriched their lives and learning as well as his own.

4.3 Conclusion

To us, Rogers' experience with leading the Counseling Center in a way that was as person-centered as possible provides intriguing insights. Firstly, it is a real example of a unit of considerable size—about 50 members—that functioned along a person-centered way of being amidst a traditional, purely hierarchical organization—a large, renowned university. Rogers nicely described the interface conditions between his unit and the encompassing one, the faculty of psychiatry. Definitely, his trusting interpersonal relationship with the dean must have been enormously helpful, if not indispensable, for Rogers to implement—*within* a traditional, hierarchical organization—an approach to management that was so different to the "norm."

4.4 Personal Reflections on Carl Rogers' Counseling Center in Chicago—A Case Study

First, David is going to share his perceptions and insights on Rogers as a leader. Subsequently, we reflect on features that, in our view, contributed to the success in the Counseling Center.

4.4.1 Rogers as a Leader

Rogers himself had the unique quality of being a hard-nosed leader with such tender, sensitive and quiet characteristics. But his strength was so darn subtle, that most of those around him mistook it for some kind of gentle, passive acceptance of whatever. Yes, Carl was very gentle; highly accepting of every aspect of humanity, even those that others might judge harshly; and appeared passive because he hardly ever confronted what needed confronting except in a questioning, receptive mode. His stance was, I may not understand what you are saying or doing, but I'm darn interested in where that's coming from. And, if you are open and authentic, I will do my best to support you in your endeavor to live as fully as you are open to learning.

4.4.2 Naming the "Elephant in the Room"

Carl was the most natural and effective leader I (David) have ever met. He led not by command or by persuasion, but rather by his authentic openness and courage to name the "elephant in the room"—the emotions hidden because of their intimate and fragile yet relevant nature—intimate because they might be based on someone's personal history, fragile because they might run against the grain of the direction of the discussion, and yet relevant because they dealt directly with the topic at hand. That's the power of person-centered leadership. But that brand of leadership can be distributed among all the members of the group, though it helps if some individual or individuals can model that for the others.

In our Western culture, especially in management, humanistic or otherwise, it is hard to imagine a totally leaderless group, though the dynamic of leadership can be pervasive among its members. The most powerful concept we got from Carl Rogers was that any group that did not deal with the underlying emotional dynamics of all the members would be unlikely to reach its maximum potential as a functioning group. In other words, attending to the people-oriented agenda in an appropriate way is vital for succeeding as a group, team or organization.

4.4.3 So How Can Leaders Transform Their Organizations for the Best of Their Members' Growth and Organizational Success?

Here is a quote from David Ryback's book, *Putting Emotional Intelligence to Work,* recalling some of the talks David had with Carl while walking the beach behind his home in La Jolla:

> "So at each step of the way," I say, "the employee needs, or at least could use, honest feedback—less hierarchy and more understanding feedback."
>
> "You see," now Carl is beginning to show signs of excitement, "that's where the magic comes in—that special feeling when two people are really communicating, when the formality is given up anda real sharing is taking place, so both people are learning."
>
> "What's the boss learning?" I ask, knowing the answer, but wanting to hear it in Carl's own words.
>
> "The magic of careful attentiveness to someone whose welfare you care about," he says with that special glint in his eyes, articulating the elegant simplicity of his theory better than an armful of textbooks. "If that employee really feels listened to and understood—deeply understood—then he will work to the best of his ability, be eager to grow and will feel intensely loyal to his company."

Feeling listened to and understood are the keystones to this new way of management. This may sound so extremely easy, however, as you, the reader, may have experienced, can pose a real challenge, if the understanding is to be comprehensive, covering what really matters to this person in the context of the organization in this moment.

4.4.4 Humanistic Management

In our view, the best humanistic leaders are those with the least ego issues. The best humanistic leaders are not ambitious for power or attention. Rather, they are fulfilled by the dissemination of power and attention among the group, in a way that feels fair, relevant and authentic. They tend to query others as to their ideas and opinions rather than advertise their own and be more likely to appear hesitant and ambivalent, even passive, as they survey all the resources in the individuals around them. Humanistic leaders are busy giving up their leadership at every opportunity (as did Rogers), but their "leadership," at the core, is precisely their determination to give each individual the safe space to risk revealing her/his option to act in a responsible and responsive manner, to offer an opinion or solution to the matter at hand, and, ultimately, to make themselves invisible in terms of power and attention, except for the sensitivity and fair-mindedness so necessary to keep things going in a humanistic direction.

Besides Rogers' personal capacities, his trusting the staff, and sharing power, some features stand out that contributed to the success of the Counseling Center at the University of Chicago.

4.4.5 Keeping Interface Conditions

From the perspective of a hierarchical organization consisting of units or departments, the way Rogers and his team chose to interface with the rest of the organization is noteworthy. Rogers and his staff kept what we would call the "interface conditions." For the sake of being compliant with the administration of the rest of the organization, they transferred their open, flexible practices to a few rigid documents. This way, they met the requirements of the organization on top, and not the other way round, namely to interfere with the encompassing, traditionally administered, big organization. In brief, the "adaptation of practices at the interface"—from the side of Rogers—served to comply with the rules of those in power.

4.4.6 Staff Meetings

Another essential feature were the staff meetings, in which all staff participated and could bring up whatever they considered relevant. This reminds us of a community meeting in the person-centered tradition that allows each to be transparent, open and yet in a respectful tone und with a deep desire to understand the other. It is a means to renew and strengthen person-centered attitudes and thus to advance personal, interpersonal, and organizational capacities to move forward, whatever forward may mean to each and their organization.

4.4.7 Cooperation Over Competition

An essential dynamic was the setup that puts *cooperation* between staff members and their moving forward on *their own* projects far ahead of competition. Nevertheless, there must have been some degree of competition since resources naturally were limited and not all staff could stay endlessly long. Also, there was no competition—in the traditional sense—with the outside world, except for excellence and acknowledgement of research and practices and for acquiring research grants.

4.4.8 Business Perspective

In any business, profit is essential if the enterprise is to survive. A humanistic business not only survives in an economic world but also creates a working space where all associates can enjoy the process of mutual togetherness in a way that we were meant to be (Ryback 1998). Empathy is the lubricant that enables groups to mesh and work together most effectively. The research reveals that such groups make more money (Spencer and Spencer 1993), have less turnover (Spencer et al. 1997), get better ratings on their management styles (Lopes et al. 2006) and, most important, find their work most meaningful (Rode et al. 2008). This, I daresay, may be the wave of the future.

4.4.9 Person-Centered Attitudes and Skills

In our view there is, however, a characteristic that applied to the Counseling Center that would be hard to achieve for other units: the very core for the "functioning" and impact of the Person-centered approach, being the *degree to which staff members already had developed their person-centered attitudes* and thus were able to live them and to pass them on in the organization and beyond. Thus, we in the next generation, we who want to promote and facilitate the Person-centered approach that we have seen can bring about unbelievable transformation and result in unbelievable productivity coming genuinely from the people without external control or regulation—are left with a significant puzzle. How can we facilitate the personal transformations needed in people to really function in a truly democratic, truly person- or people-centered unit (if not organization) and bring about the unbelievable creativity and productivity that Rogers managed to set free in his Center?

Part of further elaborating on that question will be to listen and reflect to what four colleagues-friends who embodied a humanistic leadership style experienced and were willing to share in the subsequent four chapters.

References

Lopes, P. N., Grewal, D., Kadis, J., Gall, M., & Salovey, P. (2006). Evidence that emotional intelligence is related to job performance and affect and attitudes at work. *Psychothema, 18*, 132–138.

Rode, J. C., Mooney, C. H., Arthaud-Day, M. L., Near, J. P., & Baldwin, T. T. (2008). Ability and personality predictors of salary, perceived job success, and perceived career success in the initial career stage. *International Journal of Selection and Assessment, 16*(3), 292–300.

Rogers, C. R. (1978). *On personal power*. London, UK: Constable.

Rogers, C. R. (1980). *A way of being*. Boston: Houghton Mifflin Co.

Rogers, C. R., & Russell, D. E. (2002). *Carl Rogers the quiet revolutionary an oral history*. Roseville, CA: Penmarine Books.

Ryback, D. (1998). *Putting emotional intelligence to work* (p. 28). Boston: Butterworth-Heinemann.

Spencer, L. M., McClelland, D. C., & Kelner, S. (1997). *Competency assessment methods*. Boston: Hay/McBer.

Spencer, L. M., & Spencer, S. (1993). *Competence at work*. New York, NY: Wiley & Sons.

Chapter 5
Chairing the World Association for Person-Centered and Experiential Psychotherapy and Counseling

Jeffrey H.D. Cornelius-White

5.1 Introduction and Context

This case reveals the purpose, goals, and structure of the World Association. Subsequently, I share my experience as serving as a chair, focusing on surprisingly powerless leadership activities, virtual communication around the world, and reflections on the effects of person-centered leadership.

The World Association for Person-Centered and Experiential Psychotherapy and Counseling (WAPCEPC) is dedicated to promoting person-centered and experiential perspectives internationally. Its purpose is to serve as a forum for fostering exchange of research, theory, and practice and stimulates cooperation and dialogue with other psychotherapeutic orientations. WAPCEPC operates under specific principles that relate to person-centered and experiential approaches and an openness to development and elaborations from those. It operationalizes goals related to cooperation between organizations, supporting individuals, promoting related scientific study, and sociopolitical processes, including an international conference and high-quality journal (WAPCEPC 2000).

The structure of WAPCEPC consists of individual and organizational members, regional chapters with various committees and individuals to oversee different functions, all operating within the contexts of statutes and bylaws. There are about 505 individuals and 35 organizations (WAPCEPC 2012). The general assembly occurs once every two years at the biannual conference. The board reports on specific topics to the general assembly and requires a vote for any change to the bylaws or significant new venture. The board stewards the organization in the interim and proposes policies to implement decisions of the General Assembly, and a part time paid administrator oversees routine daily tasks. The board includes a chair, treasurer, and secretary and can include up to nine people by statute though

With reflections by Renate Motschnig and David Ryback

R. Motschnig and D. Ryback, *Transforming Communication in Leadership and Teamwork*, DOI 10.1007/978-3-319-45486-3_5

other roles are often frequently held and shared by board members, such as newsletter editor and liaison to the conference organizing committee. A conference organizing committee, a scientific committee, auditors, election committee, and/or small groups provide specific functions.

WAPCEPC publishes an indexed journal, *Person-Centered and Experiential Psychotherapies* with over 2000 subscribers in both print and online versions. The journal is led by a team of co-editors and includes dozens of reviewers and other persons (book review editor, copy editors, language reviewers, etc.) who help solicit, mentor, and publish authors' work.

5.2 Leader Actions, Failures, and Successes

I served on the board of the WAPCEPC from 2006–2010, two terms, and as chair from 2008–2010, one term. What did I say and do? A lot. There were thousands of email communications. Including some I'm proud of and some I'm not. I want to highlight a few themes related to my time as chair: serving the principles and guidelines of the organization, communication frequency, means, and quality, interdependence and facilitation.

5.2.1 Servant Leadership

The first thing I felt like I learned was that leaders have limits. In a large, democratic organization like the WAPCEPC they are meant to serve more than they are to initiate. This is an inversion of typical visions of what it will feel like to be a leader, or even what it has felt like to me to be a leader in other contexts, including person-centered context. I saw my purpose as chair of WAPCEPC to serve the organization, which means to follow the voice of the general assembly and follow the principles of the bylaws and statutes. As a chair, a difference from being an individual member, organizational member representative, and board member, I felt a responsibility to understand and uphold the tenets, to represent in essence the bylaws and statutes as a party in each discussion and activity. This resulted in leadership that felt "bad" to me because it was not clearly fostering the people around me, but essentially helped the integrity of the organization; it was a responsibility to a role, a contrast to the person-centered value of not playing roles, and being true to oneself. When board members threw out ideas or developed plans to further the aims of the organization, I felt like a naysayer to initiatives by board members, a devil's advocate, voicing the limitations of the board as essentially a group meant to follow through on plans and suggest new plans to the General Assembly more than to lead or initiate directly. While I tempered my view during my term through the influence of others, my first learning was that person-centered leaders have a different constituency than other persons in person-centered organizations, the constituency of limits.

5.2.2 Communication

There was an enormous amount of email communication in the board, particularly during my time as chair. The second thing I want to highlight is that email communication is a poor way to realize the core person-centered attitudes. A small study by Grafanaki (2001) found that they were all three primarily communicated nonverbally, not verbally (from three times as much with empathy to 23 times as much with congruence). I learned this the hard way. I saw myself and others, who are frequently seen as experts at listening, do a poor job of listening within this email context. And once that poor listening occurred, resolving conflict through email was even harder. We did result to telephone and Skype conversations at times, which were pretty successful, but probably lost potential potency and productivity of board members through these failures. On the plus side, the board did recommend to the General Assembly and the future boards to have and to fund more regular face-to-face meeting through Skype and in person, in part to increase the likelihood of person-centered communication.

5.2.3 Facilitation

The third theme is about interdependence. Any group of people functions best when leaders are so transparent and facilitative that they become invisible. This may seem a contrast to the two themes above, but it should seem right at home in a discussion of person-centered practice. Leaders are chiefly facilitators, persons who listen well, and help empower those they work with to become who they can be and help foster a group's goals through individual visions and actions. In this sense, I feel humbly indebted to the other board members I served with. It was a privilege to serve with them and see how the complementary functions of a group, despite and at times because of conflict, release wisdom and inspire others. In particular I want to acknowledge the other chairs of the WAPCEPC.

5.2.4 Other Chairs

Elke Lambers had served as chair from 2000–2008, three terms, the limit, and provided invaluable motivation, responsibility, stability, clarity, and insight to the organization and to me. Susan Stephen served on the board from 2008–2014, three terms, and was chair from 2010–2013. Susan epitomizes diplomacy. Patricia McCann, on the board since 2012, two terms, and serving as chair from 2013 to the present, currently fosters the aims of the organization. I invited each of them to share a few words of wisdom with two of them providing some impressions in Figs. 5.1 and 5.2.

First of all: I (Elke Lambers) am not completely at ease with the term 'transformational' – it is not how I would ever describe my intentions as a leader/chair of the WAPCEPC. I will explain.
When I became chair, the organization was still in its infancy. We had made some progress towards raising more interest in membership, but we had to battle some prejudice and misunderstanding. There were some very negative views of the organization and its supposed aims, and some familiar longstanding philosophical differences among the wider group of members were also reflected in the board.
Board members also had different expectations of their role and responsibility on the board, and, in my years as chair, I had to manage both the board dynamic and facilitate the development of the Association-with all its ups and downs.

The word 'transformational,' to me, suggests: creating change that substantially alters something, a remake or re-modelling, perhaps a revolutionary change.
That is not what I saw as my task, nor does it fit with my experience as chair, although I do think that in my years as chair I contributed to the development and growth of the Association-and there was change. But for me, it was about helping a process along, without a huge personal investment in one particular outcome.

I will summarize in a few points the aspects of leadership that I think may facilitate change and development:

- Understanding and meeting the dynamic between both the tendency and wish for change and the reluctance and fear of change, and respecting both--but perhaps especially the latter
- Having a broad cultural understanding: appreciating differences in perspective and experience in different parts of the world and in different cultures or groups
- Being sensitive and empathic to cultural perceptions, especially where there is fear of a dominant ideology supressing a minority
- Having a 'vision,' an idea of how things could be different, a confidence in the process of change, understanding of the ups and downs of that process
- To put it in different words: having an idea of the course we are on, and keeping an eye on the horizon, but being prepared to meet whatever is there on the way
- Being clear about what is expected of others, communicate about process and tasks, show appreciation and respect, trust other people's skills, encourage initiative
- Have no big personal investment in the outcome; humility; no big ego; self-awareness--understanding my own reactions and try to understand how others may experience me. Knowing my impatience.
- Encouraging others: to take risks, explore different possibilities, trust their contribution, value their strengths and different talents.
- An understanding that change and development is not a linear process--it goes in all sorts of directions, sometimes backwards.
- Leaving before I burn out; not feel that I am the only person who can make a difference, being happy to be part of a process.
- Off all these, encouragement is the word that has most meaning for me.

Fig. 5.1 Case interview with Elke Lambers, 6th July 2015

My (Patricia McCann's) experience of working on the Board as member and now Chair is that there are many dichotomies. Previously many in the community knew each other directly or by reputation. One no longer necessarily meets the Board members at the Conference at which they are elected, may not know them from previous experiences or they may literally live in a different time zone. This is the case at present. In order to address the various issues this raises, we meet electronically. I set up a regular skype meeting across the world zones having to be aware of changes in daylight saving so all can attend. The times range from 11pm Melbourne to 6:30am Caracas at the same meeting.

The individual members of the Board have undertaken a voluntary commitment, the purpose of the Board generally is administrative and the approach is person-centered. Taking these 'competing commitments' into consideration, what approach does a Chair take when life intervenes and a member cannot complete a voluntary undertaking which is a task that has important ramifications for the Board if not completed? How does one facilitate discussion on a Skype meeting when an Internet connection is unclear and drops out periodically, interrupting engagement in relationship and understanding of an issue?

There is a responsibility with each role of the Board and traditionally that finishes with the Chair and how one negotiates completion of a task is essentially relational and fraught.

Fig. 5.2 Case interview with Patricia McCann, 21st June 2015

5.3 Transformations

The question of who was transformed is most obviously answered, "me." It is my view that the person-centered approach operates by being open to letting yourself learn and be changed by another. To accept (unconditional positive regard) and understand (empathy) another while endeavoring to unconditionally accept and/or understand your reactions to that (congruence) really is about letting yourself be transformed. It is a paradoxical process of realizing how you are frequently powerless to directly change another, but not powerless to let yourself be changed and thereby model to another how they too can be transformed by being open to themselves and others. That being said, this process is frequently messy as can be. It is about suffering. And my time as chair in particular involved a lot of suffering! I also think that modeled being transformed. Likewise, the organization accomplished many things and more importantly did so through a process influenced by the person-centered approach.

5.4 Reflective Dialogue on: Chairing the World Association for Person-Centered and Experiential Psychotherapy and Counseling

In our perception, this case brings to light the issue of how a strictly hierarchical setup influences or directs or limits leaders who are open, transparent, empathic and, furthermore, who chair an organization that espouses these values. In that sense, this is a perfect case for our consideration, as it directly deal with the issue of how leaders can maintain some degree of influence on the organization's success, while being open, transparent, and ego-free. In other words, the case addresses the questions: As a chair, can I live and act according to my person-centered value base in a large, hierarchical organization? What challenges does a leader face who himself is being open, transparent, flexible, etc., and has chosen to chair a traditional, hierarchic organization with rigid statutes and bylaws?

Indeed, this case example challenges us to look at the best example possible, as the values of this organization (World Association for Person-Centered and Experiential Psychotherapy and Counseling) appear to agree with the values we are advocating in this book. So the challenges brought before us are pure in that they are not influenced by other value systems. Yet issues, very real ones, remain.

David: The first issue that the author brings to our attention is the role of maintaining the integrity between the bylaws and the intentions of others to offer initiatives counter to the bylaws. So what about the integrity of owning his own feelings and desires for the group, he seems to ask. He occasionally felt "bad … like a devil's advocate," instead of being true to his inner feelings

Renate: Exactly, I guess he was facing the dilemma: "What is more important, my own, personal values (that the organization that I'm chairing stands for), or the organizational policies that I decided to follow when choosing to become a chair?

David: Isn't that a universal issue in leadership—to go with one's own immediate feeling as opposed to the "politically correct" option? Where is the integrity dynamic applied—to one's own self or to the organization as seen more objectively?

Renate: Seems that somehow we'd need both, wouldn't we? Following one's inner world, guided by the desire to stay congruent, and not breaking the rules, respecting the organizational strategy, perhaps culture. Seems like a real dilemma, or, as Maureen O'Hara called it in her book, the art of "Dancing at the Edge."

David: Right. And there's one more intervening challenge that Jeff mentions as well. One of the problems of modern leadership is the reliance on e-mail communication. We'd probably all agree that e-mail communication is not the best forum for problem solving. Deep awareness and understanding of what others are trying to communicate rely on non-verbal cues, such as facial expression, body language and social distance. At least we can agree on that.

"Leaders are chiefly facilitators," we are told. This is a dramatic statement, though simple enough to understand. Would we all agree that there is a difference between an "average" leader and a transformative one? If so, then leaders, particularly those who transform others, cannot be mere facilitators, or can they? As Exhibit One, I bring to your attention none other than Carl Rogers.

Rogers' uniqueness was his ability to have so much personal integrity that others seemed to resonate to his comments and suggestions. Rogers spoke from his heart. Even when he advocated something highly challenging and unfamiliar to others, he was able to do so by sharing his deep, personal feelings about his experience in coming to his thinking, so that his unusual offering of something challenging the status quo, possibly in a very transformative way, was also a very personal statement on his part. He had this apparently unique ability to encase his deep intelligence with an openness and risking of self that crashed through the walls of normal resistance. What a show of personal power!

Renate: I have several reactions to what you just said, David. First, the easy one: I feel the same about Rogers: indeed, he had a special gift, talent, skill, whatever you like to call it, to influence others in a direction toward increased congruence and "functioning." Second, you call Jeff's "Leaders are chiefly facilitators," a dramatic statement and state that leaders, particularly those who transform others, cannot be mere facilitators. If the emphasis is on "*mere,*" I think I can go along with this, and to me Jeff's expression; "Leaders are *chiefly* facilitators" (italics added) hits the point. I think that precisely the fact to be facilitative, equally for your (congruent)-self that then can expand, *as well as* the others' (and the given context) in proper balance is a kind of art. Couldn't the "magic" of transforming leadership lie exactly in the ability to co-facilitate the organization as well as yourself as a vital part of it, in other words a kind of co-actualization between the facilitative leader, those being facilitated, and the organization?

David: I agree with you completely that it is an art of co-actualizing one's inner sense of conviction and experience with the values and needs of the organization being led, just as you describe above. Ideally, the leader who is a facilitator has a keen sensitivity to the ongoing process of the organization—made up not only of the rules that structure the organization, but also of the individual needs and perspectives of the leadership team under her/him. The leadership team is like a fine-tuned orchestra sensitive to the music played by each member—particularly as it relates to shared musical passages where their instruments must totally complement one another—and where the facilitative leader is the conductor.

5.5 Personal Reflections on: Chairing the World Association for Person-Centered and Experiential Psychotherapy and Counseling

I (Renate) approached the "World Association" case with particular excitement: How would the World Association for Person-Centered and Experiential Psychotherapy and Counseling—the flagship of the Person-Centered Approach, the organization with person-centered researchers and practitioners be organized? Would this organization work entirely on the premise of person-centered principles? Would they be apparent and prove to be applicable to leadership even at the scale of a large international world organization? What would be the result? How would the chair feel, and what would he reflect on his leadership experience?

At first, I was somewhat shocked and felt humbled. Terms like servant leadership, thousands of emails, and responsibility to a role were the opposite of what I had expected! Also, hearing the word "to follow" as dominating the activity of initiating surprised me a lot. So, was there anything left from person-centered principles that a chair could live by, pass on, and inspire in a large, democratic yet hierarchically structured organization?

Gradually, I started to ask myself: Why be so surprised? Isn't what Jeff described very similar, or even a mirror image, of part of what I was going through in one of the large European Union projects I had been leading recently? Actually, being responsible for the outcome also meant being a servant to the team and the EU commission! If a colleague fell sick and unable to travel to present our work package, I had to go, regardless of anything else because none of the partners could risk losing the large amount of money we all depended on for continuing our highly exciting work together—Apparently, Jeff's valuable case study appears to throw light on a general phenomenon of responsibilities to plans in large, intertwined organizations. Perhaps before reading on you may want to find your responses to the following questions brought up by Jeff's case, either on your own or together with your colleagues:

Invitation to reflect:

Did you ever experience being a servant while leading or managing? If not, can you imagine such a situation and the way you would react to it? If yes, how was that experience for you? Do you think you spent your personal resources meaningfully? Do you think you helped the organization or project by serving as a leader or chair? Could anything be done to alleviate the servant function or in any other way make your leadership function more rewarding?

In a large organization, statutes, and bylaws are in place to provide stability and continuity at the cost of flexibility, creativity, directly fostering people and staying true to oneself that the chair perceived as "bad leadership." In this

context, do you think we could somehow have both: Inviting personal initiative of a chair/leader along with him/her directly fostering people *and* 'mechanisms' upholding the tenets, statutes, and bylaws needed to maintain the structure and mission of a world organization?
Can you think of any alternative ways of running a world organization whose mission is to promote (and research) a person-centered way of being?Do you think that different core processes and leadership activities or talents are needed for a large organization that is only forming in contrast to an organization that has been in place and running for some years? If so, what should be different?

The case study leaves me with the impression that, for sure, there is a lot that the chair can bring in and contribute in terms of person-centered principles, like shaping the atmosphere, listening, and facilitating members' or the board's contributions. But couldn't there still be more influence when keeping the soft but revolutionary power of the person-centered approach in mind, an approach that nurtures its power from the candor, integrity, or congruence of people? With too-rigid rules and bylaws, the true effect of person-centered communication seems to be heavily constrained/undermined in a democratic, yet strictly hierarchically organized, large organization. Would it be too risky to loosen the structure? Isn't there a parallel to the self-structure of a person, where it has been confirmed by research (e.g., Rogers 1961) that a too-rigid structure stands in the way of optimal adjustment and full functioning? What might be at stake when allowing for more self-organization, for example by introducing projects that would be run by small teams and would—for some specified time and objective—have a significantly larger degree of freedom, creativity, and intensity of communication?

Consistent with the items of the "people-oriented agenda," forming the atmosphere and listening to associates are core tasks of a chair. According to Jeff Cornelius-White, an essential contribution can be attributed to the way in which the chair communicates with associates and the board. Listening for true understanding is an essential basis for any further action, and it means hard work around the clock. In our busy lives, however, we increasingly resort to email and computer-supported communication. While meeting virtually through electronic media, in particular through email, can facilitate some connection and is indispensable to help sharing amongst members worldwide, it has a limited potential for solving more complex problems and conflict. Also, often it is too weak to build strong, social ties between associates. Even though video conferencing (e.g., through Skype) has proved to have some advantages in problem solving when compared with email, it has been experienced that it *cannot replace* the social richness that accompanies face-to-face meetings. These are the settings in which person-centered communication can happen in its full power and is seen as necessary to be facilitated at least from time to time. If it does not, the quality of interaction and perhaps voluntary commitment change perceivably, as Tricia McCann shared (see Fig. 5.2).

Intriguingly, it seems that the larger an organization grows and the more structure and rules there are to maintain its stability, the more the leader's/chair's facilitative communication and willingness to serve the organization are in the forefront. Promoting its espoused, specified goals is likely to take precedence over the leader's or chair's creativity, which could be channeled by democratically chosen goals. Also, the larger and more globalized the organization, the smaller the share if direct, interpersonal contact with the chair, with all the ramifying impact—No wonder, Carl Rogers did not like formal hierarchies and was looking out for means to substitute their power by more flexible, adjustable, and above all integral personal power.

References

Grafanaki, S. (2001). What counseling research has taught us about the concept of congruence: Main discoveries and unresolved issues. In G. Wyatt (Ed.), *Rogers' therapeutic conditions* (Vol. 1, pp. 18–35). Congruence UK: PCCS Ross-on-Wye.

Rogers, C. R. (1961). *On becoming a person—a psychotherapists view of psychotherapy*. London, UK: Constable.

WAPCEPC. (2000). Statutes and bylaws. Retrieved May 22, 2015 from http://www.pce-world.org/about-us/statutes-and-bylaws/statutes.html.

WAPCEPC. (2012). Minutes of the general assembly WAPCEPC (World Association for Person-Centered and Experiential Psychotherapy and Counseling). Retrieved July 9, 2012 from http://www.pce-world.org/for-members/general-assemblies.html.

Chapter 6
Managing Change, Performance Evaluation, and Controlling with Congruence and Integrity

Eva Sollárová

6.1 Introduction

This contribution demonstrates the perspective of a person as a manager/leader who, besides working with the Person-Centered Approach (PCA) as a facilitator of others, also works in a hostile environment on her own behalf. The contribution includes four stories with four different positions and roles of the Person-Centered Approach in them: The first two are about the leader in a crisis environment facing the threat. The third one reflects upon being a manager in a position of a helper, facilitator (of an individual and a group), and the relationship dynamics or performance consequences it brought about. The last one shares the actions and feelings of a manager in a position of a "bad-news messenger." The comments of the author show what the Person-Centered Approach can offer to building and managing effective work relationships as a means to achieving good results, for being effective in a difficult crisis, or even hostile environment, and for being able and courageous enough to make decisions according to one's integrity and aims.

6.2 Author's Message

The fact that client-centred therapy works is undeniable. It is less clear, however, how the Person-Centred Approach works in business relationships and specifically in organizations when viewed from the position of a leader or a manager. Why is this worth discussing? Well, the impact of the PCA and the entire humanistic psychology on organizational development and management theory has lessened since the 1970s (Montuori and Purser 2001). One of the reasons is that in turbulent and unpredictable environments, managers are more likely to prefer practical

With reflections by Renate Motschnig and David Ryback.

R. Motschnig and D. Ryback, *Transforming Communication in Leadership and Teamwork*, DOI 10.1007/978-3-319-45486-3_6

instruments and interventions focused on outcome that lead to pragmatic results, rather than "touchy-feely," group process-type interventions, as some humanistic approaches were (and still are) perceived. Even in the PCA community, you can hear opinions that the PCA is not suitable for a crisis environment and fits only for the gradually developing environment.

In my contribution, I aim to demonstrate my perspective, which, to my big surprise, is not generally perceived as a legitimate agenda for the PCA. By that I mean the perspective of a person as a manager/leader who, besides working with the PCA as a facilitator of others, works in a hostile environment on her own behalf. S/he is either threatened by the pressure from the external environment, or personally/ethically has tough messages for others that evoke resistance. If and how the PCA works in those situations is what my case study is all about.

Even if my "case study" is highly personal, it serves as a means to demonstrate the PCA in key situations related to managing or leadership roles. These situations also contributed to my PCA-inspired growth in the position of a manager and a leader, with consequences that affected me, my colleagues, and the institution.

The contribution includes four stories with four different positions and roles of the PCA in them: The first two are about me in a crisis, even hostile environment, in a personally threatening position. The first one is an accusation, and the second one is marked by pressure on my integrity. The third one reflects upon being a manager in a position as a helper, facilitator (of an individual or a group), and the relationship or performance consequences it brought about. The last one shares the actions and feelings of a manager in a position of a "bad-news messenger" who has news that negatively impact on someone else and thus evokes resistance.

6.3 Brief Personal History and Context

I was lucky many times. The following three gifts are related to what I'm about to share:

- I've gone through Rogers' ideal conditions in an offer of "the most significant other"—my father—and by receiving the values of my family which I appreciated later and used as a source of my power and courage (and also for my person-centred way of being);
- I've gone through the Velvet Revolution in 1989 at the beginning of my professional career, with an ideologically clean, non-communistic shield which created an ideal prerequisite to unlimited opportunities of building a new environment. Since then I have been managing and leading;
- I discovered Rogers at the right time. First, his book, *Freedom to Learn*, fascinated me by the concept of the title that absolutely symbolized and described what I needed. Later, I went through the Rogerian therapeutic training. "Becoming" more and more "person" in accordance with the person-centred "way of being," I naturally started to be person-centred in all roles, contexts, and situations in which I found myself. Maybe because psychotherapy has not been

my primary professional context, I became sensitive to where and how Rogers' ideas are applicable beyond therapy. As (then) a manager, I felt especially attracted to PCA applications in this context. I first met with the idea of building and managing effective work relationships via the PCA in a presentation by Ernie Meadows at the ADPCA 2000 conference in San Diego. After participating in his workshops and trainings, I started to apply and develop the PCA within my own managerial roles as well as in workshops for managers.

Today I can declare I have had rich experience with managing change, managing unsuccessful organizations, or organizations in crisis. This might have directed my attention toward those types of managerial roles and situations that were primarily derived from difficult contexts, high demands on building goals, strategy, standards, performance, and results that created a lot of pressure, resistance, and conflicts in the process of change. My belief in the "power" of PCA brought results. I have presented more detailed comments and experiences elsewhere (e.g., Sollárová 2005, 2008; Sollárová and Sollár 2013). For the purpose of this case study, I will stress the concept of being effective in a difficult crisis, or hostile environment as a means to make decisions and be able to function according to one's own integrity and also to achieve one's aims.

The following case stories are selected from my last 15 years of managing, mainly in a position **as** the dean of a faculty at one of the Slovak universities. In order to understand the context and environment, some of main characteristics are as follows. I went through changes in both the internal and the external environments:

i. I accepted the rector's task—to design, manage, accredit, and lead the new faculty. For the past two years, this work had been unsuccessfully performed by two teams. The change project was met with aversion for everybody concerned;
ii. New laws weakened the power of deans and afforced the power of rectors which, in combination with an actual autocratic boss, was the reason for my decision dilemmas;
iii. Financing public universities got worse, and new rules were made for allocating budget resources according to performance indicators of institution;
iv. There were no clear standards of first-class staff functioning, no pressure on their performance. Low-work morale was typical as well as insufficient performance, both in education and science, coupled with a low qualification structure. In spite of that, people got paid and were not threatened in any existential sense.

In this context, I tried and experimented with how to effectively function with my duties and people in the environment that had changed. Becoming more and more familiar with the PCA, it happened to be a valuable source of how not only to survive but to thrive and build a new environment for others as well. The following 4 case stories are a look into the situations, into what happened. They are structured into three parts: introduction to the context, the story itself, and my comments related to the PCA.

6.4 The Case Studies

(1) **Break point related to the experience and awareness of my own PCA competence, a story that I call "Burning Joan of Arc"**

Context: Within the university, two teams had been unsuccessful for two years in preparing the rector's strategic task—the project of establishing a new faculty, primarily consisting of the existing faculties. This met with the aversion of all concerned. I was appointed by the Rector to do the task. Within two months, I proposed a conception in a way that did not threaten guarantees or finances of the existing faculties. The Rector approved it without any changes. Even during the process of approval, there were some concerns and aversions and, after the official appointment of my role, it was I who became the target of accusations. I was summoned to the Senate of the faculty where I then had been a vice-dean.

Story: During the Senate meeting, one of the members, my colleague (frequently attacking people and causing arguments) started his 15-min-long accusation and attacking speech in a very offensive and ground style pointing it at me. Among all those attacks, he also mentioned some main concerns about weakening the faculties by moving lucrative departments. I felt as if I were at the Supreme Court, just waiting for the conviction and burning at the pyre. When he finished, I stood up and, with my hands and voice shaking, I started: "*I can see, dear colleague, you see me as a destructive rat that harms this faculty. I am sorry for that, but it is all I can do with your message right now. And now I am ready to answer your questions…*" (I briefly and clearly answered the questions.) When I finished, I sat down and to my surprise nothing more happened.

Comment I had not felt competent yet, on the contrary, I felt confused but, despite that, it worked; it was my first complex experience, where PCA "skills"/qualities worked! What I did was to listen to everything my opponent came up with, accepting his accusations and attacks, and congruently stated my position. After that I answered the questions. In my interpretation, this experience is evidence that *PCA competence can help ME to be effective when I AM facing a conflicting, threatening situation* (accusations) and also realizing what "*benefit*" the PCA provides, when I "use it" in a *threatening situation* "*on my own behalf.*"

(2) **Making and going through a serious, important decision**

Context Once the faculty was established, I was appointed the dean. Besides the fact that any new project is difficult, other circumstances made my situation even more difficult: new era (the new Law, changing conditions for organising part-time studies, with a budget based on performance criteria, and an autocratic boss with his own rules). Quite often I felt as if I was expected to go to work without brain and spine. I was sure that if no strategic changes were made, the faculty would decline… and therefore I avoided taking on responsibility. Conflicts were escalating; my discomfort was obvious; and, after 6 months, right after a three-hour monologue that my boss finished announcing he would not ask, but he would be going to decide himself, I realised I did not want to do such a job and I made a decision to quit. I flew across half the globe, so that I could talk to Ernie about my dilemmas and get reassurance in one of the most important decisions of my life.

Story I announced my resignation in a month to a totally surprised Senate and the Rector with the words: "*I was not able to enforce the strategy I consider as the right thing for the future of the faculty and for which I am willing to take responsibility.*" Neither the Senate nor the Rector wanted to accept my resignation. My reaction was: "*I'm not asking. I'm announcing my final decision.*" And that was it….

Epilogue My predictions came true, without proposed strategic changes the faculty declined (I compared it to the Titanic).

Comment The key point for me in the story is that I didn't forsake my values, beliefs, or integrity. *Thanks to the PCA competence, I was able to make a congruent decision in a serious situation with significant consequences* (one of their interpretations as to why I abdicated was that an Indian shaman had brainwashed me). As a *fully functioning leader, I was in touch with myself, being aware of everything that was happening in me and courageous enough to make a decision* according to my slogan: "I live a luxurious life. I allow myself to be myself." The story happened at the time of the first articulation of positive psychology by Seligman and Csikszentmihalyi (2000) which became a more successful psychological mainstream approach with an agenda highly compatible with the PCA. For me, it supports seeing the PCA as up-to-date.

Follow-up to the epilogue After 4 years, with a new Rector, I came back on the "Titanic" as a dean, and below I summarize the 8-year deanship. That's what the next examples are all about.

(3) **Being a PCA coach and facilitator**

Context/situations As a dean, meetings and conversations with my colleagues were an everyday routine. And they offered a massive space for listening—insecurity, fear, pressure, threats, typically hidden, or implicit in various topics, people came to me with: failures in their professional career, tensions and conflicts among colleagues, but also not knowing how to handle a child in puberty. Listening helped to identify it. I call it "capturing calling for empathy." These encounters became the most rewarding "icing on the cake."

Story But my main task as a dean in working with people was to implement the approved strategy to improve the performance of the staff so that we could meet ministerial requirements on which annual budget resources were based. Another task was to meet the requirements necessary for the accreditation of study programmes offered. All this was mostly done in direct cooperation with heads of the departments for whom it was a new situation because, up till then, they typically were organisers and administrators of tasks proposing their requests to the dean and always receiving what they asked for. They did not have to consider the economical equation of requests and needs in relation to their own performance. My plan was to make them responsible for their department's performance and become interested in achieving better results for the purpose of ensuring enough assigned financial resources according to defined methods of performance evaluation in education and science. I made my plan legitimate—I prepared the strategy, had it approved by official faculty bodies (the Senate and the Scientific Board). The goal that I presented was to get to the 100 % level of the institution, and the task for heads of departments was to create a plan on how to get to the 100 % level of their departments and to guarantee it. They understood that it was their task to design an efficient plan for the required 100 % (at average it meant increasing their performance by 20 %). After the starting phase of accepting the task, at group meetings they went from proposing vague, non-specific slogans to actually good activities and ideas on how to achieve results and inspire each other. I tried to listen more and left my colleagues to come up with ideas. I was left with the role of a moderator, listening, and making clear how exactly they were going to control and manage their specific performances. The original crisis scenario quickly changed to a growing one, just because they "came up" with their ideas.

Epilogue The results were motivating: We became the No.1 e-learning faculty at the university, with several years of repeated highest financial resources per person from research grants, and with the highest increase in qualification structure of the staff in the evaluated 6-year period. At present, our performance evaluation parameters are used at the university level. As for the results, I will quote the rector: "*From a bankrupted faculty you managed to build a stable one*!"

Comment What I did was to transform "soft criteria" to hard, measurable criteria of performance, to make the heads of the departments responsible for creating the strategy, and managing the work. The *process of how to make people responsible* for their (managing) work was to have a legitimate requirement on what to do and then let them do it their way—using their understanding of strengths, preferences, and choices of their staff. They made plans for themselves. My role was to support what they needed, such as assistance in preparing projects, education, and training in improving skills and competencies necessary for new kinds of tasks so that they had everything necessary to be able to do their part, for 100 % performance.

The evidence that the PCA works in organizations is that it *facilitates performance* via *a person-centred managerial style* that transforms a crisis context into developmental one supporting and requiring responsibility of team members. As the best strategy used to eliminate resistance and offer conditions "necessary and sufficient" for change, the No.1 is "freedom to responsibility"—also in parameters related to performance and goals. For me, the PCA does not mean a "touchy-feely" style; it is a necessary prerequisite for improving not only relationships or atmosphere but also performance.

My experience confirmed the potential that Rogers specified as a new concept of leadership (group-centred leadership) where a leader would "facilitate the distribution of leadership and would accelerate the development of a group toward the maximum utilization of its potential" (Rogers 1951, p. 333), where the members of the group have the opportunity to participate and the freedom to communicate in a nonthreatening, psychologically open climate. I would not label such a style as "therapeutic group leadership" [as mentioned by Tom Gordon, in (Rogers 1951)], but in the sense highly compatible with up-to-date concepts or models either within or beyond the PCA, such as co-actualization (Motschnig-Pitrik and Barrett-Lennard 2010), PCA coaching model (Joseph and Bryant-Jeffries 2009), authentic leadership (Avolio 2007), or transformational leadership (Schaubroeck et al. 2007).

(4) **Being a "bad-news messenger"**

Context Besides the aim to improve the performance of the staff, my second main aim was to create the environment where work morale and ethic would become the standard. In some contexts, I changed the rules—for instance, I changed the system of entrance examinations for undergraduate studies to eliminate any subjective interventions. In others, I personally watched the procedures, for instance, being a member of examining bodies. Special "above standard services" in helping special "clients" to pass examinations were quite common. Once I found evidence of preparations for one such special "service" that one of my heads of department was trying to manage. He was the one who in general had problems with accepting my requirement to do things in accordance with ethical standards.

Story The event (doctorate examinations) was going on, and he assisted the two adult students (with high positions at one of the ministries) to draw up examination questions. To the surprise of all in the examining committee, they both said they had drawn the same number of questions. I checked their numbers and saw different numbers on their cards compared to what they said. The cheating was discovered! The chair of the committee responded to it as a misunderstanding and repeated drawing examination questions—which the students were not prepared to answer. I realised that I had to have tangible proofs of the ethically unacceptable behavior of the colleague. When the examinations were finished, I called him to my office and told him: "*Based on my experience at the exams today I am aware of what I can expect from you. It is a significant message for me and I will make all the necessary arrangements.*" It was not a clear message to him, so he tried to find out more details. When he found out I would not fire him, "just" not appoint him as a member of any examining committee, he was very much relieved to hear it.

Epilogue I decided not to fire him, only to be careful of what he would do till the end of his duties (which meant one-and-a-half years) and not to appoint him as head of the department for the next term. In the meantime, he prepared a counterattack and he started a war that lasted more than a year and threatened my election for the next term.

Comment My decision not to fire the colleague was *neither congruent* nor wise. I underestimated the character of the opponent and relied on the facts I considered to be the ace of trumps. In the fight, it had no value. I do not blame the PCA for this experience. During my deanship, I typically had been able to insist on standards I considered legitimate, and in this case I was inconsistent, so I faced the consequences.

6.5 Final Comments

The person-centred way of being equips managers with competence to:

- facilitate the other person(s) to become more effective in communication and interactions;
- build and manage effective communication and interactions within his/her own team and with his/her colleagues;
- be effective in one's own communication and interactions (especially under difficult or hostile conditions).

I propose the concept of the fully functioning or psychologically integrated person in the organizational context as a prototype for an effective manager.

The perspective of a PCA coaching or facilitating "style" is quite analogous to the therapeutic way of "offering" conditions that are necessary (and sufficient) for a change of the other person in the relationship, with the consequence of a more fully functioning person whatever it might mean for a specific person in a specific context or situation. This perspective is theoretically and practically ready to be applied, and I consider the PCA coaching model (applied by coaches and managers) one of top potential areas where the PCA can gain significant impact in applied fields.

Does this perspective cover the whole potential of the PCA for a manager in the organizational context? In this context, focus on objectives, results, assessment and evaluation, crisis, and (managing) change is typical for the present economic situation worldwide, and probably most typical is competition among companies. All this creates pressure in the work environment, especially for managers. The question is whether a PCA primarily focused on interpersonal relationships can compete with different approaches that are typically result-oriented. Is the philosophy of the PCA counterproductive to orientation towards results? Is the focus on interpersonal relationships the aim in itself? Or can it also lead to good, even excellent, results within the organization?

Most definitely, it can. And what consequences can a person-centred way of being (or PCA competence) have for a manager? In managerial roles and situations, a manager's task is to manage new, usually highly demanding or unpopular tasks or goals, to make difficult decisions, or to assert high standards. In such roles, his/her focus on his/her own integrity and a congruent way of communication is primary. In situations when s/he faces resistance, conflict, disagreement, critique, his/her attitude demonstrating empathic listening, and unconditional positive regard will create conditions for constructive dialogue. Together with a congruent manner of communication on the manager's side, it creates the correct ingredients to arrive at conclusions legitimate and acceptable to both sides.

In situations that are not primarily targeted at the facilitation of the growth of others but rather focus on decision-making, problem-solving, managing change, conflict resolution, task assignment, or performance evaluation, it means situations where managerial integrity and autonomy has a significant role, the PCA can serve on the manager's/leaders behalf as well!

Thus, for its support in building and managing effective work relationships as a means to achieving good results, for being effective in difficult, crisis, or even hostile, environments, and for becoming capable and courageous enough to make decision according to one's integrity and aims, the PCA has a lot to offer, indeed!

6.6 Reflections on: Managing Change, Performance, Evaluation, and Controlling

With refreshing openness, the author leads us through significant experiences in her life as a leader in a highly responsible, autonomy *and* performance-supporting position as a dean at a European academic institution.

6.6.1 Personal Integrity as the Baseline

The first case example illustrates the effectiveness (for the holder as well as the environment) of being fully open to the experience of receiving a message from a colleague, even in a situation in which the message aims to put down the person as well as her plans. By fully acknowledging the personal attack *as well as* the content of the message for what it is—namely the colleague's perspective, no more or less —and clearly responding to the emotional part *and* factual questions, the dean took the chance to demonstrate her integrity and personal power. This situation reminds me (Renate) of Rogers' principle: "Experience is, for me, the highest authority" (1961, p. 23). While listening to others can provide worthwhile clues, one's own personal experience would matter most and provide guidance. Rogers was convinced he could trust his own experience. The same, I feel, was true for the dean in the particular situation described. To me the case example nicely illustrates how congruence coupled with the intellectual or rhetorical capacity of providing responses proves effective, even, or in particular, in situations of bullying and attack at the workplace! At the risk of sounding evaluative, I allow myself to say: "Congrats to the modern Jean d'Arc."

6.6.2 Trust Your Inner Voice and the Process

To us, the second scenario, described as "leaving the Titanic before it sinks," communicates that if the environment, in this case both from the top and from the bottom of the organization, is perceived as too difficult, adverse, uncooperative, and you feel you would need to "keep a broken ocean-liner from sinking," it seems wise to rely on one's own felt sense and not waste energy to take on or push through a hopeless task or position. Interestingly, the "inner compass" proved right and the process brought a new and better opportunity to engage. As so often, the situation changes and there is a new chance with more prospect for success if we trust the process, stay alert, and do not get lost in frustration, chaos, hurt, and defensiveness.

While most staff would have taken it for granted that the Rector decided for them and over them, the dean stood up to decide for herself. Staying true to her innermost ethical values and not letting her being pushed to act on somebody else's behalf against one's values must have taken lots of courage, but eventually proved both right and effective in the long run.

6.6.3 *The "Magic" of Leading from Bankrupt to Blossoming*

The third scenario so gracefully illustrates the power—both interpersonal (as well as performance-related) of a leader/manager who:

- Manages to empower herself by taking on responsibilities with measurable performance outcomes;
- Puts a wealth of person-centered attitudes, skills, and consequent processes into place;
- Manages to empower members of her crew (faculty) to think and feel for themselves as well as the faculty in a way that allows for maximum participation, inclusion, and self-organization;
- Includes, supports, and trusts the crew in strategic planning and decision-making instead of autocratically dictating means to achieve performance indicators;
- Acts as a facilitator for her staff and does not shy away from meeting people at both personal- and task-related levels. Better "managing" of the adolescent son at home may free enormous resources for the workplace, as many parents will testify (won't we)?

Consistent with person-centered theory, the constructive climate and caring support in meeting challenges contribute to improved performance and, we would bet, also bringing out the best in each person in both her/his social and task-related responsibilities. Not explicitly stated in PCA theorizing, but emphasized in this book, is the collaborative attitude that the dean demonstrated. This way, the whole effort became one of actually co-actualizing potentials and working and growing side by side with colleagues and as a successful organizational unit with its shared vision and unique profile.

The "bad-news messenger" scenario illustrates a situation in which there is a lot of hiding and hence lack of transparency. When the adversary is caught in the act, his illegal, unethical behavior becomes undeniable. He loses face in front of a number of colleagues and the superior. Apparently, he would fear the consequences and no longer be free from defensiveness such that the person-centered conditions would no longer be in place with all the ramifying consequence. Probably, open communication between the dean and her colleague did no longer happen, thus crucially diminishing the chances of any reasonable resolution. Probably, to defend his self-image, take revenge, and prove his power, the colleague chose a dirty attack against the dean, not rationally taking into account her sparing him from any drastic consequences such as the loss of his job and more. Once communication stops, there is an enormous barrier between people and the means to break it are difficult to envisage and still more difficult to enact. We would say: No clear communication (in the longer run) means no acceptance and no empathy and hence the opposite of a growth-enhancing climate. The question remains whether, in such situations (comparable to "Titanic" for the false player), quitting would not be healthier and more congruent than avoiding.

This scenario strengthens our awareness of what has been with us for some time: Like congruence, lack of congruence appears to be contagious. So in fact each and every interaction matters!

One other matter: There remains the option of sitting down with the "cheater" who was caught in the act and allowing him to describe, without judgment on the part of the dean (at least while he was explaining his situation), his scenario as to how he came to do something that most would consider unethical and clearly mistaken. How did he understand the setting to decide on such actions? What were the factors that took him in that direction? Did he realize that his actions were wrong, or did he have some justification in trying to do something others would consider wrong?

I (David) had an experience with Carl Rogers that I am reminded of, which relates to this principle. I was invited to give a talk to Rogers' group about what I might do for his group. I did not plan for the presentation in advance as I was invited on the spur of the moment. Sadly, my talk came across very poorly. I had no focus and just rambled on about some of my thoughts. This did not come across well at all. Instead of criticizing me, Rogers asked me, afterward, with an inquisitive expression, what I was hoping to get across. His manner was truly nonjudgmental, and seemed purely curious. Of course, I got the point, that my talk was poor. I learned to do better the next time, meaning from then on. And I became a fairly successful speaker consequently. If Rogers had been critical or angry, it might have taken me longer to succeed at public speaking. But his nonjudgmental approach possibly made my journey to success easier rather than harder.

Finally, let us remark that we consider publicly sharing a broad spectrum of scenarios from one's experience a precious gift! So let us acknowledge the rich scale of experiences in this case study—some highly successful and others deeply challenging and real—with special gratitude. All provide a valuable source for learning! Moreover, the case study author's reflective comments tellingly argue in which way the Person-Centered Approach, as a mindset and skill, can help to accompany us: Given we subscribe to a person-centered way of being, its guidance extends to difficult situations as much as to opportunities for personal growth. Thanks, Eva, for communicating this encouraging story with such clarity!

Invitation to reflect:

How would you react if you spotted a colleague's or subordinate's unethical behavior?
Did you ever experience crises in your job environment? If so, can you trace the presence or absence of person-centered attitudes (congruence, acceptance, and empathic understanding) in the most recent crises?
Were the attitudes, or one of them, missing in others or in yourself while dealing with the crisis?
Would you agree that congruence, openness, transparency, or authenticity in the other person facilitates being congruent (open, …) yourself? Can you recall an example from your workplace? Does the opposite hold true as well?

References

Avolio, B. J. (2007). Promoting more integrative strategies for leadership theory-building. *American Psychologist, 62*(1), 25–33.

Joseph, S., & Bryant-Jeffries, R. (2009). Person-centred coaching psychology. In S. Palmer & A. Whybrow (Eds.), *Handbook of coaching psychology* (pp. 211–228). London: Routledge.

Montuori, A., & Purser, R. (2001). Humanistic psychology in the workplace. In K. J. Schneider, J. F. T. Bugental, & J. F. Pierson (Eds.), *The handbook of humanistic psychology. Leading edges in theory, research, and practice* (pp. 635–646). Beverly Hills: Sage.

Motschnig-Pitrik, R., & Barrett-Lennard, G. (2010). Co-actualization: A new construct in understanding well-functioning relationships. *Journal of Humanistic Psychology., 50*(3), 374–398.

Rogers, C. R. (1951). *Client-centered therapy.* London: Constable.

Rogers, C. R. (1961). *On becoming a person. A therapist's view of psychotherapy.* London: Constable.

Schaubroeck, J., Lam, S. S. K., & Cha, S. E. (2007). Embracing transformational leadership: Team values and the impact of leader behavior on team performance. *Journal of Applied Psychology, 92*(4), 1020–1030.

Seligman, M. E. P., & Csikszentmihalyi, M. (2000). Positive psychology: An Introduction. *American Psychologist, 55*, 5–14.

Sollárová, E. (2005). *Aplikácie prístupu zameraného na človeka (PCA) vo vzťahoch. (Applications of the person-centred approach (PCA) in relationships).* Bratislava: Ikar.

Sollárová, E. (2008). Optimálne fungovanie osobnosti. Aplikácia prístupu zameraného na človeka na rozvojové tréningy. (Optimal functioning of a person. Application of the person-centred approach to developmental trainings). In I. Ruisel a kol (Ed.), *Myslenie—osobnosť—múdrosť* (pp. 237–252). Bratislava: Ikar.

Sollárová, E., & Sollár, T. (2013). Person-centred approach: Theory and practice in a non-therapeutic context. In J. H. D. Cornelius-White, R. Motschnig-Pitrik, & M. Lux (Eds.), *Interdisciplinary applications of the person-centered approach* (pp. 177–192). NY: Springer.

Chapter 7
How I Changed My Leadership Style from Directive-Confrontational to Open, Appreciative, and Person-Centered

Klaus Haasis

7.1 Introduction

In this case, I'm going to share my personal story on how I, as a CEO, transformed an innovation agency by introducing humanistic, person-centered principles into my leadership style. When I was asked to write a case example about my person-centered perspectives in management, my initial vagueness soon gave way to becoming confident to contribute some experiences about my nearly 40 years as apprentice, manager, CEO, board member, and entrepreneur. And as so often, I remembered this fascinating book by Carl Rogers, the founder of Person-Centered Therapy, *On Becoming a Person.* Carl writes at the end of the preface, To the Reader: "Stated in the simplest way, the purpose of this book is to share with you something of my experience—something of me. Here is what I have experienced in the jungles of modern life, in the largely unmapped territory of personal relationships. Here is what I have seen. Here is what I have come to believe. Here are the ways I tried to check and test my beliefs. Here are some of the perplexities, questions, concerns and uncertainties which I face. I hope that out of this sharing you may find something which speaks to you" (Rogers 1961, p. xxi). This was written in April 1961 and is, from my experience, what is still valid even after 55 years.

I want to describe experiences from the time when I worked for a public innovation agency, financed by the government of one of the most successful federal states in Germany. The goal of the agency was to foster and promote regional innovation for the information technology and software sector, media, and creative industries in the south of Germany. I worked on building up innovation ecosystems with networks for collaboration connected to a global world full of diversity. I was the founding CEO and stayed in the agency for 18 year from the start of the organization in 1995. When I ended my work as CEO, the agency had

With reflections by Renate Motschnig and David Ryback

R. Motschnig and D. Ryback, *Transforming Communication in Leadership and Teamwork*, DOI 10.1007/978-3-319-45486-3_7

around 100 employees on its payroll. My main goal was to encourage collaboration between extremely diverse stakeholders. I tried to convince federal state ministries staff, public and private institutions, and the supervisory board to collaborate more and to support innovation activities. And I tried to give meaning and structure to the employees of the agency.

7.2 My Person-Centered Transformation in Leadership

For the first 12 years as a CEO, I had a traditional style of leading and organizing the company. I relied on my previous experiences of working in a big multinational chemical company. My role models were my father, teachers, trainers, and my former bosses. My leadership style was pushy and directive. I tried to teach and convince people that my thoughts and ideas were the right way of achieving goals. I showed the employees that I was always very busy and full of tension. I created a lot of conflicts and was in a constant mode of fighting on the outside and troubleshooting on the inside. With this style, I was quite successful in building up the innovation agency and giving vital and creative impulse to the regional innovation systems and its stakeholder from science and research, business, and the public sector. But I experienced myself inappropriate and insufficient in my leadership capabilities and incongruent in the way I dealt with employees and partners around me.

After 12 years acting this way, I found myself in the emergency room of a hospital with severe bleeding into the space surrounding my brain which could lead to death. After going through a divorce too, a therapist I had known invited me to join a training course for person-centered counseling in 2008. The course ran over two years during weekends, and I managed to finish it beside my work as a CEO. This was a turning point in my life and changed my attitude of leadership sustainably. The participants of this course were women coming from the social sector, such as nurses and street workers. I was the only man with a higher leadership position. The person-centered atmosphere in this group supported me in seeing people from a different perspective, especially in my work environment. Finally, I understood that employees are not "resources" but human beings who have the potential to grow when they receive respect and appreciation. What were the important learnings?

- I learned about the transformational power of groups.
- The group dialog developed and increased my respect and my mindfulness for others.
- I learned that all human beings are "just like me" with their feelings, emotions, thoughts, sharing about losing, sadness, loneliness, and despair.
- I learned that it is much more effective to sit in a circle of chairs without a table if a fruitful dialog is what is needed.
- I understood that it is important to give an appreciative and constructive form of feedback first before making any criticizing statements.

In addition to my person-centered education, I attended a course in person-centered organizational development and a course in hypno-systemic coaching. This helped me to expand my person-centered perspective by a systemic approach. I became able to see person-centered episodes in a wider perspective of systems. I learned to understand the goals and patterns of groups, organizations, and institutions. And I liked the ideas and hypotheses of the hypno-systemic approach. One idea is that quite often we are "hypnotized" by a problem—we fall into a "problem trance." I learned how to support people to refocus and to get into a "solution trance," and I learned to apply this for myself. The great thing about this training was that I was still working as a CEO during all these courses over 6 years so that I could immediately try the new concepts in my day-to-day business and "check and test my beliefs."

7.3 Some Examples

This transformation took place at a time when I understood that the system I had been in was not fully supporting my goals, ideas, and dreams. So I decided to prepare for leaving the organization to work as a coach, counselor, and mentor. I wanted to be more helpful in a person-centered and hypno-systemic way. So I decided to utilize this transformation process for preparing my exit out of the system of the agency and out of the political system around me. When I had started the training course to become a person-centered organizational developer, I was asked to define an organizational project I want to make during the course. I was quick to understand that my project was the exit out of the agency: How could I support the organization to deal with my exit? How could I strengthen the employees to be more self-organized and constructive in challenging times? How could I prepare myself for better self-management? How could I support myself in the grief of leaving while leaving a familiar and well-known environment after 18 years?

Here are five examples of important learnings I tried to apply over and over again:

- I learned to change my body language and body posture. First, I tried to smile more. I have a tendency that the corners of my mouth, in situations of high tension, turn down. This conveys a negative, tense, and unapproachable impression. I started to train myself in raising the corners of my mouth. This had two effects: I looked much friendlier and I became more positive. Embodiment research shows that tension in the cheek muscles triggers an improvement in the mood and a positive attitude toward others. This certainly works for me.
- I started to change my way of walking through the company. I used to rush through the corridors without looking right and left—the archaic way of hunting and focusing on the next animal to kill. I had cultivated this habit because I thought this was the way an important CEO should move. Applying the

Person-Centered Approach, I tried to focus on the people I would meet before I entered the building. I tried to slow down, say "hello" to people, have a short chat, and be open and positive.

- I removed tables from the conference rooms. This led to a completely different atmosphere in the rooms. There were less felt barriers and a different flow of energy. From a person-centered perspective, I see another important reason to sit without tables. Behind tables you see only half of the person above the table top. The other half of the person is "cutoff." My belief is that it is much easier to discount others if you see only half of them.
- I changed my way of conversing in meetings and with employees. I became more mindful about the fact that in every conversation, my share of listening would become greater than my share of talking. I always tried to let the employee or partner talk first. There was always something for me to learn from employees. In my earlier years, I had formulated hypotheses about leadership coming from my experiences in my family, schools, apprenticeships, university, and companies. In my constructed reality, leadership meant giving instructions, setting goals, and controlling the results. In the groups of the person-centered training course, I saw the potential of people as Rogers describes it, "the urge to expand, extend, develop, and mature." So I became more confident in revising my former hypotheses and formulating new ones such as, for example,

  - The employee wants to achieve something positive for the company.
  - The employee often knows something important the boss does not know.
  - The employee has feelings "just like me."
  - The employee had contributed in the past somehow in a positive way to the benefit of the company and this should be acknowledged first.

- I changed my way of initiating the process of change. Change always means a modification of habits and behavior and a breaking up of familiar rules and structures. Nobody likes to do this and most show resistance first. When I tried to convince people as an innovator of change, I used to start with the threats around and felt that it was important to change habits and actions immediately. I had some successes, but it was always difficult and consumed a lot of energy. So I started thinking how to start change processes more in a person-centered way. I learned that I first had to acknowledge the status quo and the achievements of others in order to get there. Now, I always start by giving appreciative feedback first and talk about options to change later. I also tried to do this with stakeholders or members of my supervisory board whom I had wanted to convince that my organization needed to change. I call this kind of pushing to loosen overly rigid rules "person-centered rule breaking" (Haasis 2013).

  I also learned about the power of the direct relationship between positive and negative interactions: As a rule of thumb, before giving one negative or challenging feedback, an average of 5 positive feedback comments is needed to support your communication partner to help cope with the negative one.

I have not become perfect in applying these measures and still I am not. This is a lifelong learning journey. And I found myself again and again falling back into the old patterns. But I learn and improve every day, which makes me happy and congruent in my way of dealing with relationships.

7.4 The Transformation Goes on

Two years ago, I ended my work as CEO of the public innovation agency. I understood that it was time to start something new and let the "system" I had been in open up to new paths. I put a lot of effort in closing this chapter of my life in an appreciative and reconciliatory way after 18 years. I had my shares of losing and big disappointments, and I had a lot of success, enriching relationships and getting social recognition. So I organized a big farewell party. My employees had designed a farewell card for me. On the cover was written: "You came with ideas and you leave us with values." I was touched by this description. One of my favorite managers in the company, who started as a trainee in my office, wrote: "It was impressive to witness your transformation from the tense Klaus to the relaxed Klaus." This was a wonderful confirmation of what I wanted to achieve. And my latest trainee, Jonas, who was 26, gave a speech in front of 150 friends and partners from 18 years of fruitful collaboration. He stated: "I wish to see everywhere more appreciative acknowledgment and support of resources in organizations. I wish to see more chair circles with flowers on the floor instead of tables in the conference rooms and more golden Haasis Rules of collaboration. Klaus, you are super!" This helped me to be thankful and humble and gave me the energy to open a new chapter as a person-centered and systemic coach, mentor, and trainer with my new brand "ask klaus!"

7.5 Reflections on: How I Changed My Leadership Style from Directive-Confrontational to Open, Appreciative, and Person-Centered

We (Renate and David) are particularly excited about this case from a CEO who decided to participate in a full training program in Person-Centered Counseling to change the way he run his business.

7.5.1 Clear Message

We are intrigued by the clarity of the message that Klaus Haasis manages to communicate. There indeed are a few basic attitudes that we need to hold on to and bring across in order to improve the interpersonal—as well as the personal—atmosphere in our departments. And, if you are a creative CEO, you are even more likely to influence the whole organization. The most basic issue is to feel appreciation for others and express acknowledgement unequivocally—not just once, but again and again—before making a critical remark.

7.5.2 *Body Language*

The case study also reveals that embodiment, expressed through one's body language, is no less important than words and behaviors. In fact, the way we look or move reveals a lot about us. Working to reveal our appreciation of our colleagues, saying "hello" to them or rewarding them with a short smile, can significantly improve the work atmosphere by making it friendlier and more open.

Invitation to reflect:

- Can you imagine having team meetings without tables? Do you intend to try out the idea of having meetings without tables?
- What are your ways of expressing appreciation and how do you realize that it is being received by the other (s)? What is it that makes you feel appreciated?
- Even though online video conferences do not provide real face-to-face contact, is there some special value in seeing the other directly in front of you on your computer screen? How would you rate the intensity of such meetings compared with talking to the same person sitting behind a desk?

7.5.3 *Lifelong Learning*

We fully resonate with the hypothesis that the employee or other person always knows something important that we may not know. This has been helpful in valuing others as they are and approaching them with respect instead of wanting them to think as we do or to be someone else. This message is easy for us to understand since we appreciate it very much when others let us be who we are, not wanting to mold us according to their wishes or imposing something that runs counter to our values. Honest reactions are always welcome as long as the final decision rests with us.

7.5.4 *Ongoing Transformation or How Far Can Boundaries Be Pushed?*

To us, it appears that Klaus Haasis' transformation to becoming more flexible, relaxed, appreciative, and congruent at some point reached the limits of a traditionally organized agency. There seem to be rules and structures persisting in such a system that—even with realistic effort—are hard or impossible to overcome. So, while the transformation in us continues in a self-organized, actualizing direction, the system may lag behind, likely increasing the level of mismatch or lack of coherence between the person and "his/her" organization. We wish Klaus even more success and fulfillment with his choice for, and path to, more freedom and self-oriented action.

References

Rogers, C. R. (1961). *On becoming a person. A therapists's view of psychotherapy*. New York: Houghton Mifflin Company.

Haasis, K. (2013). A person-centered approach to innovation management: Experiences and learnings. In J. H. D. Cornelius-White, et al. (Eds.), *Interdisciplinary applications of the person-centered approach* (pp. 193–198). New York: Springer.

Chapter 8
Make It Personal: International Futures Forum's Approach to Community Transformation

Maureen O'Hara

8.1 Introduction

Starting in the 1970s, after his relocation to La Jolla, California, Carl Rogers explored the potential of the client-centered principles for creating healthy communities. For the next 20 years until his death, he and a group of colleagues created the Person-Centered Approach (PCA) project at Center for Studies of the Person which convened large group workshops in which basic client-centered encounter principles were applied to temporary learning communities which lasted from two to seventeen days, in locations across the globe (Bowen et al. 1979; Rogers et al. 1983; Rogers 1977; Wood 2008). Though offering extraordinarily rich opportunities to explore personal meanings, the power of personal encounter, and the magic of large group processes, these groups were at best simulations and lacked the high stakes of actions in real communities. They existed within a therapeutic worldview within which participants who were already familiar with the basic tenets of Rogers' work already identified. It remained for future studies to explore PCA principles in a real community where the stakes were high and where the people involved did not already identify with the PCA.

8.2 Community Transformation in a Scottish City

8.2.1 The International Futures Forum

In 2001, I was invited to join the International Futures Forum (www.internationalfuturesforum.com) in a project to explore how people can take effective action in a complex, liquid world that is beyond established frames of reference

With reflections by Renate Motschnig and David Ryback.

R. Motschnig and D. Ryback, *Transforming Communication in Leadership and Teamwork*, DOI 10.1007/978-3-319-45486-3_8

and for which no "best practices" are available. This gave me the opportunity to explore person-centered principles in real communities facing a huge challenge.

IFF does not identify itself as a person-centered organization. It is an international group of senior thinkers and practitioners with a wide spectrum of experience in change processes at personal, organizational, and social policy levels. It is not a consulting group; it is a learning community. Its mission is to partner with those with responsibility for organizations and communities, so they can take meaningful action in a world that is increasingly complex, uncertain and not amenable to simple direct command and control strategies. Nevertheless, the following case illustrates some important ways in which person-centered principles form a meta-story in a citywide transformation.

IFF was asked by the city manager of Falkirk Council, which administers Falkirk, Grangemouth, Bo'ness, Stenhousemuir, Denny, and Lambert, with a combined population of about 160,000, to review their five-year plan and if possible give her and her team feedback about the plan's potential to solve a looming socioeconomic crisis threatening their area. The process was actively supported by the oil company BP, both as a sponsor and participant. At the time, the company BP had announced the loss of 1000 jobs from their Grangemouth refinery—a principal employer in the area. The Falkirk Action Plan (FAP) drawn up in response described a series of initiatives that would restore the local economy and reinvigorate the community. How that might actually be achieved was not clear, and IFF was invited to enter into a collaborative inquiry process to see how this could be accomplished. The IFF principles and process are described in more detail in the book Ten Things to do in a Conceptual Emergency (Leicester and O'Hara 2009).

8.2.2 IFF's Shared Assumptions

Though group members brought knowledge from multiple disciplines, they shared a worldview that though largely tacit was very much aligned with a person-centered paradigm. This was reflected in how the team members worked with each other and in some basic assumptions about the nature of human beings, their relationships to each other, and the nature of a healthy and growth-promoting organization. These assumptions include:

- Trust the life process. There is a self-organizing vector—a "formative tendency"—inherent in all living systems from single cells, to persons to societies that moves toward greater complexity.
- Individuals and groups often have resources required to address the challenges they face and, under the right enabling conditions, these resources may be released in the direction of growth and creative development.
- Transformative change alters not only how things are done but also changes the assumptions upon which action is approached. It occurs when there is a resonance between the consciousness of individuals and the group, and an alignment exists

between the aspirations of individual participants and the direction of group creativity. When feedback loops exist that allow for reflection and learning, an emergent process may unfold that brings something entirely new into the world.
- The leader's or facilitator's role is to help establish and maintain the cultural conditions that provide a fertile environment for individuals and groups as integrities to realize the creative potential.
- The conditions which enable the emergence of a creative process include active democratic participation, congruence, unconditional respect, deep listening, empathy across diversity, and a capacity to trust the group process.
- Transformative action within complex situations occurs when focused action is built on an embodied, holistic sense of a situation (O'Hara and Leicester 2012).

8.2.3 The Inquiry Process

The IFF process in Falkirk was structured not as an "intervention" but as an inquiry. The process we undertook was developed in a collaborative conversation between IFF members and the city manager and her staff. The first step was for a group of IFF members to undertake a learning journey to Falkirk. The group comprised a team of people who were deeply informed about their own disciplines but were willing to suspend their "expert voice" to indwell in the Falkirk situation as learners to get an embodied sense of the challenges facing the city manager and her team. Once we had a shared sense of what was important, IFF undertook several more learning journeys to visit people, groups, and organizations within the region to listen and learn about what the proposed FAP looked like from their diverse perspectives. The goal was to get below surface narratives and try to hear and understand what the various local communities had to say about their future. IFF team members' backgrounds ranged across economics, chemistry, public policy, community organizing, creative arts, psychology, information management, technology, business, and government.

Over the course of our initial engagement, it appeared to members of the IFF team that, although informed by good data and careful analysis of the existing conditions in the area, the FAP appeared to have a significant weakness that could limit what might be achievable. Though the FAP generated enthusiasm among city and business leaders, it was not sitting quite as well with many of the people of Falkirk, who felt disempowered by the process. "Another top-down scheme that'll go nowhere" one person said, expressing a common pessimism. The IFF picked up an overall sense of depression among many constituents and even some of the Council staff seemed doubtful that these attitudes might change. We were told over and over that the "people hereabouts don't have much hope for the future" (An exception to this was the city manager herself who had confidence in the people of Falkirk).

Though competently done, to the IFF members the FAP reflected a conventional worldview and showed little faith in any human, messy, or creative impulse that might be engaged. It seemed lifeless, heavily focused on jobs and other economic indicators. It seemed to be missing any *genius loci*—the spirit of the place—and we came to realize later, this was a significant omission. One of the achievements local people were proud of was the imminent completion of the Falkirk Wheel—a giant boat lift that linked two canals that crossed Scotland. When people described the Wheel, they often expressed pride in Falkirk's past preeminence as an engineering town. It was a nostalgic pride, looking backwards not forward, but it was pride nonetheless and it sustained them.

Listening to citizens, it gradually became clear that the model of change embodied in the FAP disempowered the citizens. It was expert driven and considered the people of Falkirk as recipients or consumers of that expertise but with no real role to play in the plan's creation or delivery (Leicester and O'Hara 2009).

8.2.4 Listening to Everybody

We made sure we listened to everyone we met—including the doubters and the naysayers—and we helped them listen to each other. We captured their comments on large charts that incorporated art, images, and poetry as well as ideas and analysis. We also took verbatim notes of what everyone said, including school children. We followed Max Boisot's (an IFF team member) model for helping groups move from inchoate embodied tacit knowledge to articulated or "codified" meaning (Boisot et al. 2007). We provided the Council administrators with detailed feedback based on our observations, and we made sense of it together.

8.2.5 Participants in the Process

Though specialists in our respective fields, importantly, we showed up as participants not as experts. We worked together with the city manager and her administrators from a place of humility and deep respect for the capacity of the people of Falkirk to find their own solutions. We shared our puzzlement, our hope, and our trepidation that we might fail. As the IFF working group listened to people in situations as different as a women's shelter, an oil executive's office, an art center, a museum, and a fishing community, we began to hear new metaphors and themes that did not appear in the FAP.

What IFF did was to engage not with a method but an "approach"—one that was essentially person-centered. This consisted of listening to the "language, the attitudes, the processes, the structures, the mind-sets that were limiting or risked limiting Falkirk's aspirations—and ways to make sure that they did not do so in the future" (Leicester and O'Hara 2009). We did not advise, interpret, or objectify what we heard looking for signs that fit any particular theory of change the way conventional consultants might, but sought to use empathy to discern just-below-the-surface intimations of what was trying to be said and then check it out with our co-learners to make sure we were grasping the meaning. Our standpoint was not subject–object but rather subject–subject as we practiced a form of listening typical of the therapeutic culture but rare in business settings, listening not only to individual voices but also to the flows, patterns, metaphors, images, aspirations that seemed to have a creative vitality.

And the longer we listened other voices emerged which had been there all along. People began to share ideas that went beyond the most ambitious proposals in the FAP. People shared that they were concerned that their children were giving up on Falkirk, seeing their future in Edinburgh or outside Scotland altogether. They expressed resentments going back many years about what some saw as an unequal distribution of resources among the five towns. They were concerned about more than jobs. They wanted a Falkirk their children would be proud of, which would lift their spirits and energize their imaginations. Some wanted better social services, others wanted spaces where people could create art, be inspired instead of apathetic, experience beauty, a healthy environment, grow food. They wanted a vision that had room to grow and that had a "wow" factor.

8.2.6 *Moving from a Plan to an Invocation*

Based on what emerged in the multiple conversations, the Action Plan was redesigned and relaunched as the "My Future's in Falkirk" (MFiF) initiative. No longer a plan—which has a predetermined outcome conceived by experts and decontextualized from the hearts, minds, and lives of the citizens–but an invocation, "a rallying call, an invitation, a spirit" (Leicester and O'Hara 2009, p. 24) As this spirit spread within the community, IFF stayed involved as supporter and sounding board. What has happened since has been astonishing.

8.2.7 *Unleashing Collective Creativity*

We found in this case (and in other projects) that once the collective creativity is unleashed, old limits fall away and the energy and freshness is irresistible. By the four-year mark, investment had topped all expectations in the original ten-year plan by a factor of five. Falkirk had garnered numerous awards. Many of these were for projects that, after decades of dependency on petroleum industries, reflected citizens' commitment to an environmentally sustainable future.

What is important here is that person-centered cultural transformation is a long-term proposition. Initiatives often start small and, when successful, there is a ripple effect as more people are inspired to take steps in the same direction. When the IFF team returned five years later, we were told by management that we would find a place that "looks better, feels better, and thinks differently." Our task was to find out if that was actually the case by conducting a new round of listening circles with groups within the community.

8.2.8 Cultural Transformation

This time we used an approach that had been successful with other groups attempting cultural transformation. Using the actual words of the various groups, recorded faithfully over the process, we created a set of cards which captured the community wisdom and codified it into key phrases that could be easily shared with other groups. These were printed onto cards that were used as prompts for further collective inquiry. "Make it personal"; "Free some resources for the imagination of others"; "Every project is a cultural intervention" were just some of the nuggets of learning put onto cards.

But the most visible sign of the shift in consciousness from expertise to artistry came in the form of a new project—the Helix Park—which was designed in the shape of a helix—embodying the molecular structure of all life. Most astonishing was the incorporation of the mythic imagination in the final design. Thanks to the award of a huge grant to complete the project, Falkirk decided to commission the creation of two enormous sculptures of Kelpies—water horses from Scottish mythology—at the entrance to the Helix Park. These are now in place and draw attention to Falkirk and the park from miles away. The transformation of the area continues, confronting new challenges and taking on new ambition as it goes. In a 2011 poll, Falkirk was named the best Scottish city in which to live—a stunning change in less than a decade.

Principles that are consistent with a person-centered approach have become an integral part of the local governance culture without ever having been named as such. Falkirk as a community and as a jurisdiction is operating at the "visionary edge of organizational practice within a traditional political and bureaucratic culture" (Leicester and O'Hara 2009, p. 25). It is actively cultivating the new in the presence of the old. And in place of the cynicism and depression that was there at the outset of the project, a new humanistic spirit animates the conversation so that it is commonplace to hear people refer to the importance of the personal, participation, empathy, trusting the process, facilitating cultural change, and releasing the inherent creativity of people.

8.3 Conclusion

What we learned in this and other community-level projects is that people are yearning for a culture that welcomes their full selves and makes room for them to offer their creativity and service to a greater whole. They want to give their best and want to receive the best of the other. And when this happens, transformation occurs and it is exhilarating. Once person-centered principles become institutionalized as "our way," the ripples gain strength and life flows within the hearts and relationships of citizens as new projects get conceived and completed.

8.4 Reflections on: Make It Personal: International Futures Forum's Approach to Community Transformation

8.4.1 Team Effort

This case example takes us a further step forward. It manages the transition from considering one leadership person to a whole *leadership team, acting in concert* based on humanistic principles. And this is crucial since, in the given situation, it is hard to imagine that a single person could transform a whole municipal community in such a significant way as described in the telling case. A team effort is needed, and analogous principles—although on a different scale—were shown to be applicable and effective in the IFF team as well as their work with the community.

8.4.2 Collaborative Spirit

We were pleasantly surprised by the responsible and collaborative attitude as well as action by BP on the one hand and the local government on the other hand, paired with the openness of the Falkirk city manager to include the IFF. When energies join, a lot can be accomplished, and when end users—in this case citizens—are respected and included as equals, the project has a far better chance to meet the citizens' needs and sustenance. It seems that the sustainability of the community's transformation was also an effect of the deep listening and consequent encompassing understanding that the IFF team accomplished to gain due to the high level of skill and experience of its members.

8.4.3 Shared Principles and Vision

The case example also illustrates the elaboration of a complex, shared vision that had "natural/cultural" roots in a broad base of the local population. It thus could exhibit stable growth and even surpass the expectations of economic experts. The case herewith confirms that trusting the process is a principle that could be relied upon, however, not without some risk. The size of the risk is hard to calculate, though, but the same would hold true when implementing the original, well-specified, predominantly economy-based plan. All in all, the IFF team was aware of the risk and certainly did not blindly trust the process but instead put their heads and experiential wisdom together to *collaboratively* facilitate the interventions and co-create the "My Future's in Falkirk" initiative.

☕ Invitation to reflect:

Can you exemplify how (some of) the basic assumptions listed in the case are mirrored in the working of the IFF team? For example, can you trace the feedback loops and reflections as the process continued? Which of the changes do you attribute to the "self-organizing vector"?
Do you have people around you with whom you feel you could collaborate to some transformative project that seems meaningful to you?
Did you find inspiration in this case study for trying to initiate some transformation in your context? If so, which one would you go for first and with whom would you team up?
Can you spot any items of the "people-oriented agenda" being realized in the IFF team's intervention?

References

Boisot, M. H., MacMillan, I. C., & Keong, S. H. (2007). *Explorations in information space: Knowledge, agents and organizations*. Oxford: Oxford.

Bowen, M., Miller, M., Rogers, C. R., & Wood, J. K. (1979). Learnings in large groups: Their implications for the future. *Education, 100*(2), 108–116.

Leicester, G., & O'Hara, M. (2009). *Ten things to do in a conceptual emergency*. London: Triarchy Press.

O'Hara, M., & Leicester, G. (2012). *Dancing at the edge: Competence, culture and organization for the 21st century*. Axminster, Devon, UK: Triarchy Press.

Rogers, C. R. (1977). *On personal power*. New York, NY: Delta.

Rogers, C., Wood, J. K., O'Hara, M. M., & Fonseca, A. H. L. D. (Eds.). (1983). *Em busca da vida*. São Paulo: Summus.

Wood, J. K. (2008). *Carl Rogers' person-centered approach: Towards and understanding of its implications*. Ross-on-Wye: PCCS Books.

Part III
For the Manager and Team Member

Chapter 9
The Interpersonal Relationship at Work: The Preconditions of Transformative Communication

I have learned, however, that realness or genuineness, or congruence—whatever term you wish to give it—is a fundamental basis for the best of communication.

Rogers (1980, p. 15)

This chapter focuses on:

- Factors that make up a constructive climate and why it is crucial
- Qualities and skills that facilitate a constructive climate and progress at work, including listening for understanding, a nonjudgmental attitude, respect, facilitative openness, and inclusion
- How these qualities are perceived by team/group members, what tendencies they usually invoke, and which problems may occur despite the constructive intent to provide these qualities at the workplace
- The directions managers and team members tend to develop in a person-centered climate
- What person-centered managers often struggle with, such as external regulations, conflicts between team members, lack of transparency of stakeholders, tight, rigid schedules, and an incompatible culture of the encompassing organizational unit or system
- Coherence, or lack thereof, between the organization's or project's objectives and person-centered attitudes.

9.1 Introduction

Much has been written about what furniture, shape, size, and arrangement of tables, room size, color, light, food, smell, etc., contribute to shaping the atmosphere of a room. Far more sophisticated, though perhaps less visible, is the contribution of people and their relationships on creating a constructive atmosphere. In this chapter, we shed some light on the oft concealed factor of interpersonal relationships and their essential contribution to keeping people motivated and making meetings and

R. Motschnig and D. Ryback, *Transforming Communication in Leadership and Teamwork*, DOI 10.1007/978-3-319-45486-3_9

Table 9.1 Directions of transformative communication

The direction of change is from	To an increase in
Rigid organizational structure	Flexible structures, based on flow of communication
Rigid policies	Policies interpreted according to particular challenges
Rigid personnel policies	Flexibility to account for unique situations
Personal considerations being discouraged	Personal considerations being encouraged
Individual achievement only encouraged	Group achievement also encouraged
Sharp boundaries between boss and employee	Individuals being supported to move to their level of potential
Customers on the other side	Customers being seen as partners
Strictly fulfilling the contract	Customer satisfaction

projects succeed, or, equally, on the opposite side—leading projects to failure. Intriguingly, for example, in the realm of IT projects, the predominant problematic factors are not methodological or technological issues but rather people issues such as lack of clear goals, missing executive support, and poor or inadequate communication among project stakeholders and the project team (Standish 2016).

In order to reveal the essentials of a constructive, collaborative atmosphere, we are going to take up the ubiquitous challenge of good listening. This is because, first, it is still lacking in so many people (see also Chap. 17). Second, its function is being repeatedly underestimated and not taken seriously enough, in particular in hierarchical organizations that believe in maintaining strict control. Third, we have some evidence that young managers, in particular, consider it a key issue and perceive listening well to be a challenging yet crucial component of competent leadership (iCom Team 2014) needing perfection!

The second part of this chapter focuses on interpersonal qualities and skills that facilitate a constructive climate and progress at work. To illustrate and appreciate the impact of these qualities, several concrete cases and dilemmas from the work context are provided aiming at useful, personal insight for both managers/leaders and team members. The resulting direction of changes by transforming communication to encompass the qualities discussed in this chapter is sketched in Table 9.1.

9.2 Active Listening in the Workplace

Before recalling Rogers' groundbreaking work on active listening, let us share some excerpts from students' reactions to Renate's recent course on communication and soft skills at the masters level of computer—and service science.

"An activity that I appreciated the most was 'active listening.' From my own experience, I can tell that it is applicable in every area of life, when there are problems in communication. I am a bit introvert and I never had high confidence in communication with people or in presenting some topic in front of the crowd. I was expecting that it could improve in this course somehow, but I didn't know how much. Now after completing this course, I can honestly say that it did work."

"I would probably say that the most valuable skill is active listening—it's part of all the other skills and very useful in both personal and professional life."

"I have learned a lot of interesting stuff, like the importance of active listening and that the spoken words are just a minority of information revealed."

"I hated/liked the active listening activity. I hated it because it was by far the hardest thing from the whole course. I have terrible listening skills and I have to try REALLY hard to listen. If I think of something else, or even just look elsewhere I'm lost in the conversation. But I know it's not polite to ignore, and it isn't even good for my learning abilities, so I liked it because I had the opportunity to work on it, realize how bad I am at it, and now I know I have to work on it later too. We often shared how important we experienced it to be even in other aspects of our lives."

"We processed very good topics, and we gained a lot of knowledge from each topic. We learned how to listen, how to speak, how to empathize with people, how to become a leader, motivator… It's very hard to choose only one thing. But if I have to choose I will choose listening. The REAL careful listening is most important and best way to communicate with other people."

Almost half a century ago, Carl Rogers and Richard Farson published their famous article on active listening in a business journal (Rogers and Farson 1987). In their article, they present the attitudes as well as do's and don'ts in a most compelling fashion. This is why the Resource Box 9.1 heavily draws on Rogers' and Farson's work.

Resource Box 9.1 Attitudes, do's, and don'ts of effective active listening at work

Active Listening: Attitudes, insights, do's, and don'ts

- To be effective at all in active listening, one must have a *sincere interest* in the speaker. We need to convey the idea: "I think that what you feel is important. I respect your thoughts and, even if I don't agree with them, I know they are valid for you. I feel sure that you have a contribution to make and I want to understand you."
- If we are only making a pretense, the speaker will quickly pick up on this.
- Developing an attitude of sincere interest in the speaker can happen only by willing to *risk seeing the world from the speaker's perspective*.
- Active listening tends to lead to *constructive changes* in the listener. It is a source of rich information and deep, positive relationships. For the speakers, it makes clear what they are feeling and thinking. It need not

pose a threat to the individual's self-image. He or she does not have to defend it but can freely explore it and then may be in a position to change.

- To ensure *good communication between associates* up and down the line, *every* person who feels the responsibility can set a pattern of active listening and the tone of the interaction. The behavior exhibited by one person will eventually tend to influence similar behavior in the other person.

To do:

- *Create a climate* which is neither critical nor evaluative nor moralizing. It must be one of equality and freedom; permissiveness and understanding; and acceptance and warmth. It is a climate in which the individual feels safe enough to assimilate new experiences and new values.
- Listen for the *total meaning* of the message for greater understanding. Besides the content, it entails the underlying feeling or attitude that gives the message meaning.
- Get inside the speaker's point of view and try to *understand* what they are communicating. The speaker can get a sense that we are seeing things from his or her point of view.
- In some instances, the content is less important than the feelings underlying it. In those cases, to catch the full flavor of the meaning, one must *respond particularly to the feeling* component.
- *Note all cues*. Besides verbal expression, we need to become aware of several kinds of communication such as voice inflection, points of hesitation, facial expression, body language, eye movement, and many more. In online communication, these cues are reduced and in part substituted by various symbolic expressions.

To avoid:

- Avoid trying to *change* the other's way of looking at things the way we see the situation.
- Avoid passing *judgment*, whether positive or negative, as it makes free expression difficult.
- Avoid fast and easy *advice*. Advice is often seen as an effort to change a person and thus serve as a barrier to free expression. Moreover, such advice is seldom taken, unless explicitly asked for, and based on prior listening and effort to understand the often complex situation of the person seeking advice.

To provide readers with an up-to-date perception of junior leaders of IT teams, Table 9.2 lists the potentials as well as problems of active listening as recalled by a group of 14 team leaders during an international workshop on person-centered communication in spring, 2015.

Table 9.2 Potentials and problems of active listening as indicated by junior team leaders

Potentials/benefits of active listening	Problems of active listening
Establishing connection	May seem artificial
Getting deeper understanding	May not be rewarding for the listener
Better insight as a basis for a solution	Hard, if little interest in the subject matter
Feeds patience	Costs time
Speaker gets space to express himself/herself	Can be exhausting
Improved relationship	
Feeling valued	

It is over half a century since Rogers and Roethlisberger wrote about barriers and gateways to communication in the renowned journal, *Harvard Business Review*. Nowadays the value of active listening is widely acclaimed. Nevertheless, there remain several challenges to good and effective communication at work. Resource Box 9.2 summarizes some evocative ideas.

Resource Box 9.2 Active listening in business: Necessary but not sufficient. Items in part inspired by John J. Graham's retrospective commentary to Rogers and Roethlisberger (1991).

Active listening in business: Necessary but not sufficient.

- In a time of tough competition and job insecurity, the process of establishing trust is not as linear as opening up and being listened to by the manager. When one fears losing a job and the others are obliged to downsize their teams, open conversation would rather be avoided by either side.
- Establishing trust happens through a complex process in which a person's behavior, character, managerial competence, etc., all play a role beside their capacity to listen. Thus, whether or not an employee opens up depends on several aspects of confidence.
- An ever-increasing barrier to good communication is the pressure of time. In a culture with emphasis and valuing of speed, we need to embrace this criterion and learn to communicate effectively in particular when time is of the essence.
- We need to appreciate that understanding is essential for decision-making and conflict resolution. However, understanding does not necessarily mean a good decision or resolution. Furthermore, it is a mutual more than a one-sided understanding that is needed. Thus, we are always dependent on the other side and their capacity for understanding as well as on capacities for decision-making, conflict resolution, collaboration, negotiation, etc.
- Managers, in particular, face a double challenge. On the one hand, they need to be able to listen nonjudgmentally; on the other hand, they are

constantly called upon to evaluate and make judgments about projects, budgets, strategies, etc. Thus, they crucially need the capacity to live the two-agenda metaphor, namely to be capable of non-evaluative listening while also being able to judge and make good decisions based on all the evidence gained from their multiple senses and information channels.

But how well does listening work in today's organizations? In a recent study (see Part 4 of this book), the vast majority of human resource professionals experienced deficits in listening in their workplace. A telling sample response was: "If I've really got a problem, there's no one to turn to."

While positive examples tend to inspire constructive attitudes, often realizing what's going wrong and making the problem evident from the viewpoint of an observer can be illuminating too. It has the potential to illustrate adverse behavior from the safe perspective of an observer and hence can avoid personal defense mechanisms to block out the experience as something threatening our self-image. Thus, we invite you to participate in the following three vignettes:

Vignette 1: *Different frames of reference, standpoints, and paths to reach the goal or "Whom should I trust more, an experienced colleague or myself?"*

As an experienced manager in the USA, you have invested lots of energy and time into a gifted, junior marketing expert—let us call her Tina. In the past, she had worked with you on a project that went quite well, but in your view she could have done even better, if you had had more experienced colleagues to support the marketing. Tina is responsible for the marketing strategy of your new event-management system that shall be rolled out soon. While you are convinced that the major market for the system is going to be your company's contacts and the close surroundings, she thinks differently. She is very sympathetic with Asian culture and wants to market the system in the Far East, assembling evidence that this would bring much more revenue. She is really eager to travel to a fair in Shanghai and present the system there. She seems bored with the local market and stakeholders, arguing that the new system is just a tiny bit better than others, and hence, she is not sure she could convince local customers to buy it.

So, how to deal with the dilemma? Recently, each day you come to work you feel some tension about the difference. While you cooperate successfully on other issues, you feel the difference is always there, "remains in the air," and is consuming some of your mental resources. A solution needs to be reached soon.

Vignette 2: *Rigid external requirements or things turn out to be different than originally perceived*

A project proposal for a project with seven international partners was accepted. Each partner contributed to putting the proposal and the work-breakdown structure together, based on the best of every partner's knowledge. Throughout the project, slight adaptation of the proposal needed to be made in order to meet the prospects of reality. For example, skill-training exercises had to be implemented, not just interlinked, since existing ones were found to be missing some key criteria. Due to extra work, at the end, time became very limited and the project needed to be validated. One partner started validation in time and strictly based on the project proposal, since this would be the only way to finish the validation process on time. However, other partners optimized the validation process to better suit the adaptations made throughout the project and claimed that their validation protocol needed to be followed by all partners! No one was prepared to step back from their position, since that would have rendered part of their work irrelevant and they could not validate the product.

As a consequence, some partners were upset at the others and stopped communicating, since they felt the others did not hear them and were harming the project's success.

It is not hard to find variations of the examples given above in managers' practice. We assume that you will have your personal reaction and tips on how to go about resolution. But before we share our thoughts; let us turn our attention to the following conversation between a team member and his manager.

Vignette 3: *Running out of time—a problem-solving dialogue*

Manager	We need to deliver the code tomorrow; otherwise, we will have to pay a penalty as it is written in the contract. Any ideas?
Team member	Yes, tomorrow is the scheduled date of delivery. No doubt, we could deliver the software and mask a few mistakes that we won't manage to fix till tomorrow. So we're going to fulfill the formalities. However we'll need much more additional time for re-installations and bug-fixes once the system is delivered and this affects both the customer and us. I guess it would be wise to talk to the folks at the customer and let them know that we'd need two more days for thorough, systematic testing that would help to save time in the longer run. Would that be an option for you?
Manager	Not quite, since they arranged everything for the installation and the training to happen the next few days. So they might really be annoyed to hear about the delay on such a short notice and insist that we pay the difference
Team member	Right, I haven't considered that.—O.k., [pause] let me see if there isn't an option to run the training on our servers– for the training. the software is fine and an occasional bug could be tolerated and logged. So part of our team could still work on fixing the sophisticated bugs and we wouldn't block our customer. What do you think?
Manager	This starts getting a bit complicated and definitely bears some risk on our side. Hmm. [pause]—But why not, it really does make sense! Well, … if you think this would help us to deliver first

quality software finally, without paying the penalty and annoying the customer, I feel you should go ahead and talk to them. Let me know if I can support you in any way. Good luck!

What all three vignettes have in common is that expectations are not met. The perceived reality at hand differs from some preconceived, planned state, like finishing on time, and achieving consensus. Differences come to the surface more or less clearly, more or less annoyingly, and more or less as being perceived as threatening—like having to pay penalty for a delay—or acceptable and natural—like needing to talk to arrange for the best possible solution under given circumstances. In times characterized by a very fast pace and almost instant communication cycles, change is inevitable. Hence, in our view, it is essential to be able to deal with change—which means—to be as open as possible to the current reality and to communicate and collaborate toward meeting the reality as it is perceived at the given moment. However, this requires one to listen very well to oneself and to others and to try to understand the essence of what is going on. There seems to be no way to achieve this without good, precise, and deep empathic listening as well as responding. How else could the manager and team member in the third vignette above come to a solution that is agreeable to both parties and furthermore uses both parties' resources sensitively and meaningfully?

You may interject, why we should care about using the other's resources sparingly. Why should we care, isn't it *their* job? Sure it is; however, if we want to stay in business with the other, ignoring their side may become costly and, sooner rather than later, will make them withdraw. This is totally different, if we accept the others as partners and acknowledge their issues as our issues as well, joining energies to find a solution that fits both. The same holds true for us. If the other side ignores our needs, we might take the first opportunity to quit the business.

Note the inherent reciprocity between (business) partners. One's communication and behavior does not stand alone, and it tends to be intricately intertwined with the other. We can have a strong influence on the other partner and the atmosphere. However, if our partner stands in constant opposition, our person-centered, constructive attitude cannot (fully) unfold and may be even swallowed by authoritarian, directive practices. But if we get a handle on our partner, for example, if the team member in our vignette is understood in his message to look for the most agreeable solution for both parties, then the trust can grow and the business relationship can become more transparent and mutually respectful.

Invitation to reflect:
If you were the manager in the vignette Running out of time how would you deal with the situation? Would you tend to turn to your customer or would you rather deliver the (still faulty) software product? What would your course of action depend on? What would you say?

After having illustrated a few examples in which flexibility and an effective flow of communication within a constructive climate are needed, let us investigate into some more depth the foundations of a constructive, interpersonal climate.

9.3 Three Interpersonal Attitudes as Cornerstones of a Constructive Climate

Rogers postulated three attitudes for a relationship to be growth-promoting. These attitudes (or "ways of being") need to be lived by at least one person and be perceived by the other person(s):

- Empathic understanding (sometimes briefly but imprecisely termed "empathy")
- Acceptance or unconditional positive regard
- Congruence or genuineness, authenticity, and transparency.

According to Rogers (1980, p. 115), these attitudes form the basis of a constructive climate that enables a largely unbiased perception of any situation, and *significant learning*—learning that makes a difference to one's life. If these attitudes are perceived at least to some degree, then people can become the best they can (Rogers 1961). Since many of us devote the majority of our time and effort to our work–life, it seems essential to consider what Rogers' three attitudes mean for interpersonal relationships at work and how they influence the interplay of the 2agendas@work

9.3.1 Empathic Understanding, Empathy

Empathic understanding originates in the longing for a deep understanding from the perspective of the other person. Rogers describes the respective feeling as follows:

> … I feel a continuing desire to understand—a sensitive empathy which each of the client's feelings and communications as they seem to him at that moment. Acceptance does not mean much until it involves understanding. It is only that I understand the feelings and thoughts [..]—it is only as I see them as you see them and accept them and you, that you feel really free to explore… your inner and often buried experience… There is implied here a freedom to explore oneself at both conscious and unconscious levels (Rogers 1961 p. 35).

Rogers defines empathy as follows:

> The state of empathy, or being empathic, is to perceive the internal frame of reference [i.e., the realm of experience which is available to the awareness of an individual at a given moment] of another with accuracy, and with the emotional components and meanings which pertain thereto, as if one were the other person, but without ever losing the 'as if' condition (Rogers 1959, p. 210).

In a recent survey, Seyhan Güver (Renate's Ph.D. student) asked managers of intercultural projects what empathy meant to them (Güver 2016). We were pleasantly surprised at the accuracy of the managers' understanding and will share selected responses in a later chapter on multicultural teams.

The following examples illustrate empathic and less-empathic responses in work-related conversations.

Case scenario, part 1

The employee says: "When I hear the word 'assessment,' I always think of something really upsetting."

(1) Less-empathic responses:
Aren't you exaggerating a little? (judgemental)
Why's that? There must be something to it. (diagnosing, analyzing)
You need not be upset, you'll do fine. (saying how one should not feel)
If you always think negatively, you'll never become successful. (generalizing, instructing)

(2) Empathic response-variants:
You tend to feel upset about what would happen?
Just the term makes you anxious.
So you would like to avoid it.
"Assessment" comes with something really unpleasant for you.

Case scenario, part 2

A team member says: "I can't help thinking that the coordinator looks down on me."

(1) Less-empathic responses:

Many colleagues experience this, but you'll get used to it. (generalizing)
This is your fantasy! Here nobody is looked down upon. (teaching, instructing)
Oh, don't take it seriously, the best thing you can do is to ignore it. (giving advice)
The more you think like this, the worse it will be. (moralizing)

(2) Empathic response-variants:

You would like to be taken seriously.
You feel patronized.
You indeed miss an eye-level contact with the coordinator.
There is something that makes you feel inferior in this particular relationship.

Case scenario, part 3

An employee shares with his team leader: "Finally I've finished that damn software upgrade."

(1) Less-empathic responses:

"So we may continue with the setup of the device." (ignoring the emotional part of the message)
"You should be happy you have a job at all in these tough times!" (teaching, instructing)
"Damn software upgrade? There's always something you need to criticize!" (generalizing, blaming)

(2) Empathic response-variants:

"Had a pretty rough time with this task?"
"Relieved to have it finished, huh?"
"Well, I guess you don't feel like doing another upgrade in the near future."

The case scenarios are intended to reveal that it does matter to listen for total meaning of a message rather than just the content and that attending to the feeling part; in particular, it matters to feel more thoroughly understood. Moreover, sensitive listening can facilitate the relationship (Rogers and Farson 1987). Suppose the team leader were to respond by directly giving another task. Would the employee feel that he had gotten his message across? Would he feel better about his job, more motivated to do good work on the next task?

On the other hand, the empathic responses communicate that the team leader heard and understands. This does not necessarily mean that the next task need be postponed or altered or that he must devote an extensive listening session to the employee complaining about the problems he encountered. Alternatively, he may react differently in light of the shared information he has acquired. It is first of all the perceived sensitivity on the part of the team leader which can transform an average team climate into a superb one (Rogers and Farson 1987).

Invitation to reflect:

What would your response be to the following statement? "If something goes wrong, I'm always the first one who gets blamed!"

As sketched in Fig. 9.1, empathic understanding encompasses attitudes as well as skills. It has both cognitive and affective components (Cain 2010, p. 92) such that empathic responses take on a variety of forms. Based on David Cain's description (Cain 2010, pp. 95–100), we summarize the straightforward forms of expressing empathic understanding in the Resource Box 9.3. Readers interested in the complex expressions are referred to Cain's book.

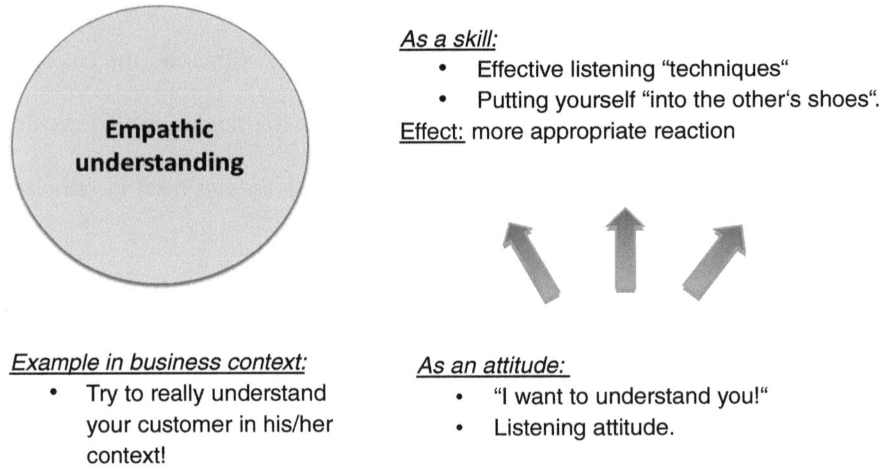

Fig. 9.1 Empathic understanding as an attitude and skill

Resource Box 9.3 Varieties of empathic understanding according to Cain (2010) with examples adapted by the authors. "E" stands for Employee, and "M" stands for Manager

Varieties of empathy

- *Empathic understanding* responses attempt to grasp and accurately communicate the other person's basic message. Examples:

  E I'm just done with the damn data import.
  M Seems it needed a lot of effort to finish it.
  E Indeed, it seemed like an endless endeavor, the system wasn't working properly, and we had **to** repeat the procedure over and over. I'm totally exhausted now.

- *Clarifying* responses attempt to articulate clearly what the other person is trying to say by struggling to find words, or offering just a vague expression. Examples:

  E I'd really like to get up and walk out.
  M You seem to be angry.
  E I believe I am. We aren't making any progress in this meeting and nobody is listening to me.

- *Affective* empathic responses focus on the other person's emotions or bodily felt sense of a problem, going beyond the content of the message and articulating the feeling being expressed or implied: Examples:

E I just can't believe that our director signed the contract for the merger.
M You're feeling cheated and scared about the future of your workplace.
E Exactly. I've no idea what is going to happen to us.

- *Explorative* empathic responses engage a probing and tentative style to assist the other person to locate, explore, unfold, examine, and reflect on unclear or hidden aspects of experience. Examples:

E I can't quite put my finger on it, but I feel worried about the upcoming strategic meeting.
M So there's some vague sense that something may go wrong in the meeting?
E Yes. Like I'm not sure that my boss and I have the same sense of direction and expectations for the coming period. I can't agree with his strategies, they stand in opposition to what I'm aiming for.

- *Affirmative* empathic responses validate the other person's experience of sense of self, whether positive or negative. To be effective, they require credible evidence from mutual knowledge or sharing. Examples:

E I am so proud of how my team is performing. I think I'm a good leader.
M You are a good leader. All team members respect you as a leader and like their work.
E I think I've been neglectful of my family.
M From what you've said I can see that you have been neglectful lately.

Invitation to reflect:

Studying the examples in this book, which kinds of empathic responses can you identify? Did you encounter empathic responses that do not match any of the categories listed above?
In your responses, do you prefer certain response patterns to others to express empathic understanding?

9.3.2 *Problems in the Context of Empathic Understanding*

Occasionally it happens that paraphrasing is not received by the other person, often the one in charge, as a means to clarify understanding but instead as a weakness, a sign of "stupidity," maneuvering, or even attack on the side of the listener. Let us illustrate this by a few examples.

Case example 1 for problems with empathic understanding:

Manager to employee	"The report needs urgent revision as there are many errors and the style is really poor. Also, the report has to be submitted to the commission as soon as possible in order not to miss tomorrow's deadline. I don't know why these things take so much of my energy and I never get to doing anything meaningful."
Employee	"You feel exhausted by having to take care of all those details, I'm wondering how I could …"
Manager (annoyed, interrupting)	"That's my issue and how I feel. Better take care of the quality of the work you deliver. Style is not an option—it's essential!"

Case example 2 for problems with empathic understanding:

Manager to employee	"The report needs urgent revision as there are many errors and the style is really poor. Also, the report has to be submitted to the commission as soon as possible in order not to miss tomorrow's deadline."
Employee	"You mean, I should revise the report by correcting errors and improving the style, then …"
Manager (interrupting)	"Of course, that's what I said. Instead of repeating my words, better go and do it!"

At a more subtle level, empathic understanding is sometimes avoided because the risk to be changed or feeling obliged to take action is too high. In fact, direct interpersonal contact including honest eye-contact tends to intrigue the partners in a conversation so that, as a genuine manager, you may feel the need to react to the person who shares his inner world with you. Just listening, with our mind made-up to definitely not react to the message in a genuine manner, would fail its purpose and soon be recognized as a shallow ploy. Reciprocally, a sensitive employee would also recognize realistic limitations to what a manager/leader could do to support him or her in a situation of distress and communicate this in her message. He or she might say something like: "I appreciate you listening to me and it feels good to know I've got someone who cares. This will help me to move along, and should I get stuck on the road, I hope I can call on you again." However, any response learned in advance would miss the subtleties of the situation and relationship at hand, so readers, be warned about using the example just for orientation and feel called upon to form your own authentic response.

Summarizing, empathic understanding is the ability and choice to put yourself in the other's perspective as if you were seeing the world through the other's eyes. You look for the words that would best express the other's struggle to express her/his point of view in challenging situations and when emotions are not clear enough to be expressed simply and directly. At best, empathy is a shared experience as we allow the other to correct our best guess as to his/her ongoing feelings in the moment. As empathic understanding is crucial to communicating in the workplace, it has been included in item 4 ("Trying to understand and be understood comprehensively and thoroughly") of the people-oriented agenda.

9.3.3 Acceptance, Respect

Synonyms here include: *unconditional positive regard, caring, prizing, acknowledgement, warmth.*

Rogers describes acceptance as follows:

> I find that the more acceptance and liking I feel toward this individual, the more I will be creating a relationship which he can use. By acceptance I mean a warm regard for him as a person of unconditional self-worth, of value no matter what his condition, his behaviour, his feelings. It means a respect and liking for him as a separate person, a willingness for him to possess his own feelings in his own way (Rogers 1961, p. 34).

To be accepted exactly the way we are—not needing to disguise, justify, endlessly explain, perform or hide anything but being fully received as we are—is a precious gift. It helps us to accept ourselves more fully. Paradoxically, feeling accepted puts us in a state in which we are open to change (Rogers 1961), not needing to defend anything about ourselves.

Mutual acceptance or respect has the potential to connect people, to build rapport. Being accepted means that the other person perceives us with all our potentials as well as limitations and provides space to us—a characteristic of *inclusion* in the sense of making space in one's inner world for the other. Acceptance, however, does not mean agreement. This is another issue. Indeed, it might be a lot harder to accept a colleague whose work style is totally different from ours than one whose style is in tune with ours.

The consequence of acceptance is a nonjudgemental attitude that can evolve to a *mutual* appreciation of one another, not depending on any conditions and giving us the safety to experience the feeling that is present to us in the moment.

Accepting the other nourishes trust. Consequently, our interaction will grant the *maximum possible space* to the other, without ever compromising our own congruence. In a job situation, this would mean that we follow our business goals and the maximum possible free space we can grant the other may be minimal. However, even this minimal freedom—like a small choice or question regarding a preference—if communicated genuinely, may help others to feel accepted rather than ignored and motivate them to collaborate as well as possible. Consequently, acceptance must neither be confused with not caring about what the other feels or does, nor with giving up one's direction and blindly letting the other take over control.

Rogers clarifies that a nonjudgemental attitude does not imply the need to stop expressing reactions. On the contrary, it may grant the freedom to react without the fear of being judged:

> … to cease evaluating another is not to cease having reactions. It may, as a matter of fact, free one to react. "I don't like your idea (or painting, or invention, or writing)" is not an evaluation, but a reaction. It is subtly but sharply different from a judgment which says, "What you are doing is bad (or good), and this quality is assigned to you from some external source." (1961, p. 358).

In fact, the judgement tends to put the speaker at the mercy of the evaluators' forces who evaluate from their position of authority and often prompt defensive or justifying reaction from the speaker to counterattack. All this is very much in line with the notion of *autonomy support* in Self Determination Theory (SDT) (Ryan and Deci 2000). As recent research shows, psychological well-being is increased when being with an autonomous supporting partner (Lynch et al. 2009).

Invitation to reflect:

Do you have a pattern along which you tend to react in response to being positively or negatively judged by others? How do you feel in such situations? How do you react?
Do you tend to judge others? Do you think that judging others is (not) necessary? Can you say why you think so?

Considering the two distinct dynamics of personal reactions (also referred to as "I-messages") and judgments, we have experienced that in some situations it is worthwhile to perceive judgement as a sort of reaction and not to let oneself react to the evaluation but rather to stay with oneself. "I see, you (don't) concur with…" and show interest in the reaction: "What is it that causes your dislike/liking/opposition/….?" With such an attitude we can creatively influence the course of the conversation more often than we might expect.

Rogers expressed an intriguing relationship between receiving positive regard from another person and one's own need *for* positive regard. The need for positive regard "is reciprocal, in that when an individual discriminates himself as satisfying another's need for positive regard, he necessarily experiences satisfaction of his own need for positive regard" (1959, p. 223). We conjecture that this relationship lies at the roots of social and collaborative behavior—contributing to a positive experience in you satisfies me too.

Invitation to reflect:

Do you remember any work-related situation in which you have felt:

- ignored, overlooked, judged, or
- genuinely accepted

How did you react in each of the situations? What was the effect on your motivation to engage in your job?

The vital importance of acceptance can be painfully recognized in situations in which it is missing—we are judged, rejected, ignored, excluded, etc. This tends to signal inferiority, at times feeling useless and is often mirrored in the loss of motivation to contribute. Such a strong, negative reaction to a lack of acceptance points to the fact that being accepted by others is a pervasive, deep need in humankind.

> Invitation to reflect:
>
> For the manager or leader:
> Do you feel you accept your team? How do you express this attitude?
> For the team members: Do you feel you accept your peers and the team leader? How do you express this attitude?
> In case you cannot accept someone: What is it that would need to change in yourself that would allow you to be more accepting? Is there any facet of the other that you like?

Acceptance and its opposite make themselves known by the way we act as well as the words we use. For example, we can express acceptance by responding quickly and carefully to our associates' calls or emails, or by including them in activities or decisions, by listening to them, and a lot more that lets them experience that they matter to us. While this may sound and also be easy, it can become challenging in situations of conflict when the other is mad at us or shares a view that is totally at odds with something that matters to us. However, meeting this challenge can be decisive as to whether a conflict becomes an opportunity for constructive change or escalates in a destructive way (Rogers 1959). Figure 9.2 sketches essential features of acceptance as an attitude and its active expression.

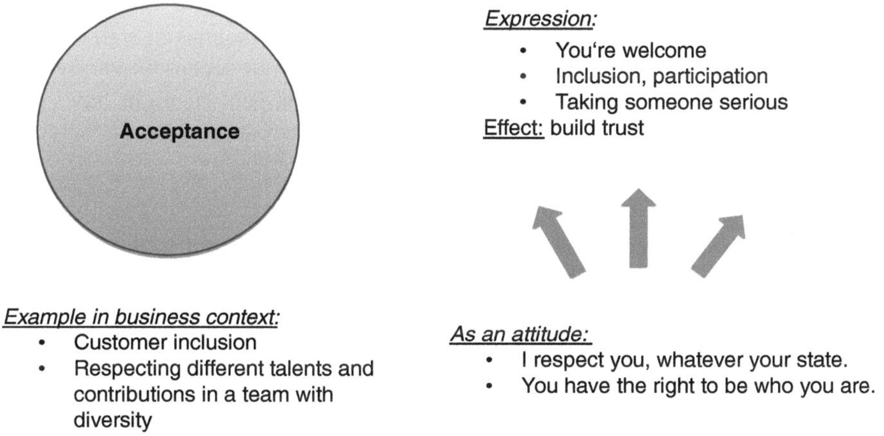

Fig. 9.2 Acceptance as an attitude and its expression

Example from experience building upon vignette 2: *Rigid external requirements or things turn out to be different than originally perceived*
Situation: One project partner started validation in time and strictly based on the project proposal. The other two partners responsible for the validation work-package revised the validation process to better suit the adaptations made throughout the project and claimed that their validation protocol needed to be followed by all partners! No one was prepared to step back from their position; communication stopped.
One project partner specializing in the design process strongly felt that all wanted the best for the project but the paths were different. She expressed this in an email sent to all project partners and carefully tried to identify differences and commonalities between the original and the revised validation protocol. Based on a transparent analysis, she suggested considering the validation study to be designated as incremental, with the "fast partner's" results serving as a first step on which the revised validation activities had been built. This was exactly how the revised procedure had been generated and it seemed so simple to accomplish, just needing—on the task-based level—effort to look into what exactly had been done at each of the sites. But foremost, it needed—on the basic interpersonal level—trust and acceptance of the individual partners and an unbiased approach to their different values and viewpoints.
The validation work-package was accepted by the commission but some dents in the relationships between project partners remained, showing that genuine acceptance is something that needs to evolve.

9.3.4 Problems with Receiving Acceptance or Respect

Occasionally it happens that our acceptance of the other person is not well received. This can happen if, for example, the other person does not accept him/herself and hence raises suspicion that being accepted by another person might have some manipulative intent.

Example 1 for problems with acceptance:

Manager to employee	"I appreciate how carefully you prepared the meeting room."
Employee	"I just do my duty, that's what I'm paid for!"

Case example 2 for problems with acceptance:

Manager "In my view, your critical remark hit the point and brought the discussion back to essential issues!"
Colleague "I know that people don't like my criticism, but that's how I am. I just can't listen to so much stupid stuff so I have to say something. Sorry."

Case example 3 for problems with acceptance:
Alternatively, accepting feedback can be interpreted as evaluation or judgement and evoke a rejecting response, such as in the following exchange:
Manager "In my view, your critical remark hit the point and brought the discussion back to essential issues!"
Colleague Y "I know I'm good at grasping the essence; you don't have to tell me."

These case examples may provide some flavor on the subtleties of expressing respect and the fact that it needs to be received by the other person to contribute to a positive work atmosphere.

There are other situations, too, in which acceptance is missing. An apparent one is the case that we lose respect toward others by judging what they have said or (not) done and feel that their behavior is inappropriate (bad, wrong, harmful, etc.). Effectively, confronting the person with the effect of their behavior could even be regarded as a kind of acceptance, namely caring about the person enough to share our honest reaction and giving them a chance to respond. However, a person's defenses may be too strong to let them perceive the situation on a broader context other than their own.

A less apparent situation in which acceptance is missing is one in which our (cultural, often unconscious) values make us blind to, or unaware of, the fact that we are ignoring another person's values. A situation as simple as one in which a person's being late for a meeting is received with negative emotions can illustrate this misunderstanding. In some cultures, such as those in South European and South American countries, it is more important to finish a (preceding) task than arriving on time. A manager unaware of this would easily destroy a positive climate by showing his/her frustration because of late attendance.

In summary, experiencing acceptance toward another person and oneself is a very powerful and versatile attitude. In the people-oriented agenda, it is integrated as item 3 ("Respect toward the other, oneself, and the environment."). Expressing as well as receiving it appropriately may lie at the core of healthy interpersonal relationships at work and in all social contexts, regardless of our position, nationality, or religion. In particular, intercultural settings rely on a great deal of acceptance as well as cultural awareness to fully receive others from diverse cultures.

9.3.5 Congruence

Some synonyms for "congruence" are *realness, transparency, genuineness, authenticity, openness*. Rogers (1961, p. 33) describes congruence as follows:

> I have found that the more that I can be genuine in the relationship, the more helpful it will be… Being genuine also involves the willingness to be and to express, in my words and my behavior, the various feelings and attitudes, which exist in me… It is only by providing the genuine reality which is in me, that the other person can successfully seek for the reality in him. I have found this to be true even when the attitudes I feel are not attitudes with which I am pleased, or attitudes which seem conducive to a good relationship.

This vital attitude is so basic on the one hand yet complex on the other hand that one term hardly suffices to capture the whole meaning. This is why a number of terms are being used interchangeably, each bringing core assets for any given context into the foreground. In the context of communication, for example, "transparency"—the 2nd item of the people-oriented agenda—is a key to delivering a message without any hidden aspects. In leadership, it is "honesty" or "integrity" that is what people look for and admire in a good leader in the first place (Kousez and Posner 2002). In their book, *Transformational Leadership*, Bass and Riggio (2006) advocate being straightforward, honest, and open with others if we want to achieve effective leadership.

Since the notion of congruence is so complex, let us break down the complexity of the concept at least to some degree and see which parts or levels can be congruent (matching) or incongruent in us. The easier part is the one which we can control consciously, namely our expression of what we feel is going on inside us. If we willingly say something that is not what we feel inwardly, then we presumably lie or cheat. The more difficult part of congruence which we cannot fully control willingly is whether our inner world (feeling and meaning) is in tune (congruent) with our perception of this inner experience. Lack of congruence in this sphere can happen if we do not perceive our feelings accurately and if our perception of them is distorted, for example, to protect us from difficult feelings or to disguise them in order not to lose the acceptance of some significant other person. For example, if it would be too risky to admit being angry at a superior, one's feeling might be distorted to signal sadness and depression. Yet this renders us incongruent because, while we would consciously express sadness, part of our organism would signal anger.

In brief, we are congruent or genuine only if our inner world (feeling and meaning) is in tune with the perception, as well as the communication, of our experience. Rogers emphasized many times that the development of congruence is a process that *spans our whole lifetime* and is never accomplished completely. This can be understood such that the environment tends to bring us into situations, for example, new ones, in which we need to establish congruence from initial disorientation. And, according to neuropsychologist Ainley et al. (2012) of the University of London, this ability to have access to our inner world depends on whether we have, what she calls, high or low *interoceptive awareness*, the high being more accurate.

☕ Invitation to reflect:

Try to recall a person in your professional or school life whom you consider significant in their relationship to you. Do you think of this person as real, genuine, or authentic?
What is it that makes you think/feel like that? Did that person influence your further personal or professional growth? If so, how does this influence live on in you or help you in your way of being right now?

At any given point in time, we cannot consciously establish a complete match between our inner world and the way we perceive it, since not all aspects of our inner world are accessible to our awareness. However, the candid, congruent expression of what we perceive as going on inside us depends on what we want to share with the other person. Rogers (1980, p. 115) clearly states that an open, inner reaction is *shared only if* this is deemed *appropriate*. In this statement, the connection between congruence, acceptance, and empathic understanding becomes apparent, since the latter two variables would co-inform us about the appropriateness of an open, transparent reaction. In any case, we agree with Rogers that a high degree of congruence facilitates mutual understanding. If we do not even know what the boss, colleague, or customer is feeling because they hide their emotional reaction, how can we respond to their needs? Alternatively, when they express what they think and feel, we have an opportunity to receive them more fully and react appropriately.

Examples of being present with one's own needs that are counter to those of the other person or organization are not rare. Imagine, for example, an organization which was born out of a merger of different organizations with diverging opinions as to which business strategy seems most promising and should be followed. In such cases, there is a major challenge to move on and not to get stuck with the differences, and, as the leader personality, to sense one's own needs as well as those of the others and to act in a way that reflects one's congruence in addition to acceptance and empathy. More detailed examples and resolution proposals can be found in Motschnig and Nykl (2014). In any case, congruence is an attitude that goes deep and needs real first-person experience to be acquired. It is primarily our whole-person interaction through which our transparency or façade, authenticity or being a marionette, comes to light and is passed on to our social environment.

In a nutshell, seeking congruence—as a pivotal aspect of the people-oriented agenda—can optimally support us to behave appropriately, even in new, complex, unfamiliar settings. In such situations, a congruent, undistorted access to all inner resources from knowledge about feelings to intuition is crucial for appropriate behavior (Rogers 1983; Damasio 2000). In order to show some of the dynamics of congruence, Fig. 9.3 summarizes essential aspects in a clearly simplified form.

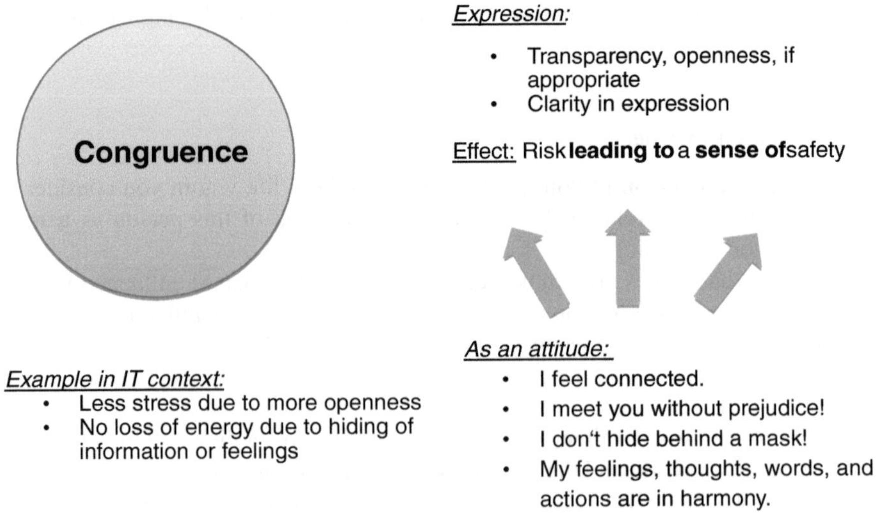

Fig. 9.3 Congruence as an attitude and its expression

Rogers (1961) discovered that realness in one person frees the other to be real too. Openly addressing an unclear situation, a weakness, a misunderstanding, a revelation tends to stimulate openness in the other person. They may respond by sharing their thoughts and feelings signaling their understanding. More of the whole becomes revealed and hence available for thoughtful consideration. Furthermore, openness can lead to trust (Ryback 2013; iCom Team 2014). Others meet us without hiding, taking the risk of being uncovered and even attacked, so by opening up they demonstrate trust that their revelations will not be used against them. Should openness be misused, trust will be lost immediately (Motschnig and Nykl 2014). While this is likely to come with negative consequences, we can certainly learn from the interaction directly and timely and re-orient ourselves immediately.

9.3.6 Problems with Congruence

Congruence is an inner state in which we reside, more or less, and that we endeavor to re-establish once environmental or inner influences cause incongruences that often can be perceived as some kind of tension or stress. Let us consider a few examples:

Case example 1 illustrating environmental conditions challenging congruence: As the leading senior architect of your small town, you love your job and are made the head of a jury to select and award the best architectural designs for the renewal of the city center. Suddenly, you get a new boss who is politically biased and requires you to focus on strategic, political criteria in the architectural design proposals above all. As a consequence, you have to turn back the ingenious proposals and accept those that meet the political criteria, all this clearly against your sense of integrity. Because of your age, you cannot simply quit the job, as this would likely render you unemployed and cause a threat to your economical existence. You are under extreme pressure.

Case example 2 illustrating inner conditions challenging congruence: Through a conflict in the team we are leading, we realize that our leadership style that we cherish is inadequate in some situations and largely has contributed to the conflict that is about to escalate. We feel we need to change our approach significantly to accommodate for situations such as the one in which we are currently involved.

*Case example 3 illustrating incongruence in **a** relationship:* While you cannot pinpoint the problem exactly, you feel you cannot be yourself in the relationship with a superior whom you respect and do not want to disappoint. In order to keep the relationship going, you need to hide aspects of yourself, which feels awkward, puts a load of stress on you and causes some decrease of your energy and vitality.

Intriguingly, there is no simple recipe on how to resolve incongruence. Typically, the solution differs from person to person and from situation to situation. Some say (e.g., Helgoe 2008) that introverts have a somewhat more difficult time, being more critical and analytical about their inner feelings. Nevertheless, according to Carl Rogers, receiving another person's unconditional acceptance, empathic understanding and genuineness, at least to some degree, are the core "ingredients" of an atmosphere in which each person tends to move to a higher degree of congruence. At the end of this subchapter, we invite you to accompany Richard Weylman, the author of *The Power of Why*, in his reflection on what it really means to be open.

Case example by illustrating openness in a sales context

Seriously, Do You Really Think You Are Open-Minded?

Jan 26, 2016, 08:00 am

When I was General Sales Manager for a Rolls-Royce dealership in upstate New York, we had converted an old grocery store into a luxurious showroom and service facility. We installed mirrored walls framed with mahogany paneling, baccarat crystal chandeliers, and even Sherle Wagner bathroom fixtures. We became a tourist attraction nearly over night. But given the demographics of the region most of our business was generated by our innovative and personalized marketing campaigns to major metro areas such as NYC, Boston, Washington D.C., Philadelphia, Miami and Palm Beach.

We were known as the place to receive great service, a personalized approach and that we would take most anything in trade. We even were the first to create 7-year financing to leverage tax advantages then available and to maximize the ROI on a Rolls-Royce which contrary to any other brand was an appreciating asset. I constantly heard how creative and open-minded we were as we seriously out performed other dealers nationwide. We were so proud of ourselves!

One afternoon, an older couple came into the showroom, I greeted them and then they began to look at several of the Rollers we had on display. They looked like the looky-loos we saw several times per week. He had on bibb overalls and she had on a dress that most would categorize as a "house coat." They walked around several cars until they stopped at one and he said to his wife, "What do you think?" She said, "I like the color, what do you think?" And he said, "I like the color too darling."

I smiled and walked back to my office and a few minutes later he walked into my office and said, "How much would that one we like be?" I said, "Well come in and sit down and I will add it up for you," while giving him my best don't you wish you could afford it smile. They both sat down and I quoted them the full near 6 figure price and smiled again. He looked at her and said "Well what do you think Darlin'?" She said "Well I like the color."

He then stood up pulled down the flap of those bibb overalls (no shirt on, lots of body hair-scary looking), pulled off a money belt and counted out the full price in CASH! Then he leaned over my desk and said "Do you think you can get off your judgmental butt and deliver this car to my house downstate by 8 am tomorrow morning?" I jumped to my feet and said, "Yes sir, I will be there at 8 am sharp!"

When I pulled up the next morning, he had an average looking split-level house but it was adjacent to his massive wholesale construction company warehouse with at least 40 trucks getting loaded for the day's deliveries. When he came out to meet me he had on a Fioravanti-tailored suit that was $6,000 if it was a dime. He looked me straight in the eye and said "What threw you off big boy—was it the bib overalls or was it my wife's house coat?" I sheepishly said "Well actually it was both."

He then said, "I came to see you because I had heard how nice it was to do business with you, but a word of advice—you're nice but you're not very open-minded and frankly you have a long way to go in that department!" That hard to hear lesson has guided me all the years since.

I think of this story often because so many sales people and leaders talk about how open-minded they are, but in reality they are not. They talk about being open-minded but their immediate response to most anything new or different is "but," as in "thanks, BUT we already have that pretty well handled" or "Yes BUT, I am pretty good at that already." Business suffers because the tendency is to prejudge new ideas, new approaches, or even how to find new prospects. Consequently they do not invest in themselves, their team, or their business.

The marketplace is changing rapidly. Keep doing what you have been doing and you will NOT keep getting what you have been getting, rather you will slowly go into decline. You never know in advance how much you can

improve or where your next sale or referral will come from if you prejudge the outcome or the person in advance.
We learn two ways—from experience or from education. Take a moment now and learn from my experience so you do not make the same mistake I did. Or as Isaac Asimov said so well, "*Your assumptions are your windows on the world. Scrub them off every once in a while, or the light won't come in.*"

–Richard Weylman, author of *The Power of Why*

9.3.7 The Confluence of the Three Person-Centered Attitudes

In order to be truly facilitative, the three Rogers' variables—at any time—need to form a balanced configuration in which one or the other is in the foreground and neither of them is missing completely. Figure 9.4 sketches this situation.

To give an example, let us follow up on Vignette 1: *Different frames of reference, standpoints, and paths to reach the goal or "Whom should I trust more, an experienced colleague or myself?"* So the question is: How do we see holding and expressing all the three variables in the context of Vignette 1?

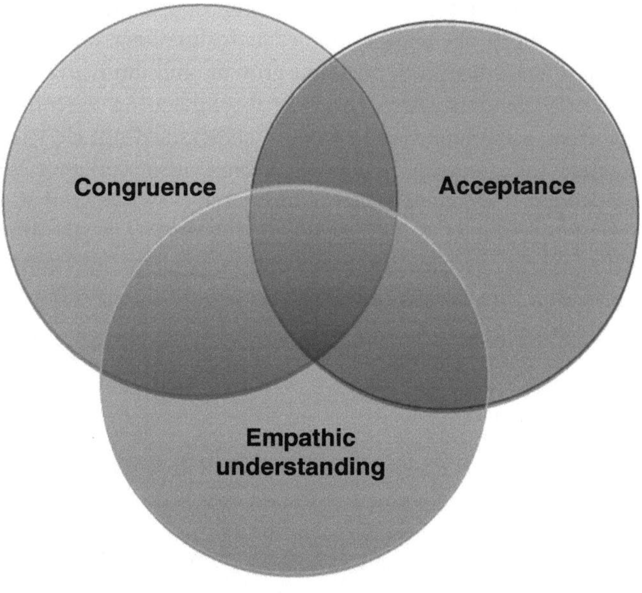

Fig. 9.4 Confluence of the three Rogers' variables

First of all, how can we (or, in Vignette 1, the experienced manager and the junior expert) regain congruence? How can each admit to himself or herself, first of all, that one is feeling stressed, possibly somewhat angry at this particular difference in standpoints, and even sad that one's ideas and plans are not received by the other and blocked up? By admitting this to ourselves, we can more easily convey to the other that there is something that lies between us and needs attention, whenever the time is right. While admitting to oneself the difference in this one specific issue, it would be important to also emphasize the otherwise successful cooperation and good relationship. Possibly, consulting with others and thoughtfully describing to them each of the positions might help to meet this one challenge. Or both stepping back from their positions and exploring the interest behind the positions might help to re-establish some flow in this area.

Furthermore, listening for deep understanding of the other's perspective would be of highest priority. Would it be possible to sit down with her/him, without distraction, and really get into one another's perspective, one at a time, and understand his/her motivation from an authentic level? What is the logic in the other's perspective from that frame of reference, putting our own values and prejudices aside, at least temporarily, so that the other feels fully understood? This includes asking all the questions we need to in order to feel totally satisfied that we understand that perspective fully, remembering to keep our own values in check.

In this vignette, acceptance appears to be in place already, judging from the otherwise good relationship between the "players." So, having fully understood the other's perspective, we are now in a much more comfortable position to move on in collaboration without letting ourselves get stuck in the perceived difference. Feeling fully received, even in the difference, the other will be much more receptive to hearing our view and look out if there is some compromise that can be made or some third option to be taken. In the authors' view, such situations, indeed, can be turned to ones full of significant learning, personal growth, and innovative solutions.

As early as 1959, Rogers (1959, p. 215) formulated an essential relationship between congruence, acceptance, and empathic understanding. He wrote that a part of the congruence of a person is the experience of acceptance and empathic understanding (Rogers 1959, p. 215). He considered congruence that encompasses the experience of acceptance and empathic understanding as the basis of highly appropriate behavior. In our view, such perception, reaction, and behavior are fully in tune with including the people-oriented agenda and this is what (not only) our business world needs urgently.

Invitation to reflect:

Let us reflect on the three core attitudes in the interaction between the manager and team member interacting in the third vignette at the beginning of this chapter. At which places do congruence, acceptance, and empathic understanding enter the conversation and what effect do they have?
What effect does the lack of congruence have?

In particular, how, in your experience, is realness expressed that lacks acceptance and empathic understanding? Have you ever experienced such a situation?

9.4 Coherence

The basic idea behind this concept is simple. It means that, at each moment, a person can integrate Rogers' three attitudes with following the organization's goals. In other words, he/she manages to follow two agendas such that the (inter-)personal and organizational aspects are coherent to each other, resonate, or fit in with each other. This constellation can create synergy between the flourishing of people and the moving forward in the organization or business. However, as with congruence, coherence needs to be re-established again and again. It is a process in which incoherent states are dissolved as coherence is approached. In music, this process can be compared with tuning which needs to be done each time a new instrument joins the orchestra or when one needs to make sure all are in tune before playing a piece together and avoiding dissonant tones.

Carrying the music metaphor further, the various attacks on coherence can be compared with the causes for acoustical dissonance. For example, one instrument can get off-tune—much as people can become incongruent/overstressed in their work. Moreover, the orchestra can get confused and stop functioning smoothly due to some instruments playing too loudly or fast, etc. This is comparable with some internal problem in an organization, such as unrealistic claims for higher salaries. Yet a further scenario deals with external causes of dissonance or attacks on coherence: Imagine that the orchestra cannot perform well because of environmental noises and disturbances, etc. Transferred to issues causing incoherence, a comparable scenario is the organization being threatened by new governmental demands. All these reasons can cause incoherence, and it is apparent that coherence needs to be re-established if employees and organization are to work productively, efficiently, and with the satisfaction of all concerned.

Evidently, once we are interested in people in the context of their work, Rogers' socio-environmental conditions of personal growth need to be complemented by their relationship to an organization's objectives so that the person as such *and* as part of the organization can unfold psychologically and positively contribute to the dynamically changing organizational objectives. This aspect of coherence is sketched on the left-hand side of Fig. 9.5 as an inclusion of person-centered attitudes in the frame of organizational objectives. In other words, it can be expressed as following the 2agendas@work.

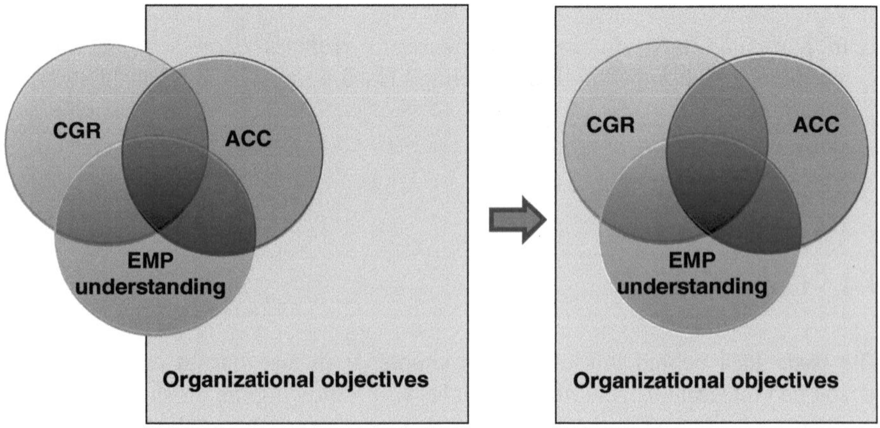

Fig. 9.5 Sketch of moving from an incoherent state to a coherent one in which the person-centered attitudes resonate with the organization's objectives

9.5 Conclusion

Congruence and coherence are highly desirable but complex and not easy-to-reach goals. Even though they can be acquired in a multitude of complementary ways, a proven path to higher congruence is a direct, interpersonal relationship to a person who embodies a high level of congruence, acceptance, and empathic understanding. This is because these attitudes are expressed through a complex mix of words, feelings, and actions.

If we can manage our person-centered attitudes to be consistent with the goals of the organization or team that we are part of or aspire to, the state of coherence is reached—in our view the best precondition of motivation for mindful action at work.

Let us end this chapter—but not the further development of our attitudes—with a quote by Carl Rogers:

> Perhaps the most basic of these essential attitudes is realness, or genuineness. When the facilitator is a real person, being what he or she is, entering into relationships with the learners without presenting a front or a facade, the facilitator is much more likely to be effective. This means, that the feelings the facilitator is experiencing are available to his or her awareness, that he or she is able to live these feelings, to be them, and able to communicate them if appropriate (Rogers 1983, p. 121).

References

Ainley, V., Tajadura-Jimenez, A., Fotopoulou, A., & Tsakiris, M. (2012). Looking into myself: The effect of self-focused attention on interoceptive sensitivity. *Psychophysiology, 49*(11), 1504–1508.

Bass, B. M., & Riggio, R. E. (2006). *Transformational leadership*. Mahwah, NJ: Lawrence Erlbaum Associates.

Cain, D. J. (2010). *Person-centered psychotherapies.* American Psychological Association (APA).

Damasio, A. R. (2000). *The feeling of what happens: Body and emotion in the making of consciousness*. London, UK: Vintage.

Güver, S. (2016). *Communication in multicultural project teams: Developing a communication model* (Ph.D. thesis concept, submitted to the Faculty of Management). University of Vienna, Austria.

Helgoe, L. A. (2008). *Introvert power*. Naperville, IL: Sourcebooks.

iCom Team. (2014). *Constructive communication in international teams.* Münster: Waxmann.

Kousez, J. M., & Posner, B. Z. (2002). *Leadership challenge* (3rd ed.). San Francisco, CA: Jossey-Bass.

Lynch, M., La Guardia, J. G., & Ryan, R. M. (2009). On being yourself in different cultures: Ideal and actual self-concept, autonomy support, and well-being in China, Russia, and the United States. *The Journal of Positive Psychology, 4*(4), 290–304.

Motschnig, R., & Nykl, L. (2014). *Person-centred communication: Theory, skills, and practice.* McGraw Hill, UK: Open University Press.

Rogers, C. R. (1959). A theory of therapy, personality, and interpersonal relationships, as developed in the client-centered framework. In S. Koch (Ed.), *Psychology: A study of a science* (Vol. 3). New York: McGraw-Hill Inc.

Rogers, C. R. (1961). *On becoming a person. A Therapist's view of psychotherapy*. London: Constable.

Rogers, C. R. (1980). *A way of being*. Boston: Houghton Mifflin.

Rogers, C. R. (1983). *Freedom to learn for the 80's*. Columbus, OH: Charles E. Merrill Publishing Company, A Bell & Howell Company.

Rogers, C. R., & Farson, R. E. (1987). Active listening. *Communicating in business today.* http://www.gordontraining.com/pdf/active_listening_article_rogers-farson.pdf

Rogers, C. R., & Roethlisberger, F. J. (1951, 1991). Barriers and gateways to communication. *Harvard business review* (*HBR*) (pp. 105–111). November–December 1991. First published in 1952, with retrospective commentary republished in 1991.

Ryan, R. M., & Deci, E. L. (2000). Self-determination theory and the facilitation of intrinsic motivation, social development, and well-being. *American Psychologist (APA), 55*(1), 68–78.

Ryback, D. (2013). A brief history of trust in society. In E. Hammer & N. Tomaschek (Eds.), *Vertrauen* (pp. 11–23). Waxmann: Munster, Germany.

Standish. (2016). Website with yearly Chaos reports. https://www.standishgroup.com. Last recalled on January 16, 2016.

Chapter 10
Methods for Transforming Communication: Dialogue

> *"I go along with Martin Buber and the ancient oriental sages: "He, who imposes himself has the small, manifest might; he who does not impose himself has the great, secret might." "*
>
> Rogers (1980, p. 41–42)

This chapter focuses on the following:

- The interplay of attitudes and practices resulting in effective communication,
- Dialogue according to David Bohm as a stance and a method that supports transformative communication,
- Case examples and reflective practice regarding dialogue,
- The four dialoging practices according to Isaacs (1999):
  - Listening
  - Respecting
  - Suspending
  - Voicing
- Theoretical soundness of dialogue with the Person-Centered Approach.

10.1 Introduction

In counseling, the pivotal criterion is that any intervention be in the best interest of the client (Cain 2010). This single, primary focus cannot always be maintained in the context of enterprises and project work, where stakeholder needs and interests need to be maintained along with other objectives that address the organization's moving forward and accomplishing its mission. In brief, multiple objectives and needs coexist and need to be balanced. In order to address this situation, the two-agenda approach has been introduced in Chap. 2.

In this chapter, we summarize a method that optimally fits into the core of transformative communication: dialogue, according to David Bohm. It

R. Motschnig and D. Ryback, *Transforming Communication in Leadership and Teamwork*, DOI 10.1007/978-3-319-45486-3_10

complements the two-agenda approach by providing a method that supports the unfolding of a holistic view out of individuals' expressed partial, subjective knowledge, and experience. If facilitated properly, genuine dialogue has the potential to help communicative exchanges to acquire a quality of moving beyond what is already known and reach states of increased knowledge and improved understanding. These are essential for shared visions, good decisions, and an organization's success. As with active listening—the common root to all the methods presented in this and the following chapter—it is not the techniques that stand in the foreground but rather the attitudes that people hold and express in complex, verbal, nonverbal, and behavioral way that matter most. Thus, pure training of techniques would be meaningless if constructive interpersonal attitudes were missing. On the other hand, some situations are too complex to be handled by expressing our attitude only. This is where methods can come in handy, in particular, if assimilated into our way of being and applied mindfully, be it in face-to-face sessions or online. Hence, rather than just writing about dialogue and inviting our audience to read about it, we call upon you to explore, select, and use the resources and to introduce them to your colleagues for unfolding inherent potentials collaboratively.

10.2 Dialogue According to David Bohm

Historically, the term "dialogue" has focused on diverse aspects of the communication among two or more people and can be traced back to the ancient Greeks. William Isaacs nicely summarizes the etymology of the word dialogue (1999, p. xvi). "For the Greeks, *dia logos*, flow of meaning, was seen as the cornerstone of civic practice, inseparable from self-governing. The *polis* or gathering place for governing, the root of our modern politics, was nothing but a physical space that designated and enabled the conversational space required for true self-governing. The capacity for talking together constituted the foundation for democracy [...]."

Interestingly, even indigenous cultures share the habit of sitting in the circle, often around a fire, and talking such that this can be considered as a universal practice among humankind. Why not rediscover and adopt it for effective communication in today's workplace? In doing so, we advocate the notion of dialogue according to the physicist Bohm (1996). Bohm was convinced that thinking together would deepen and intensify a conversation and, in a transformative sense, bring the fire of genuine conversation back. His own words characterize the spirit of dialogue:

> If the spirit of the dialogue is present, the picture [...] is of a stream of meaning flowing among and through us and between us. This will make possible a flow of meaning in the whole group, out of which may emerge some new understanding. It is something new, which may not have been in the starting point at all. It's something creative. And this shared meaning is the "glue" or "cement" that holds people and societies together (Bohm 1996, p. 6).

As such, dialogue seeks to harness the "collective intelligence" (that can be thought of as the collective intelligence quotient "CQ") of people involved, such that together we can be more aware and smarter than we are as single beings (Isaacs 1999). As a consequence, together we can discover new opportunities and directions more clearly than on our own. In particular, leaders who engage their teams in dialogue can uncover the thinking of others that otherwise would not even reach the surface. They can adjust their direction that then may be followed with more meaning and devotion since it is transparently shared and backed by the whole team or unit.

Example: Excerpt from a dialogue between David Ryback and Carl Rogers

"If only we could bottle that level of trust that enables people to work together so effectively, and sell it," I say playfully. Then, more seriously, "There must be a way to train leaders for that kind of trust, to teach people how to be open and persist through the initial awkwardness and confusion."
"Yes, I agree," says Carl. "My experience in groups is that there is almost always some awkwardness and confusion at first. As a matter of fact, I would even go so far as to say that a group never really gels until the leader deals honestly with it. It really remains superficial until that initial confusion—about less structured leadership and organization—has been dealt with."
"So how could you teach that?" I ask.
"All I can do is be myself in any group," he replies, "my total, honest self. If people can trust me, my honesty and openness, my frankness, then maybe they'll take a risk on being open themselves."
I then ask him how he does this, when it is so difficult for others.
Carl is silent for a moment. "I don't exactly know," he says finally. "All I can say is I share my feelings as honestly and straightforwardly as I can, particularly those that persist in me for a while.... And that isn't as easy as it sounds, David. I find that, as time goes by, I have to keep working at it, finding new horizons for my awareness of what's happening within me, as well as around me." (Ryback 1998, pp. 30–31).

In dialogue, as in encounter, the flow of thought and feelings is not forced by anything. Bohm and Peat (2000) wrote:

> In a true dialogue there is the possibility that a new form of consensual mind, which involves a rich and creative order between the individual and the social, may be a more powerful instrument than is the individual mind. Such consensus does not involve the pressure of authority or conformity, for it arises out of the spirit of friendship dedicated to clarity and the ultimate perception of what is true. [...] fixed and rigid frames dissolve in the creative free flow of dialogue as a new kind of microculture emerges (p. 247).

Invitation to reflect:

Can you imagine that consensus in your team or division or organization is reached without the pressure of authority or conformity?
If no, why do you think it is not possible?
If yes, do you think that it is always important to reach consensus without the power of authority? Do you want to invite your team members to try to have a dialogue on this (or any other) issue?

From a practical perspective, Isaacs (1999) points to the need for assimilating the theory and practice of dialogue into our way of being rather than applying it as a method to achieve something. He writes: "It [dialogue] is a method or theory that, once learned and incorporated into our conversations, must be dropped completely so that we can live and speak naturally again" (p. 78). Equally naturally, the ensuing changes then become irreversible. As Isaacs points out, "Once people rediscover the art of talking together, they do not go back. This rediscovery seems to awaken something deep within us, some recognition of what we have lost as our societies have drifted away from the core practices that can make them healthy" (1999, p. xv). As Isaacs points out, people who engage in dialogue are ready for surprise and learning:

> Dialogue is characterized by people who surprise themselves by what they say. They do not have all of their thoughts worked out in advance but are willing to be influenced by the conversation itself. They come with questions to which they do not yet have answers. And they do not demand answers from others (Isaacs 1999, p. 126).

10.3 Four Practices Enabling Dialogue

Isaacs (1999) proposes four practices as key, interdependent components of dialogue, namely listening, respecting, suspending, and voicing. To be effective at establishing the deep connection between us and the wider world with which we interact, we first need to both understand and develop the practices within ourselves. But what do we mean by practice? Usually it is rooted in theoretical principles and requires repetition over years in the sense that one is always learning, becoming better at it (see Rogers' statement in the previous example). Continuous reflection tends to facilitate improvement and develop a better understanding. Intriguingly, each of the practices requires underlying attitudes, understanding, as well as skills. Isaacs views each of the four practices as something that can be developed if we actively and repetitively go for it.

In the following, we aim to capture the essence of the four practices underlying the capacity for dialoguing, drawing mainly on the thoughtful description in Isaac's book (1999, pp. 80–176) and establishing some cross-connections to the person-centered theorizing and practice.

10.3.1 Listening

Good listening forms an indispensable ground for dialogue. No listening, no dialogue however, besides listening, dialogue has a strong component of reciprocal sharing, symmetry, and often a shared third item that matters, such as the planning of a primary area of work, organizational change, and problem solving. The attention that one person is receiving is reciprocated by the other. We gradually collect and follow each move and mutually accompany one another.

Barrett-Lennard (1998), Carl Rogers' former PhD student, colleague, and close coworker in Chicago, speaks up for the quality of mutuality in natural conversation and describes the ensuing process as follows:

> Yet, one-way listening, of whatever depth and impact, lacks the mutuality found in some complete natural dialogue. A two-way flow in which each closely shares and listens, that is, a symmetrical dialogue, must involve a somewhat different inner process. This process would seem to depend on an easy fluency in running two closely linked, interweaving channels at once: close listening attention to the other while also forming and expressing one's own thought and feeling; and an inner building toward a next response as one is reading further signals and sensing below the surface of the other and self. There is no fear in easy and full dialogue, either of inability to express and communicate self or of implying any lower valuing of the other when not concentrating on them wholly (p. 360).

Listening can be seen as an expansive activity. As others open up and share, we can connect to them and build up a channel through which we perceive more directly the ways we participate in the world around us. Thus, as Isaacs put it: "Listening can open in us a door, a greater sense of participation in the world. […] The principle of participation builds upon the realization that individuals are active participants in the living world, a part of nature as well as observers of it" (1999, p. 87). Transferred to the work context, managers, leaders, and employees certainly need to participate in a project or organization! So, ideally, listening would have a significant share in making the participation clearer, more thoughtful and effective. As described in the chapter on the interpersonal relationship at work, the superior who reacts sensitively to the employee's statement, "Finally I'm done with the damn database upgrade," can turn an average work climate into a good one.

The capacity to listen can be developed by first recognizing how we are listening now, what we attend to, how we react when we do not agree with what we hear, etc. In addition, we can begin to listen more consciously to ourselves, to our own reactions and feelings. Moreover, it is important to be aware of what we add from our memory to what is actually expressed such as not to get caught in the web of our memories and interpretations. More ideas on how listening can be developed are summarized in Resource Box 10.1 that adds aspects to the do's and don'ts of active listening elaborated on in the previous chapter.

Resource Box 10.1 Helpful listening resources enabling dialogue according to David Bohm elaborated on the basis of Isaacs (1999).

Listening resources

- Ask
  - How do I listen now? What do I attend to?
  - What is it that I tend to respond to?
- To be present, one must notice what one is feeling in the present moment.
- Listen to yourself
  - What do I feel? Where do I feel it? How does this feel?
  - What are the different inner "voices" trying to convey?
  - What "voices" are marginalized here?
  - Listen to your actions to see how you deal with others.
- Stay relaxed
  Metaphorically: Calm the surface of the waters (or currents of your experience) so that you can see below the surface.
- Stick to the facts rather than making interpretations.
- Listen while noticing resistance.
  Listen while consciously noticing your ongoing judgment that influences and may distort what is said. Simply watch what comes up.
- Follow the disturbance
  Some expressions may trigger strongly negative emotions that tend to color the communication for a while. Rather than feeling angry and staying with the frustration, try to listen for the sources of the difficulty (in you or in others) and for evidence that may challenge your view. Ask: How can we get beyond this?
- Reflect on how others are experiencing the situation.

Invitation to reflect:

Compare the resource box on active listening with the one presented in this chapter in the context of dialogue. Do you realize different focal issues or practices? In your view, are they consistent or can you spot incompatibilities?

While active listening focuses on the interpersonal relationship between the speaker and the listener and acts more to support the speaker in making sense of his or her experience, the dialogical listening practice takes a more symmetric function. It is targeted at collaboratively generating knowledge and improving the understanding of the whole situation in order to facilitate problem solving. Consequently, the listening practice in dialogues appears to emphasize thought and awareness of what is going on in the present and how this is going to influence the future, whereas active listening is more concerned about the momentary feelings and deep understanding of the speaker from his or her perspective. Thus, while understanding is pivotal to both listening practices, dialogue emphasizes knowledge construction while in active listening the (inter-) personal experience is crucial.

10.3.2 Respecting

Isaac's practice of respecting is a close kin to acceptance in the Person-centered approach and can be seen as contributing complementary aspects. Like acceptance, Isaacs' practice of respect means to consider and support the potential that the others carry within themselves, and to respect their boundaries. To respect someone implies not to intrude and not to impose. At the same time, it often implies not to withhold oneself or distance oneself and leave the other completely alone. It is definitely more than tolerance. What can become challenging, indeed, is seeing people as whole beings and to legitimate them even if we do not agree with what they say or how they act.

Respecting is based on the principle of *coherence* (Bohm 1996). It implies embracing an already existing wholeness in life, such that we are more likely to look at how an existing system works and what aspects we wish to sustain rather than searching for what needs to change. When dialoguing in situations of disagreement, we learn, in particular, to conceive that what is happening is unfolding from a common source. This helps us to develop the capacity of respect for oneself, for others, and for diversity. It also helps us to refrain from looking at single aspects, views, or people in isolation without considering the context and interconnections (Lago 2013).

A touching (in the true sense of the word) idea is that respect requires us to perceive a problem that comes from outside as a part of ourselves, to co-own it, to empathically sense it in our bodies in order to be able to connect to it more than just superficially.

We were moved by the experience of Peter Garrett who conducted dialogues with imprisoned dangerous criminals and shared his view on the crucial function of respect (see box below).

Invitation to reflect:

What does the following quote tell you? Do you want to share the message you got with your colleague(s)?
"The impulse behind intentions is pure, even though the intention may be distorted and the impact not what was intended. Inquiring deeply enough to reach the original impulse will always reveal wholesomeness. This provides the confidence to enter the loudest confrontation and the darkest territory without fear that it will get forever worse." P. Garrett quoted by Isaacs (1999, p. 121).

What managers may appreciate is that Garrett was speaking of more than conversational skill for inquiry. He was referring to the stance of deep respect and inclusion that must lie behind inquiry for it to have any real effect. Behind this stance is the appreciation of the principle of coherence.

While respect is an attitude that is deeply ingrained in our personality, there are ways to develop it gradually. Resource Box 10.2 below draws substantially on the writing of Isaacs (1999) who elaborates on multiple ideas on how to become more respectful.

Resource Box 10.2 Some resources for building respect in the context of dialogue elaborated on the basis of Isaacs (1999).

Resources for developing respect

- Ask
  - What can I learn from this person? What is best in this person?
  - How does what I'm seeing and hearing here fit in some larger whole?
  - What must be sustained here that others are missing?
  - What is happening right now?
- Try to understand what is happening without resorting to accusation and blame.
- Honor the other person's boundaries and not to intrude.
- Neither completely distance yourself from the other nor ignore him/her.
- Become centered: Stay rooted but flexible. Take a deep breath and then another. Let yourself come to rest, letting go of any tension that you might feel, any intruding thought.
- Don't try to "fix others." Use the disturbances you feel with others as a means of including those factors and providing them with space to be who and what they are. This requires a willingness to meet the difficulty outside of ourself, in ourself in order to allow it to connect to something in us.
- Learn to hold creative tension.

- Look for someone who is as different from you as you can imagine and spend a couple of hours with him/her. To your amazement, you probably will discover how much you have in common.

Example from experience:

The first question: "What can I learn from this person?" has a particular (hi) story with me (Renate). Since I first had been confronted with this question (during a church service in my adolescent years), I started asking it in various school, work, and private contexts and cultures. I feel most thankful for the effects it has had on my listening capacity and attitude toward others.

10.3.3 Suspending

Suspending starts with becoming aware of the contents of one's consciousness so one may more accurately sense what is going on. This can lead on to awareness of the processes that generat**es** the thinking. Reflecting on those processes generates the opportunity to transform them. This becomes possible as we allow our attention to include more and more of our immediate experience that can help us to come to grips with what is happening as it is happening (Isaacs 1999, pp. 142–144).

The word *suspend* has the Latin root *suspendere*, which means "to hang below." Literally, suspending reminds us to put on hold what goes on in the forefront of our awareness so that we can inquire into what we observe and gain a richer meaning and understanding.

Suspending emphasizes the putting aside of one's own thoughts and reactions in order to achieve openness for what else might be there, for what lies beneath the surface, what else is unfolding in me, what questions come to mind and what the other(s) may want to share. If we aim to fully and exactly understand another person and his or her opinion and meaning, and respect that person, we will tend to put our view to the side for some time, to suspend it, in order to be able to more fully attend to the other person and the whole context. Practically, suspending acknowledges the *self-organizing tendency* inherent in the universe. This implies that, unlike a mechanic who works to fix a broken article, for example, as a manager you would not seek to "manage" an organization but rather invest your effort in cultivating the conditions under which it might evolve and prosper. Interested readers will find more resources to develop their suspending practice in Resource Box 10.3 below.

Resource Box 10.3 Resources on suspending in the context of dialogue elaborated on the basis of Isaacs (1999).

Resources for suspending

- Ask
  - What are my thoughts right now? What could underlie them; how could they have arisen?
  - Why am I so convinced about this? What is leading me to hold on to it so tightly?
  - What would be at risk if I let go?
  - What is my own part in what I'm dealing with or exploring?
  - What am I missing right now?
  - What are the forces at work that have produced this problem? What are the currents that keep the system alive?
- Put on hold the temptation to immediately fix, correct, or solve a problem. Begin to imagine or sense yourself into what you observe and how it connects to you.
- Build conscious awareness. Being aware allows our attention to expand and to include more facets of our experience. This provides more access points to the situation.
- Suspend certainty. By relaxing our grip, we open up to new insight.
- Mine for the questions: Identifying one good question can be vastly more significant than offering many partial answers.
- Look at the situation from a different angle; see it in a different light; describe it in different terms or let others describe it.
- Look for the bigger picture and acknowledge some inherent order.

10.3.4 Voicing

There is a simple question underlying the practice of voicing, namely "What needs to be expressed now?" (Issacs 1999, p. 159). To find an answer, we need to listen to ourselves. This may not be so simple, since, too often, we are taught how we ought to behave, what we ought to do or say, etc., so that it is hard to identify what lies at our core and would benefit from being unfolded and shared. For example: Now—during a phone call—should I tell my managing partner who had prepared a meeting very carefully, proposed a detailed agenda, and was sharing, that she had a sense that it was really productive that my sense was pretty different? Even though I considered it strategically appropriate to conduct the meeting the way we did, I actually found it quite tedious and would have preferred more space for dialogue?

OK, should I tell her right now, or will there be a better occasion to share my perception, for example, when preparing for the next meeting? What is it that I want to change and how would the steering committee react to a less structured meeting with the goal of spontaneous expression?

To discover what we feel and think can bring us closer to our genuine being and make our expression more unique, authentic, united, and hence trustworthy. One path toward learning more about oneself is to reveal aspects of oneself through expressing them. In this way, they rise from the implicit core in you and take on explicit form that both you and others can perceive through multiple channels such as tone and rhythm of voice, words/sentences spoken, body language, gesticulation, etc. The implicit in you becomes explicit, apparent, and shared such that others can perceive it, react to it, and let you know and feel how your message was received.

Isaacs (1999) notes:

> Our organizations give us many mixed messages about expressing our own voice. On the one hand we hear about endless "empowerment" programs, transformation initiatives, and development plans in companies large and small. On the other hand we are expected to toe the line and defer to the authority figures who reign supreme. [...] Despite the democratic climate in which most modern corporations have arisen and function, in many ways life within them is a direct denial of the freedoms that guarantee their survival (p. 181).

To speak one's voice, determination is required and some risk needs to be taken. Only if we admit to ourselves the possibility that what we think might be valid for others do we tend to find the confidence to share it. As one student reflected in one of our seminars, it may be easier to speak up if you are asked by another. This is why voicing would include inquiry as much as articulation and is intricately connected to listening.

Voicing can be considered as an expression of the principle of unfoldment which denotes the constant potential waiting to unfold through and around us. This principle follows from Bohm's notion of the implicate order that

> ... is based on a premise about the nature of "unfoldment and enfoldment," where reality unfolds from a patterned invisible level to the visible world that we see, and then folds back up again into the invisible state. Reality consists both of a surface level "explicate order" which has a relative independence like the individual notes of a piece of music, and a deeper implicate order out of which the explicate flows (Isaacs 1999, p. 186).

Bohm goes on to link ideas and perceptions which appear as distinct things to us as the explicate versions of some more implicate order "in which there is both an underlying wholeness and relative independence of the external parts" (Isaacs 1999, p. 187). Thus, voicing—in the sense of speaking my authentic voice—would ultimately flow from the underlying implicate order, explicating aspects of it.

Now let us ask: What value would appreciate the notion of the implicate order and learning about it has for a manager? Given that Bohm's theory reflects part of our reality, voicing would indeed provide an invaluable tool for allowing us to share and see aspects of our organization that hitherto had been concealed and join efforts to deal with them, rather than remaining blind and overlooking aspects that are on the edge of unfoldment anyway. By the way, who would risk shutting down information channels willingly? Yet, it seems that in several organizations, voicing is underdeveloped (as is listening) and this may be one of the major reasons why their performance is less than optimal.

Practically, voicing, much like listening, has a key function in all the methods contributing to transformative communication that are going to be presented in this chapter. Despite the enormous value of silence for allowing thought to form, voicing ultimately facilitates sharing and explication of the implicit. And, whoever has experienced a situation of not understanding (the language of) the other will witness the enormous value of speaking and understanding (the language of) the other as well as the frustration when understanding cannot be reached.

In the context of dialogue, in particular, Isaacs (1999) suggests how one can learn to find one's voice. A helpful metaphor he uses is music, asking the reader to ponder what our music might be and who would best play our music. Finding our music and giving ourselves the permission to "play" provide the core energy of our voice.

Another helpful question is to ask ourselves what we would like to be known for and to allow oneself to look for—and to explicate what we *truly care about* most. If you find yourself deliberating whether you can fully appreciate the idea of voicing what you care about most in any work context, you'll be in company with the authors of the book you are reading now. Both authors are extremely devoted to the understanding of the potential benefits of the person-oriented approach to the world of business. While we fully agree that it would be crucially important to be aware of what we really do care about, giving the proper voice to it in the work context would also require us to listen, respect, and take into account the current situation encompassing people, organizational/project objectives, and the current context. Readers interested in further hints on learning to find and express their authentic voice are referred to the Resource Box 10.4 as well as the remainder of this chapter.

Resource Box 10.4 Resources for the practice of voicing in the context of dialogue (Isaacs 1999).

Voicing

- Ask
  - What needs to be expressed now? By me? By others? By the whole?
  - What purpose would this pattern serve if it was designed with intention?
  - What is trying to emerge?
  - What do I want to stand for? What do I want to be known for?
  - What might be at risk if I don't speak up now?
  - What do I risk when I speak up?
- Overcome self-censorship and risk to find and express your voice without planning.

- Discover and integrate more of yourself: Part of the discovery process in dialogue is the integration of all the different aspects of oneself.
- Find your "melody" and share it with others. If you don't speak up and stand for your destiny, who else should do it?
- Connect. There is a deeply communal dimension to speaking together that is often lost but can be overcome when our words emphasize connection rather than sustaining separation.

Example from experience:

To illustrate the usage of Resource Box 10.4, let us mutually ask "What do I want to stand for? What do I want to be known for?"
I (David) am fully invested in manifesting the people-oriented aspects of communication for the workplace. I had a chance to collaborate with Carl Rogers on this issue several years ago. Now I'm still destined to work in that direction—to make the person- or people-oriented aspect more available through research, practice and writing, such as this book.
I (Renate) have been standing up for my destiny—namely to strengthen communication and teamwork skills in academic education—several times. Initially, I seem not to have been heard, but gradually my message reaches its recipients and influences new curricula and staff. As a team with three colleagues, we just won this year's (2016) Teaching Award of the University of Vienna. So I hope the upward spiral, though slow in its beginning, will continue and the collaborative effort in this book will reach people around the globe. Good to join effort!

10.4 Limitations of Dialogue Practices

While the four practices were presented in sequential order, one following the other, it is vital that they are lived and practiced in proper balance with each other. What "proper balance" means would depend on the particular people involved in a dialogue as well as on the particular situation at hand. If, for example, one person dominates others by skillfully voicing one idea after the other without ever listening and suspending, this "monologue" surely would not qualify as dialogue. By the same token, if I practice suspending for too long a time, I may get frustrated not to contribute what I'm thinking and feeling.

Further noteworthy limitations to the practice of dialogue are rigidly held beliefs or positions and fear of consequences. In particular, in a business context, for example, people holding power may be unwilling to change their view and/or strategy unless forced by some risk or losses in the market. Similarly, we may be in fear of the consequences of giving up some proven (organizational or personal) patterns that work and have always worked for us well. Why should we risk giving it up and walking into the unknown? *What if we couldn't bear the chaos or void that inevitably can't be excluded and would need to be overcome*? Do people bring with them the necessary collective intelligence and interpersonal attitudes to find the new, better order that could unfold through being in dialogue?

10.5 Dialogue Versus Discussion

Ellinor and Gerard describe the objectives of dialogue and contrast them with just wanting to win an argument: "Dialogue occurs when people are trying to learn from one another, to understand from a larger perspective rather than defending and justifying from a personal perspective" (1998, p. 20). We believe that dialogue can help us to see the bigger picture and thus enrich each individual view. While, ideally, this coincides with what we expect from any good conversation—often informally termed "discussion"—in reality this is not often (or should we say rarely) the case. In order to better discriminate different conversational settings and their underlying goals and strategies to achieve them, Table 10.1 provides a continuum between dialogue and discussion derived from Ellinor and Gerard's conceptualization.

According to Bohm, the essence is the ability to think together what we cannot if we need to defend our opinions. It means to suspend our opinions, to listen to others' opinions, to suspend them, to see what all that means and to voice what we think and feel. In a dialogue, ideas flow back and forth between people, rather than "each trying to persuade or convince the others [...] everybody is quite free [...]. So there is both a collective mind and an individual mind and the flow moves between them." (Bohm 1996, p. 31).

Table 10.1 The discussion/dialogue continuum (Ellinor and Gerard 1998, p. 21)

Dialogue	Discussion
Seeing the whole among the parts	Breaking issues/problems into parts
Seeing the connections between the parts	Seeing the distinctions between the parts
Inquiring into assumptions	Defending/justifying assumptions
Learning through inquiry and disclosure	Persuading, selling, and telling
Creating shared meaning among many	Gaining agreement on one meaning

Invitation to reflect

Where on the dialogue/discussion continuum would you position the conversation

- that took place in the most recent meeting you attended/headed?
- typically is happening in your organization or most recent project?

Do you think discussion (in the sense of Ellinor and Gerard) is ever needed? If so, in which situations do you consider it important?
Do you think dialogue (in the sense of Ellinor and Gerard) is ever needed? If so, in which situations do you consider it important?
Do you think there is a value to distinguishing between dialogue and discussion? Should the two conversational forms be combined in problem-solving sessions and if so, which form should precede the other?

10.6 Conclusion

The practices of listening and respect are akin to the capacities of empathic understanding and acceptance as presented in the previous chapter. Intriguingly, as expressed by Isaacs (1999) and Rogers (1980), both are connected such that real respect requires one to encounter an issue that is outside at the inside in order to be able to connect to it. In other words, acceptance without understanding would be void. For managers or leaders, this means that they need to encounter and truly feel their coworkers' issues, problems, challenges, etc. and include them in their own "inner agenda" if they want to be truly helpful. For team-members, symmetrically, it would be most helpful if they could put themselves in the shoes of their superiors to truly sense their issues, like taking on risks and being responsible for decisions. The practice of dialogue can help to achieve this, given people's commitment to hold person-centered attitudes.

Suspending calls upon us to put our own thoughts aside in order to become open for what the other person expresses at whatever level of clarity or consciousness. If we aim to fully understand others and respect them, we will tend to put our view to the side for some time, to suspend it, in order to be able to more fully attend to the other persons. Finally, the practice of voicing can be seen to be aligned with the expression of what is conscious at the moment and matches the person's present experiencing. In this way, multiple facets of the current situation are explicated, can be perceived, examined, and collaboratively be joined together to deliver an image that is as realistic and accurate as possible. This holistic image, we believe, would be the best possible basis for mindful and rational decision-making (Rogers 1961; Ryback 1998).

References

Barrett-Lennard, G. T. (1998). *Carl Rogers' helping system: Journey and substance*. London, UK: SAGE Publications.
Bohm, D. (1996). On dialogue. In L. Nichol (Ed.), *London*. UK: Routledge.
Bohm, D., & Peat, D. (2000). *Science, order and creativity*. London, UK: Routledge.
Cain, D. J. (2010). *Person-centered psychotherapies*. American Psychological Association (APA).
Ellinor, L., & Gerard, G. (1998). *Dialogue: Rediscover the transforming power of conversation*. New York, NY: John Wiley and Sons.
Isaacs, W. (1999). *Dialogue and the art of thinking together*. New York, NY: Doubleday.
Lago, C. (2013). The Person-centred approach and its capacity to enhance constructive international communication. In J. H. D. Cornelius-White, R. Motschnig-Pitrik, & M. Lux (Eds.), *Interdisciplinary handbook of the Person-centered approach: Research and theory*. New York, NY: Springer.
Rogers, C. R. (1961). *On becoming a Person—A psychotherapists view of psychotherapy*. London, UK: Constable.
Rogers, C. R. (1980). *A way of being*. Boston: Houghton Mifflin Co.
Ryback, D. (1998). *Putting emotional intelligence to work*. Boston: Butterworth-Heinemann.
Wood, J. K. (2008). *Carl Rogers' Person-centered approach: Toward an understanding of its implications*. Ross-on-Wye, UK: PCCS-books.

Chapter 11
Transforming Communication Through Intensive Group Experience, Communication Workshops, and Open Case

> *The intensive group experience the encounter group—whatever you wish to call it—is when well managed well facilitated I think one of the most significant inventions of this century. I think it has had—and still continues to have—a tremendous impact.*
>
> Rogers and Russel (2002, p. 194)

This chapter focuses on

- Attitudes and competences at the core of effective communication;
- Selected settings that support and tend to accelerate the development and practice of transformative communication;
- Including
  - Person-centered intensive groups;
  - Communication workshops;
  - Open case;
- Case examples and participants' reflections regarding the settings;
- Resources for communication workshops and the open case setting; and
- Comparison between settings and their acquaintance with the Person-Centered Approach.

11.1 Introduction

This chapter presents three settings that stand at the core of transformative communication: the intensive group experience (Rogers 1970; Wood 2008), communication workshops (Motschnig-Pitrik 2012, 2015), and the open case setting. If facilitated properly, these settings have in common that they support community and team building and have the potential to improve participants' dialogical and problem-solving capacities. They help communicative exchanges to acquire a quality of moving beyond what is already known and reach states of improved

R. Motschnig and D. Ryback, *Transforming Communication in Leadership and Teamwork*, DOI 10.1007/978-3-319-45486-3_11

understanding, taking several perspectives into account. As with active listening, it is not the particular techniques that stand in the foreground, but rather the attitudes that people hold and express through words, body language, gesticulation, intonation, and behavioral ways that matter most for co-forming an atmosphere in which people feel safe to learn significantly, experientially, and sustainably. Thus, pure training of skills would be insufficient, unless it can build upon interpersonal attitudes that underlie the people-oriented agenda.

Due to the significance of experiential learning (Rogers 1961), rather than just writing about methods and settings, we provide case examples, exercises, and participants' reactions and call upon readers to explore, select, and use those resources that they consider most meaningful in their own context. Optimally, teams within or across organizations would practice and reflect collaboratively and thereby mutually learn from each other.

11.2 Intensive Group Experience and Communication Workshops

After having introduced dialogue as a way of thinking together, let us turn to the intensive group or workshop as a way of being, focused on improving interpersonal relationships with oneself and the other. In this sense, self- and group experience can be seen as a means of unfolding, among others, the personal capacities of people for dialogue, collaboration, and working with groups or teams. Consequently, (inter)personal substratum for management, leadership, teamwork, and dialogue can intensively be nourished by participating in intensive groups. In order to allow readers to form their own view and optimally also motivate them to experience an intensive group or workshop, the following paragraphs provide a first introduction to the phenomenon. Needless to say, reading about it can never substitute for a real-life experience of actually participating in a group or workshop.

Historically, at about the same time, two distinctly different objectives gave rise to the movement toward an intensive group experience in two different places, though in the same continent. Around 1947, the psychologist Kurt Lewin, from the Massachusetts Institute of Technology (MIT), realized that the development of human relation skills was a crucial but underdeveloped area of education. Thus, at the National Training Laboratories (NTL), he and his colleagues started to conduct so-called T-groups (T standing for training) in which top personnel from industry was taught to observe their interactions with other members in order to better understand their own functioning and to better cope with difficult situations (Rogers 1970; Motschnig-Pitrik and Nykl 2014).

At about the same time (1946), Carl Rogers and his team at the University of Chicago were involved in training personal counselors for veterans returning from World War II. As they felt that cognitive training would not be sufficient to prepare them, they experimented with integrating a cognitive and an experiential approach.

The "trainees" met for several hours each day in order to better understand themselves and to relate to each other in ways that would be helpful and could carry over into their work (Rogers 1970). It turned out to be so successful that the concepts were gradually further developed to include various orientations and forms (Natiello 2001). A quite recent one that acknowledges the faster pace in our time (in most cultures) and the availability of Internet services are person-centered communication workshops (Motschnig-Pitrik 2012, 2015). The second part of this subchapter is going to describe them as time-effective successors of intensive groups that provide a loose structure, helping participants and facilitators to focus on the main goal: to transform communication.

Resource Box 11.1: Intensive groups: Features and tendencies according to Rogers (1970, p. 6)

Features of person-centered intensive groups (Rogers 1970, p. 6):

- The group tends to be small (8–18 participants—there are, however, reports about quite successful large groups as well), relatively unstructured and choosing its own goals and directions.
- The group experience often, though not always, includes some cognitive input—some content material to be presented to the group or some particular direction to focus on.
- In almost all instances, the leader's responsibility is primarily the facilitation of the expression of both feelings and thoughts on the part of participants. The group leader and the members focus on the process and dynamics of immediate personal interactions.

Tendencies in intensive groups (Rogers 1970 p. 6):

- A facilitator can develop a psychological climate of safety in which freedom of expression and reduction of defensiveness tend to occur. In such a climate, many of the immediate feeling reactions, meanings, and thoughts of members tend to be recognized and expressed more freely.
- A climate of mutual trust develops out of this mutual freedom to express genuine feelings, both positive and negative. Each member moves toward greater acceptance of his/her total being—emotional, intellectual, and physical—as it is in the moment, including transformative potential.
- With members less inhibited by defensive rigidity, the possibility of change in personal attitudes and behavior, in professional methods, and in administrative procedures and relationships becomes less threatening. Individuals can hear each other more clearly and can learn from each other to a greater extent.
- There is a development of feedback process, such that members learn how they appear to others and what impact each has on interpersonal relationships.

- With this improved communication, new ideas, new concepts, and new directions emerge. Innovation can become a desirable rather than a threatening possibility.
- The learnings in the group process tend to spill over, whether temporarily or permanently, into relationships with spouses, children, students, subordinates, peers, and even superiors following the group experience.
- After initial uncertainty and tension, an atmosphere develops that invites the free expression of feelings, meanings, and ideas. However, this tendency cannot be perceived through an intellectual approach alone; it requires the personal experiencing of such an open atmosphere.

11.2.1 Transformations Facilitated by Participating in Person-Centered Intensive Groups

Viewed from the perspective of a participant or client, Rogers (1961, pp. 37–38) describes the self-organized direction of personal development in a person-centered atmosphere as follows. He and social scientists in his field conducted research that allowed them to measure the changes described (Rogers 1961, 1970; Barrett-Lennard 1998; Cain 2010):

If I can create a relationship characterized on my part:

- by a genuineness and transparency, in which I am my real feelings;
- by a warm acceptance of and prizing of the other person as a separate individual; and
- by a sensitive ability to see his world and himself as he sees them;

then the other individual in the relationship:

- will experience and understand aspects of himself which previously he has repressed;
- will find himself becoming better integrated, more able to function effectively;
- will become more similar to the person he would like to be;
- will be more self-directing and self-confident;
- will become more of a person, more unique, and more self-expressive;
- will be more understanding and more acceptant of others; and
- will be able to cope with the problems of life more adequately and more comfortably.

☕ Invitation to reflect:

Do you consider developing yourself into the direction described above worthwhile or even desirable?
Would you like to provide a person-centered atmosphere to your team or colleagues such that they could develop in the direction described?
Do you think that providing a person-centered atmosphere to your boss or superior would be possible and could have any effect? If not, why? Is yes, what effect do you imagine it could have?

Regarding organizational change, Rogers encountered individuals who were greatly changed, while their institutions did hardly undergo any change. Some group participants even resigned from their jobs, having decided to work for change outside the institution rather than within it because of the courage gained. In another case, interpersonal communication transformed an enterprise (Rogers 1970, p. 79). This illustrates that intensive groups tend to foster openness and interdependence and may encourage changes. Interestingly, the changes that intensive groups tend to bring about highly correspond to respective attitudes and competencies captured by Peter Senge in *The Fifth Discipline* (Senge 2006). Prominent examples of these transformative changes are “a more encompassing and sensitive perception of the environment, the loosening of rigid mental constructs, the capacity and readiness for dialogue and many more” (Motschnig-Pitrik and Nykl 2014, p. 192).

Speaking personally, we (the authors) are experiencing again and again that these changes are deep and lasting and never totally disappear from one’s attitude base. Nevertheless, the social environment in which we live and work does have a considerable influence on how intensively the transformed attitudes and their communication can be expressed and thereby deepened and unfolded further. Often, the hierarchical working and tone in organizations or the rigid planning and assessment required in large projects reduce the opportunities and make it difficult “to be the transformation” we internally become. If such adverse conditions dominate, we long for the renewal of some kind of intensive encounter experience in order to keep the transformation alive and nourish it. In other cases, if we are lucky to work in an organization or team employing flexible structures and people who master transformative communication, then we love to deepen these capacities together and “apply” them, foster them, and pass them on to our environment. This, for example, is happening right now for us while collaborating on a book for you and us. It was happening throughout the iCom project (www.icomproject.eu) in intensive cooperation with more than ten interactive workshops between industry and academic partners (iCom Team 2014). The personal effect is that we feel immensely motivated to be on the outlook for opportunities in which we can work and live with constructive, transformative communication. This can happen, for example, when working with people who appreciate and assimilate this kind of communication. It can also happen through facilitating groups or workshops for students and/or managers who want to improve their communication and, as a concomitant to this, become more effective in their jobs and lives.

11.2.2 Potentials, Limitations, and Need for Adaptation to Changed Conditions

We go along with Rogers in seeing intensive groups as a particularly powerful means for facilitating the living and working together of people, in particular in situations characterized by tension, change, high customer orientation, and diversity, without having to resort to the application of power or formal authority. Part of the power of the encounter setting might stem from the fact that, at any moment, the group invites each member of the group (implicitly) to contribute to the moving forward of him-/herself and for the group by utilizing the talents each of them brings to the table. This is *the* task, so full concentration is on one's feeling, thought, meaning in the concrete, present moment, providing ample opportunities for participants to listen to and get to know themselves, perceive their and others' interactions, and share whatever comes to mind and seeks expression. Consequently, the personal growth spans a broad rather than narrow scope and the particular area in which it happens depends on a myriad of situational factors. Also, the overriding self-organized processes going on need time to unfold and their effects to be assimilated.

This is part of why pure intensive groups—despite their unique and unexpected potentials—have lost some attraction as a means for business-related personal development. In our competitive (western) society, it seems understandable for an employer to ask why he/she should invest in the broad personal development of an employee who might be leaving the company soon. Also, people who have not yet experienced an intensive group tend not to be able to imagine what it could be like since the group experience differs a lot from the traditional, structured educational offerings we consume for thousands of hours in our educated lives. Why then should they invest a considerable amount of time for something unknown and put some of their current, often urgent activities on hold?

In sum, there appears to be a demand to overcome the uncertainties typical of intensive groups and yet retain many of their powerful potentials. The "solution" that one of the authors is experimenting with for more than a decade is person-centered communication workshops.

11.2.3 Person-Centered Communication Workshops

The primary objective of these workshops is to improve participants' communication rooted in their interpersonal attitudes and polished by appropriate skills. This happens, in the first place, by providing them with an atmosphere based on congruence, acceptance, and an effort to deeply and empathically understand them. Unlike intensive groups, however, the facilitator proposes a loose structure including some exercises or elements geared toward specific aspects of constructive communication. These elements are never imposed, and it is always suggested to participants that they may prefer just to listen and not take part actively if this is what they prefer. In general, once some element is performed, participants are invited to reflect upon it in the group such that both the merits and the criticism on the elements' rules and constraints are voiced. If the group seems ready—which can be determined by directly asking participants—one whole session can be offered as an encounter session while clearly stating that "it will be up to us what we make out of the free space" and that the facilitator would participate as an experienced group member rather than someone structuring the session. Some groups like the free session so much that they decide to have more of these sessions; however, in the authors' experience, participants prefer some structuring and guidance in addition to sufficient time for free interaction. Sometimes, participants are split, some sensing the deep learning and creative potential of encounter, while others are keen to learn something more "crisp" through the exercises. Several of the students' "voices" are captured in Motschnig-Pitrik and Nykl (2014) with a whole chapter on intensive groups and person-centered workshops (Motschnig-Pitrik 2015).

In order to let readers imagine what elements have qualified to be suggested to participants of person-centered communication workshops, Resource Box 11.1 describes the most frequent ones.

Resource Box 11.2: Some favored elements proposed during person-centered communication workshops

Name of element or exercise	Goal	Description
Active listening exercise	Improve listening competence	Participants form triads in which one person acts as speaker, one as listener, and one as observer. The speaker shares something that matters to him or her right now, and the listener listens actively for about seven minutes. The observers may take notes about what they observe and give brief feedback after the speaker has finished. Then, people in the triads change roles and repeat the exercise. This happens until each participant has tried out each of the three "roles." Afterward, all share their experiences and insights in the plenum

(continued)

(continued)

Name of element or exercise	Goal	Description
Sharing active listening experiences in real life	Transfer of competences; expressing one's experience; finding out whether participants try out new skills outside the seminar	The facilitator expresses his/her interest in whether participants tried out their acquired listening skills in real life and what their experience was
Summarizing the essence	Listen attentively and experience capturing the essence	Facilitator suggests trying out the following: Before the speakers express their point (e.g., their experience with active listening in real life), they should paraphrase the essence of what the person ahead of him/her had expressed
Enacting barriers in communication	Identifying barriers and enacting them in role-play; introducing some physical movement into the setting	Participants form small teams (about 4–5 persons) and elaborate on communication barriers. Then, they choose one barrier and design a role-play in which they illustrate the barrier. Finally, they perform the role-play and receive feedback from the group. Afterward, the barriers are listed, compared with the literature and the match, and/or difference is elaborated
How would you react if …?	Finding out one's response preferences and becoming aware of alternative response options and reactions	Example: How would you react if your employee said: "finally I'm finished with that damn data report"? Participants share their responses and perceive their own reaction to each response variant. Participants reflect feelings, thoughts, and insights in the plenum
Self-evaluation regarding the 3 person-centered conditions and giving feedback	Self-exploration and articulating direct feedback	Finding personal strengths and weaknesses regarding the 3 person-centered conditions. Which one is easiest/hardest for me? Participants break into small groups according to their strengths and weaknesses. They share in small groups and reflect their "findings" in the plenum

(continued)

(continued)

Name of element or exercise	Goal	Description
Reaction sheets (Rogers 1961; Motschnig-Pitrik 2014)	Giving a written personal reaction; giving written feedback	Typically, participants are expected to post their reaction to a workshop unit onto some Web space that can be accessed by the group but not by the general public. The reactions provide a virtual bridge between sessions and make it easier to find out where we are in the group. Written reactions may help participants to realize people's different perspectives and sometimes totally different reactions to one and the same element/situation

11.2.4 Summary and Outlook on Intensive Groups and Communication Workshops

Research on person-centered intensive groups and communication workshop indicates that they deserve a place in management education—far beyond the study of psychology. In a survey at the University of Vienna, Austria, the vast majority of students mentioned retrospectively that it was the intensive or encounter groups that they had perceived as most meaningful out of three elements: structured workshops, online support/materials, and intensive groups (Motschnig-Pitrik and Nykl 2005). Moreover, the inner flexibility and interpersonal attitudes that tend to unfold in well-facilitated intensive groups and communication workshops appear particularly relevant in two contexts that are moving to foreground: agile management and intercultural teams. Both are going to be in the focus of a case study summarized in the research section of this book.

However, in order to properly integrate the intensive group experience into educational portfolios, it is essential that experienced facilitators and carefully designed and transparently communicated concepts for the respective workshops or seminars are available. Also, the vast potential but also the possible risks such as harsh conflicts or very slow processes that may happen in intensive groups need to be understood and taken into account. This is because self-organization and the actualizing tendency are inherent tendencies but not imperatives taking over each and every instance of a group from the first moment onward. In any case, research results point to the fact that intensive groups and structured, interactive workshops provide a powerful potential to develop those disciplines, which Senge (2006) propagated as the “disciplines of the learning organization.” They promote the constructive advance of both people and organizations. So even though our Internet time may require some creative and sensitive adaptation to the basic concept of the intensive group experience, we fully agree with Rogers and Russel (2002, p. 194) that “a well-facilitated intensive group which relies on the potential that resides in the group is, and continues to be, a very powerful experience for personality change, for behavior change, for laying the basis for solutions of social problems.”

The following books and articles contain further “material,” ideas, research, participants’ reactions, and reflections on person-centered groups and workshops: Rogers (1961, 1970, 1978, 1980, 1983), Schmid (1994), Barrett-Lennard (1998, 2003, 2005), Lago and McMillan (1999), Natiello (2001), Nykl (2005), Nykl and Motschnig-Pitrik (2005), Wood (2008), Cornelius-White et al. (2013a, b), Motschnig-Pitrik and Nykl (2007, 2014).

11.3 Open Case

Open case is a workshop setting for interactively exploring experiences, attitudes, thoughts, and solution strategies regarding some specified, predetermined, or participant-selected case. While resembling some established settings such as world-café, open space, marketplace, dialogue groups, and person-centered encounter and supervision groups, it can be distinguished from these settings by a unique set of features. Open case is most prominently characterized by the presence of a person who supplies a real, authentic case and the precondition of a facilitative climate based on the attitudes of congruence or authenticity, respect, and empathic understanding. Open case employs small teams (3–7) typically meeting in two phases and emphasizes participants’ personal expression in a person-centered climate, listening, and dialogue in approaching the case rather than pure brainstorming for new ideas.

The open case setting was developed in the course of the EU project iCom (constructive international communication in the context of ICT) in which European academic partners cooperated with small- and medium-sized enterprises with the focus on improving and researching communication in project teams and at the interface between industry and academia. The project team under the scientific lead of Renate Motschnig soon realized that pure intensive groups would pose too large a challenge on people’s time resources and thus looked for a setting that would:

- Include as much of the spirit of person-centered communication as possible,
- converge faster to meeting the business partners' objectives, namely to get some recognizable results, and
- be possible to be included as part of some (project) workshop, meeting, or educational offering.

Several experiences of conducting open case sessions reveal that even though the open case format cannot compete with person-centered intensive groups in terms of depth of experiencing, community building, breadth of learning, self-experience, insight, and personal development, it nevertheless can provide significant learning in terms of:

- Practicing active listening and sharing in a constructive atmosphere without having to go through the often laborious and time-consuming early phases of the group process;
- Helping the case-provider move forward in their particular current challenge, due to the combined creative energy of the team being focused on the case-provider and their sharing; and
- Appreciating the vast repertoire of ideas and thoughts being expressed as people think together.

11.3.1 Preconditions

Since the open case setting springs from a person-centered mind-set, the most essential precondition is that participants communicate in a genuine and mutually accepting way, trying to understand each other empathically and comprehensively, and refrain from judging each other. No less important is that they trust in the personal resources of the case-provider to move forward and see their function as resourceful peers facilitating the case-provider's process, along with shaping their own capacities for problem solving. Another precondition is the willingness of some participants (at least one) to share their case. Participants can be supported in finding cases by sharing some of the characteristics of a good case and giving examples. In our experience, the following features characterize cases that are particularly suitable for an open case setting. The case:

- Is something that currently occupies its holder and has meaning for him/her;
- Can be influenced by its holder at least to some degree; and
- Can be described in a few sentences and is not too complicated.

Cases that led to exciting insights are a creative designer who was not cooperative in a team at all, a boss who often dismissed the work of his employees but had good visionary capacities worth following, the difficult situation of a newcomer into a department, the tough decision on whether to continue working or enroll in a study, the question as to whether to wait for the promised job of one's dreams in a particular company, etc.

11.3.2 Process

Participants are invited to think about cases they are interested in sharing. The facilitator keeps track of them and subsequently helps the group in the selection process. If there are more than 7 people available to participate in open case, they are then asked to form small teams around cases the group can imagine getting involved in. This can happen, for example, by letting participants gather around the case providing volunteers and move around the room until each has found a place. Once the teams have formed, they are given the handouts (provided in Resource Box 11.3 a and b) that describe the individual steps in the process that should be followed. The facilitator presents these guidelines and offers to clarify any unclear issues.

The first phase focuses on recalling and sharing personal experience and on understanding the "forces" or currents being at work in the case. The second phase emphasizes the collaborative development of moves and solution strategies, however without necessarily solving the case. In order to maximize participants' learning from the whole experience including the level of the subject matter (case), process within oneself, and process in the team and in the group, we end the workshop with a reflective phase and then invite later reactions by means of online communication.

Resource Box 11.3a: Handouts for the first phase of the open case setting

OPEN CASE

Handout 1st session

The **goal** of this session is **to present and collaboratively elaborate on the case(s).**

All confirm their promise of confidentiality in group!

Participants may want to use the following items to guide them through the session.

1. (Before splitting into small groups) Find individuals to assume the following functions:
    - Case-provider
    - Moderator
    - Interested peers
2. **Case-provider describes his/her case** and proposes 1–3 questions of interest.

Case-provider may want to express his/her personal **feelings** about the case, what moves them in the case.
The case is given a **name** and, if appropriate, a symbol/**image**/metaphor.

3. **Peers reflect their understanding** by trying to capture—in their own words—the essential meaning of what the case-provider has revealed.
   Peers may ask questions regarding what has been said. It is essential that **peers stay with the case-provider and try to understand his/her message** (e.g., You said you felt stressed, so do you still feel stressed now?)
4. **Peers** may **ask whatever is of interest to them** in the context of the case. (e.g., Did you already talk to the department head?) **Peers** may **share their reactions** to the case.
5. All try to identify the currents or "**forces**" at work in the given case.
   - Forces immediately related to the case (within the person and the system)
   - Forces from/to the environment
     Can you name some of the forces and/or draw a diagram?
6. Based on what happened in this session, the **case-provider** reflects his/her **feelings and meanings** about the situation. In particular, he/she identifies any **significant, highly important events** in the case; others listen actively.

Optional: Before going into a short break, teams briefly share the names and essence of the cases. If peers want to switch to different teams, they may do so.

Resource Box 11.3b: Handouts for the second phase of the open case setting

OPEN CASE

Handout 2nd session

This session's **goal** is to further elaborate the case and open up new perspectives. The improved understanding of the case can possibly lead on to finding solution strategies.

Decide for keeping the **moderator** or switching to a new moderator.

7. **Change of perspective**:
   Peers take on the perspective of the case-provider and potentially other functions that are central and **share their feelings and view of the case**, case-provider, and context.
   Do you feel like staging some conversations that may go on?

Peers suggest various options that might be helpful to consider in the case.
Case-provider gives feedback.

8. **Rogers' core conditions**
   Peers make an effort at identifying **connections** (if any) between the **case and**

   - the three **person-centered core conditions** (congruence, acceptance, and empathic understanding)
   - the **talks** during the **break**

   Case-provider listens and may take notes.
9. **Reflection of case-provider**
   Case-provider explores the contributions of peers' perspectives and **reflects** in how far anything/any person in the workshop contributed to **moving the understanding of the case forward**.
   Case-provider explores what it is that he/she would most wishes (or fears) to happen.
10. **Reflection in small group**
    Small group reflects upon their process, insights, and solution strategies in the case.

Optional: Sharing in plenum
Each small group may produce a **flip-chart** with the following structure:
CASE-NAME

- Description (3–5 adjectives)
- Effects of case
- Case in context of 3 core conditions
- Solution strategies: first steps and long-term perspective
- The open case setting was ……………………………

11.3.3 Open Case as Perceived by Participants

An advanced student of "Service Science Management and Engineering" from the Masaryk University in Brno, Czech Republic, who also worked as a team leader reflected the following after his first participation in an open case session:

> @Open case - such an impressive thing! Most of you might be familiar with a thing called "intervention" - when a group of friends prepare their opinions on their common friend's life situation (alcohol, drugs, bad habits, other problems) and then […] try to change him by forcing him to see things from their point of view. Open case seems to be exactly the same thing but with a completely opposite polarity in a sense, that in an intervention - friends are trying to impose themselves, their opinions and their needs upon him, trying to foist a new

> behavior upon him. There is a force from people into a case inside somebody. In an open case the situation is opposite, one has an issue, with which he wants some help and others try to see as well as they can his point of view. So there is a lot of listening and understanding in an open case as opposed to a lot of talking and forcing in an intervention. At first, my expectations were such that people would be less understanding and more trying to enforce their own ideas and points of view onto the person whose case was elaborated. However, I was surprised by the momentum the resolution of the raised issue had gained. Not only did the person who brought the case – at least as it appeared to me– feel understood quickly and could help others understand more and more details about the situation, but the reactions and questions asked helped the person to see things from a new perspective and find new solutions. Yes, there were moments when advice and suggestions were provided before the case was really deeply understood, but I – and I think others as well – felt that the case was moving in a better direction when the understanding deepened, … I certainly hope people could help each other this way more often than only on such special occasions as our person-centered communications course.

> So many times, when people come to share a problem that they have - people mistake it for an opportunity to start an intervention. It is pulling and pushing a person, not respecting his being with the case. Open case, however, is just that - opening it, allowing it to be, to give it space and understanding - the inherent aspect of people to be constructive, then drives the case to move towards resolution almost by itself under such conditions.

To also share the perception of the open case session from the case-provider's perspective, here is an excerpt from her reaction sheet:

> Since I was one of those whom the open case was about, I enjoyed people listening to me. [...] Yet it was a bit strange for me to talk in front of so many people about a kind of a problem that I had and it was a bit of a shock for me that those people looked like they cared and tried to help and bring their perceptions and advice. I could feel a huge relief inside when I was listening to others′ reactions because many times they formulated what I had on my mind and they just made me see my answers more clearly. So thank you for that. I think that we went a bit off-topic because we rather tried to give an advice than focus on thoughts and emotions so maybe I would be glad to do more of this in the next class. It might be more beneficial not only for the one having the open case, but also for the rest.

Interestingly—as follows from the reactions above—even though the process guidelines were not followed precisely, the participants found the session a valuable experience and wanted to have further open case sessions.

11.3.4 Discussion and Variations

The way open case sessions are designed does not allow them to provide the full creative potential and space for self-exploration inherent in intensive groups. Rather, they focus on offering a person-centered atmosphere in the context of a perceived problem or challenge. This makes open case sessions particularly suitable for workshops and meetings in the context of work: Rather than personal development in general, it is the moving forward in participant-selected situation that stands in the foreground. As frequently noted by participants, this clear orientation and the deliberate structure make open case sessions easier to oversee and make sense of than the full-blown, more sophisticated and potentially more powerful intensive group.

Also, as with all interactive settings, their success crucially depends on the willingness and capacity of participants to share their case and to listen. If, for some reason, the climate does not fit and participants are unwilling to share real issues, the best guidelines are useless. Some diversity across participants proved to be helpful to span a larger space of ideas and approaches. In particular, inviting people across organizations or teams or even nations to participate tends to support openness of sharing and the repertoire of thoughts, ideas, and experiences.

If participants are experienced in listening and dialogue, the function of moderator is typically more or less shared among them and hence not so outstanding. However, in groups with inexperienced participants, the moderator tends to have a crucial function. If he or she does not monitor the process, people tend either to stay with an item too long or to skip items and talk across them, not keeping the suggested order. This often leads to a less than optimal process. Also, if the moderator lacks empathy and sticks to the guidelines too strictly cutting off unfolding ideas, this tends to inhibit the process. Consequently, the less experienced the participants, the more important is an experienced and empathic moderator.

In some workshops, the available time might be too tight to conduct both phases of the open case. In this case, just the first phase would be performed thoroughly with an option to go into some of the items in the second phase for the faster groups. Definitely, we do not advise participants to rush through the items too quickly as both the group and the case need time to unfold, and hastening through it too quickly would be counterproductive, leaving valuable aspects undiscovered.

11.3.5 Summary and Outlook

A junior team leader summarized his experience with the open case setting as part of a workshop on person-centered communication as follows:

> I liked that this block had a clearer “form.” I didn’t mind that it didn’t always go as intended, for example, with splitting up for the open case. I enjoyed the cases very much and the fact that it was kind of a bit more firmly set activity was pretty much enough for me. During the open case I’ve noticed that sometimes we got a bit off topic, then a more firm moderator would work for me. Still, I think the open case activity served its purpose and, even when we get off topic, we can still get the correct “learning value” from the dialogue.

Definitely, thoughtful research is needed to find out more about the dynamics, cost, and benefits of open case sessions in the context of management, leadership, and teamwork.

Besides dialogue, intensive groups, person-centered workshops, and the open case setting, there are several other methods and technique that can contribute to transforming communication at the workplace. Since they are well documented in the literature, we decided to just mention some prominent examples along with sample references, such as appreciative inquiry (Cooperrider and Whitney 2001; Bushe 2007), coaching (Van Zyl and Stander 2013) focusing (Gendlin 1978), and various approaches to mindfulness practice (Kabat-Zinn 2001), etc.

11.4 Conclusion

Even though person-centered intensive groups remain "one of the most significant inventions" (Rogers and Russel 2002: 194) of the previous century, in the authors' experience and research, some adaptations have been perceived as welcome by participants in the context of their working lives. In particular, they appreciate some flexible structuring proposals by the facilitators leading to less "just sitting in the circle and talking" and more versatile arrangements with pairs, small groups, activities like role-play, or physically interactive games such as throwing a ball to determine whose response is invited next, etc.

A participant in a course on person-centered communication that combined phases of pure encounter with structured offerings wrote the following that can be seen as representative for several similar reactions:

> This time I saw a lot of effort from Renate to help others feel better about the whole course. She involved feedback and prepared some structure, which we anyway didn't use so much, but we had a little plan, which kept us awake about what's going on in the right moment. That I found very helpful for me, because I was not totally uninformed and there was no information hidden in what we were doing which would not be the case without this plan.

Another student characterized the effects of provision of some flexible structure on himself:

> I had a much better feeling about this block, because I knew what's going on and I had more fun, I participated more and I also experimented with intensity of my involvement.

Nevertheless, in a survey at the University of Vienna, Austria, the vast majority of students mentioned retrospectively that it was the intensive groups that they had perceived as most meaningful out of three elements: structured workshops, online support/materials, and intensive groups (Motschnig-Pitrik and Nykl 2005).

The newest setting described in this chapter—open case—is also the most firmly structured and least time-consuming one. It was designed with the scarce time resources of leadership people in mind, yet trying to preserve as much as possible from person-centered intensive groups and communication workshops. In a nutshell, the design objective was to fold the wisdom of the group process into a loose agenda and process guidelines. More research is urgently needed to confirm or disprove the initial positive effect voiced by participants.

References

Barrett-Lennard, G. T. (1998). *Carl Rogers' helping system: Journey and substance*. London, UK: SAGE Publications.

Barrett-Lennard, G. T. (2003). *Steps on a mindful journey: Person-centred expressions*. Ross-on-Wye: PCCS-Books.

Barrett-Lennard, G. T. (2005). *Relationship at the centre: Healing in a troubled world*. Philadelphia, PA: Whurr Publishers.

Bushe, G. R. (2007). Appreciative inquiry is not (just) about the positive. *Organization Development Practitioner, 39*(4), 30–35.

Cain, D. J. (2010). *Person-centered psychotherapies*. American Psychological Association (APA).

Cooperrider, D. L., & Whitney, D. (2001). A positive revolution in change. In D. L. Cooperrider, P. Sorenson, D. Whitney, & T. Yeager (Eds.), *Appreciative inquiry: An emerging direction for organization development* (pp. 9–29). Champaign, IL: Stipes.

Cornelius-White, J. H. D., Motschnig-Pitrik, R., & Lux, M. (2013a). *Interdisciplinary handbook of the person-centered approach: Research and theory*. New York, USA: Springer.

Cornelius-White, J. H. D., Motschnig-Pitrik, R., & Lux, M. (2013b). *Interdisciplinary applications of the person-centered approach*. New York, USA: Springer.

Gendlin, E. (1978) *Focusing. New York*: Bentam Books.

iCom Team. (2014). *Constructive communication in international teams*. Münster, Germany: Waxmann.

Kabat-Zinn, J. (2001). *Mindfulness meditation for everyday life*. London, UK: Piatkus.

Lago, C., & McMillan, M. (1999). *Experiences in relatedness: Groupwork in the person-centered approach*. Llangarron, Ross-on-Wye, UK: PCCS Books.

Motschnig-Pitrik, R. (2012). Agile management needs agile persons—Developing inner flexibility. In Sushil, G. Chroust, & R. Bieber (Eds.), *Systemic flexibility and business agility. Twelfth Global Conference of Flexible Systems Management* (*GLOGIFT 12*) (pp. 1–10). New Delhi: GIFT Publishing.

Motschnig-Pitrik, R. (2014). Reaction sheets pattern. In Y. Mor, H. Mellar, S. Warburton, & N. Winters (Eds.), *Practical design patterns for teaching and learning with technology* (pp. 73–82). Rotterdam: SensePublisher.

Motschnig-Pitrik, R. (2015). Developing personal flexibility as a key to agile management practice. In G. Chroust & Sushil (Eds.), *Systemic flexibility and business agility* (pp. 131–141). India: Springer.

Motschnig-Pitrik, R., & Nykl, L. (2005). Was hat Carl Rogers Wirtschaftsinformatikern im Zeitalter des Internet zu sagen? [What can students of business informatics in the Age of the Internet learn from Carl Rogers?] *Gruppendynamik und Organisationsberatung, 36*(1), 81–102.

Motschnig-Pitrik, R., & Nykl, L. (2007, September). The application of technology enhanced learning in person-centered education including encounter groups. In: Proceedings of ICTE'07, international conference on information and communication technology in education, Rožnov, Czech Republic.

Motschnig-Pitrik, R., & Nykl, L. (2014). *Person-centred communication: Theory, skills, and practice*. McGraw Hill, UK: Open University Press.

Natiello, P. (2001) *The Person-Centered Approach: A passionate presence*. Llangarron, Ross-on-Wye, UK: PCCS Books.

Nykl, L. (2005). *Beziehung im Mittelpunkt der Persönlichkeitsentwicklung* [Relationship in the center of personal development]. Münster-Hamburg-London-Wien: LIT Verlag.

Nykl, L., & Motschnig-Pitrik, R. (2005). Encountergruppen im Rahmen des ganzheitlichen Lernens an den Universitäten Wien und Brünn - Motivation, Kontext, Prozesse, Perspektiven [Encountergroups in the context of whole-person learning at the University of Vienna and the Masaryk University in Brno—Motivation, context, processes and perspectives], *Zeitschrift für Hochschuldidaktik 4*, 36–62.

Rogers, C. R. (1961). *On becoming a person—A psychotherapists view of psychotherapy*. London, UK: Constable.

Rogers, C. R. (1970). *Carl Rogers on encounter groups*. New York, USA: Harper and Row.

Rogers, C.R. (1978) *On Personal Power*. London, UK: Constable.

Rogers, C. R. (1980). *A way of being*. Boston: Houghton Mifflin Co.

Rogers, C. R. (1983). *Freedom to learn for the 80's*. Columbus, OH: Charles E. Merrill Publishing Co.

Rogers, C. R., & Russell, D. E. (2002). *Carl Rogers: The quiet revolutionary: An oral history*. Roseville, California: Penmarine Books.

Schmid, P.F. (1994). Personzentrierte Gruppenpsychotherapie, 1. Solidarität und Autonomie [Person-centered group-psychotherapy, 1. Solidarity and Autonomy]. Köln, Germany: Edition Humanistische Psychologie—EHP.

Senge, P. M. (2006). *The fifth discipline, the art & practice of the learning organization*. USA: Currency Doubleday.

Van Zyl, L. E., & Stander, M. W. (2013). A strengths based approach towards coaching in a multicultural environment. In J. H. D. Cornelius-White, R. Motschnig-Pitrik, & M. Lux (Eds.), *Interdisciplinary handbook of the person-centered approach: Research and theory*. New York, USA: Springer.

Wood, J., K. (2008) *Carl Rogers' person-centered approach: Toward an understanding of its implications*. Ross-on-Wye, UK: PCCS-books.

Chapter 12
Integrating the Two Agendas in Key Situations

One of the basic things which ... I am still learning is that when an activity feels as though it is valuable or worth doing it is worth doing. Put in another way: I have learned that my total organismic sensing of a situation is more trustworthy than my intellect.

Carl Rogers (1961, p. 22)

This chapter focuses on

- Transforming communication in typical management/leadership situations such as:
  - Meetings,
  - Developing a shared vision and customer inclusion,
  - Negotiation,
  - Conflict,
- Case examples and reflective dialogue,
- Providing resources for the key situations,
- Putting the people-oriented agenda to work in each of the key situations.

12.1 Introduction

This chapter aims to illustrate how communication can be transformed in a handful of frequently occurring situations in the workplace. This is approached by recalling key situations in management/leadership, reflecting upon them and aiming to enrich the experience by a novel perspective—the careful inclusion of the items of the people-oriented agenda. This is expected to lead to new, valuable insight regarding the integration of the task-oriented and the people-oriented agendas in key situations, such as meetings, developing a shared vision, negotiation, and dealing with conflict. Significant, experiential learning in this chapter can happen either by reflecting upon the cases and examples individually, or, even better, by going through them with a trusted colleague, friend, or team.

R. Motschnig and D. Ryback, *Transforming Communication in Leadership and Teamwork*, DOI 10.1007/978-3-319-45486-3_12

12.2 How to Make Meetings Truly Engaging

Even though communication can be transformed to become more meaningful and effective in any kind of meeting, it is the smaller, interactive team meeting where essential communicative features can be put into practice most apparently. This is why, in the following, we focus on team meetings of, say, 3 to 9 persons. However, much of what is said is applicable—in an adapted form—to larger meetings as well. Resource Box 12.1 provides some practical hints on how to bring life back into meetings and make them a meaningful experience for all involved.

Resource Box 12.1: Features contributing to successful team meetings
Making meetings engaging

Meetings need preparation—at least to some degree: What is the goal? Why are we coming together? Which formal or informal, implicit outcomes do we want to achieve? Who/what could help us to move forward in our project or mission and as a team?

Suggesting a simple, flexible agenda and asking participants to complement or adapt it in the beginning of the meeting can help to include participants more actively. Moreover, each gets a picture of what is expected to happen.

The process and moderation of the meeting may be at least as important as the content and outcomes to be designed and thought through beforehand. In particular, being thoughtful on how to include participants actively can change a passive "surviving the meeting" to an engaging and enriching experience for all!

Not all responsibilities need to stay with the department head or project manager. Sharing responsibilities for subtasks among participants can help to empower these people and take some load off the manager/leader. The team will more likely feel co-responsible for their project. Moreover, participants will experience "the other side," namely what it means to be in charge of a task and thus have more understanding for leadership functions.

A constructive and convenient atmosphere such that participants feel well helps to prevent tension and facilitates being open to what is going on.

Length and frequency of meetings depend, among others, on how often you meet between the meetings, how many people participate, and how interactive the meetings are meant to be.

Meetings cost time; however, they are a valuable means for reducing the risk of people running off into different, uncoordinated directions or introducing unwanted redundancy.

Invitation to reflect:

Which of the elements do you already apply actively?
Which elements do you think don't fit in with your particular meeting culture?
Which elements would you add to the resource box for your institution or project? Can you describe the dynamics of any of these, sharing why in your view they work so well?

In Resource Box 12.2, we suggest how the five items of the people-oriented agenda can show through in meetings: The Resource Bow can also be used as a checklist for evaluating the interpersonal quality of meetings. Items that do not apply at all tend to point to issues that block or restrict the people-oriented agenda of transforming communication. Their careful investigation can point us to what is going wrong and what could be changed to improve it.

Resource Box 12.2: Putting the people-oriented agenda to work in meetings.
The people-oriented agenda in meetings
Contact:

The invitation to a meeting already can set the tone and expectations. Participants can prepare if not explicitly so at least inwardly.
Welcoming participants, if felt honestly, can make a huge difference.
The first moments set the tone and initialize the atmosphere. Thinking about the opening, in particular, is essential.

Transparency of goals, vision, and participants:

The goals and agenda of the meeting are transparent.
Participants express themselves as openly as appropriate.
Participants can sense what is going on in them and express themselves clearly.
Whenever appropriate, feelings are expressed in order to increase transparency and improve understanding.
Disturbances, if any, may be followed, but participants take care that the disturbances do not swallow everything else that is on the agenda and leave participants' expectations unmet.

Respecting the other, oneself, and the environment:

Participants feel invited and included in the process of the meeting.
Attendee's experience that their presence, attention, participation, and candidness are welcome.
Any effort to find and schedule a meeting slot that is feasible for all participants is appreciated.

Coming prepared for the meeting signals respect as it mirrors that coming together is considered important.
A brief, honest explanation why I couldn't prepare for the meeting tends to be clearer than pretending that I am prepared while I'm not.
A meeting that does not last too long or a speech that is concise signals respect regarding the participants' limited time resources.
Speaking a language that the others understand helps to build common ground even among diverse participants.

Trying to understand and to be understood comprehensively and thoroughly:

Active listening is crucial for understanding participants from their perspectives.
Besides trying to understand other persons' feelings, meanings, and statements, it is decisive to understand the context too.
Besides trying to understand individual persons in their context, it is essential to sense where the group is as a whole. For example, how do others engage or not engage while I am in conversation with one other person? Is there a way to include others too?

Collaboration and sharing:

Participants make the meeting's agenda also their agenda and contribute their resources appropriately. They are responsive to questions, participating actively.
Sure there may pop up some urgencies from the outside world that need participants' attention. However, a meeting where participants are looking into their laptops most of the time would certainly be lacking collaboration and sharing, perhaps even respect.

☕ Invitation to reflect:

Recall the last meeting that you attended. How do you feel about it?
Which of the items of the people-oriented agenda were present for you? Did you miss any of them?
Was acceptance expressed? If so, how was it expressed? If not, how did you realize this?
Did you understand other participants and did participants try to understand each other? If so, how was this communicated? If not, can you describe the source of the lack of understanding?
Do you feel there was appropriate openness and transparency in the meeting? How did you feel about this?

Example from experience: What is missing here?

The group who was assigned to a particular department met regularly each week on Wednesday morning, from 9 a.m. till about 10 or 11 a.m. Occasionally, there was an agenda that was sent out for people to prepare, but typically there was no agenda and people could talk about whatever. Often the department head shared informally what happened in various committees and executive meetings in which he had participated. Sometimes participants shared experiences from courses, conference trips, examinations, etc. Some participants dominated the talks, and others stayed quite silent. Typically, the atmosphere was relaxed and the staff had coffee/tea and cookies together.

Personally, after the meeting, it took me a while until I (Renate) could concentrate on getting some original work done, like elaborating a course unit or doing research. Part of the reason may be that already during the meeting I realized that I felt nervous about the waste of time but nevertheless thought to be obliged to participate and pay attention. This rendered me torn and incongruent. Consequently, despite the cozy atmosphere, I didn't like the meetings at all. My suggestion to have them in the late afternoon was kindly declined by the majority of peers. Well, I didn't give up and used the next best occasion to propose to divide the meetings into two parts, while important issues needing everyone's attention would be dealt with in the beginning. The second part would be more informal with participation being optional. This idea was welcomed and adopted and helped me and in fact also others to appreciate the meetings.

Invitation to reflect:

What do you think and feel about the meeting practice at the department described above? Can you imagine how you'd feel in such meetings?
Which of the five items appear to have been largely missing in some of the participants?
What meeting culture dominates at your institution and how do you like it? Is there anything you'd like to change?

Example from experience: Project jour fixe

The project team from two collaborating departments was dispersed between two locations being about 10 min walking distance apart. Besides team members arranging for smaller meetings between two or more members, the team decided during the project kickoff meeting to meet regularly each week for a "jour fixe" (consistent day). Participants looked carefully to find a suitable time slot such that every member would have 1.5 h available, or at least 1 h at the minimum. After a busy search, the team agreed to have the meetings at 2 p.m. each Tuesday. In one of the first meetings, the team also agreed to deal with organizational issues first and with the scientific ones second, such that administrative team members would not need to participate in the scientific parts and could immediately start working on tasks that emanated from the meeting.

If someone wanted others to attend to some issues in advance, he or she could send an e-mail and propose agenda items. Otherwise, the upcoming agenda items for the coming week were indicated at the end of the meeting and reiterated and complemented dynamically at the beginning of each jour fixe. We (Renate's team) used a whiteboard to assemble and arrange/prioritize the items and frequently also a flip chart to sketch and document ideas or tasks/plans. Frequently, the meeting stared by briefly sharing what had happened in the meantime for each member. This procedure developed more like a useful habit than any prescribed procedure and was optional. A statement like "nothing special, just continuing the data analysis" would be OK as much as a team member could voice problems or conflicts they encountered, for example, once a colleague who was responsible for collecting workshop inputs voiced her frustration since participants did not submit anything on the sheet she had prepared. Fortunately, this omission could be compensated almost immediately since we collected the inputs directly during the meeting and even could prioritize them.

Invitation to reflect:

What, in your view, distinguishes the two examples sketched above? Is there anything they have in common?

Which of the two meeting cultures would you prefer? Can you share why?

In your view, which of the items of the people-oriented agenda can you trace from the short description of the project jour fixe given above?

12.3 Developing a Shared Vision and Customer Inclusion

Many projects or ideas are too complex as to be followed or accomplished by a single person. Moreover, whether directly or indirectly, they almost always address other persons often referred to as the addressees, customers, or end users. In all these cases, it is essential that others are included early in the process such as to maximize their motivation to participate and engage. Since actualization of one's inherent potentials is such a powerful and overarching motive, it seems only natural to tap it. This happens best early in the process when there is still open space for forming and fitting in the others' inherent directions or "vector" resulting in a multidimensional space. The project or idea will become ours *and* theirs and will be co-owned rather than being mine and asking others for compliance and support. There is a big difference between these two modalities, since once the core idea is external to someone, it will not receive the intrinsic motivation and actualizing direction that can only unfold from inside.

Peter Senge notes:

> Yet, there is a world of difference between compliance and commitment. The committed person brings an energy, passion, and excitement that cannot be generated by someone who is only compliant, even genuinely compliant. The committed person doesn't play by the rules of the game. He is responsible for the game. If the rules of the game stand in the way of achieving the vision, he will find ways to change the rules. (Senge 2006, p. 205)

If we want to develop a *shared* vision among stakeholders, it is essential that the stakeholders each hold their vision in awareness, so they know their direction. Without personal visions, there is no "substance" for a shared one! At the same time, each person needs to hold their vision *flexibly* as to be sufficiently open to the thoughts and ideas of the others. The alignment of visions is hard to achieve if any of the stakeholders stubbornly holds to their position and does not trust others to contribute meaningfully. A truly shared vision, however, is feasible if stakeholders are seeking dialogue with peers and respect them as partners in the "game" of creating something that is in some sense "more" than one's own vision because it is held in common with others. The word "more" does not necessarily mean larger or more extensive, but it means primarily more complex, more creative, perhaps more valid, etc., emanating from a richer base of perspectives or even cultures than a single person could ever offer.

Peter Senge explores the power of a shared vision and grounds it in people's feeling connected in something they care about deeply:

> A vision is truly shared when you and I have a similar picture and are committed to one another having it, not just to each of us, individually having it. When people truly share a vision they are connected, bound together by a common aspiration. Personal visions derive their power from an individual's deep caring for the vision. Shared visions derive their power from a common caring. In fact, we have to come to believe that one of the reasons people seek to build shared visions is their desire to be connected in an important undertaking. (Senge 2006, p. 192).

We would add that people become transformed when the actualizing process of one joins with the actualizing process of the other in striving to accomplish something of shared, high significance. Interpersonal relationships which make this mutual actualization possible have been referred to as *co-actualizing* (Motschnig-Pitrik and Barrett-Lennard 2010).

In the following, we give an example that illustrates the building of a shared vision in a small team, including the use of digital media. Thereupon, Resource Box 12.3 summarizes the features that contribute to building a shared vision, and

Resource Box 12.4 traces the items of the people-oriented agenda for creating a shared vision.

Case Example: Creating a shared vision for a small project in health care

Kathy, an organizational developer, and Tom, head of the IT department of a big organization, talked about the possibility of starting a series of round table talks. Their aim was to bring together stakeholders in the field of health care, Information and Communication Technology (ICT), and academia in order to improve and innovate communication in the field of health care. Soon after the idea was born, they invited Susan, a long-year colleague from academia, highly interested in interpersonal communication, asking her if she wanted to join their effort. Susan agreed basically, and as she was very busy at that time, they arranged for a 2-h brainstorming meeting in a nice coffeehouse in three weeks' time, a period that was feasible for Susan.

The weekend before the meeting, Kathy sent out an e-mail to Tom and Susan. She wrote: "Below I'm sharing my preliminary draft of the round table series, intended as a resource for our meeting. You may want to include you resonant, complementary, or contradictory thoughts, or create a separate document. My non-binding first draft is open to any changes … I hope I'm not interrupting any creative process ☕."

Indeed, when Susan received the mail, she had sketched her notes and wanted to continue explicating her own vision before letting herself be influenced by what she expected would be brilliant ideas from Kathy's perspective and background. So Susan felt kindly called upon to prepare for the meeting and complemented her own notes, before editing most of them into Kathy's file. Apparently, the styles differed, but there was trust that both would be valued.

When all three partners met in person, each had read the draft and brought copies for the others. Susan, being the person who had joined the "project" last, started inquiring into the ideas with questions such as: "What idea is there behind the bringing together of stakeholders in the field? Why do we need/want them to talk to each other? Shouldn't we focus on a specific aspect within the broad field, which aspect is pivotal to (each of) us?" Then, Tom asked Susan which value these round tables would have for universities and listened carefully to what Susan was figuring right at the moment. Later, he asked Kathy about the logistics and her experience with similar projects. In brief, we spent the two hours with sharing ideas from different perspectives and agreed to arrange for a next meeting after taking some time to ponder about what started to develop between us. For sure, we would also use a shared Web space for collecting intermediate ideas to make sure they do not get lost!

Invitation to reflect:

In your view, was this a good start of building a shared vision? What would you do differently?
Can you identify the steps taken to build a shared vision?
What role does the Internet and new media have in building and sustaining shared visions in the example and in your experience?
Do you think virtual communication and digital media can support:

The creation of shared visions substantially?
The maintenance of shared visions substantially?
The enhancement of shared visions substantially?

Can you appreciate the power of a truly shared vision? What have you experienced as the biggest obstacles of building a shared vision? Could the use of new media compensate for them in some way?

Resource Box 12.3: Factors contributing to creating a shared vision

Factors supporting shared visions:

- A *climate* that encourages personal visioning and collaboration
- People with *personal visions* and an ability to *communicate* them in a way that others are encouraged to *share* their visions
- Awareness of what it is that I *care for deeply*
- *Awareness* of: "I can't accomplish it all alone!"
- Interest in and *listening to* people's visions without judging them
- A *collaborative* attitude paired with trustful interpersonal relationships
- Capacity and time for *dialogue*
- Since shared visions are built from personal visions (Senge 2006, p. 198), holding one's vision *flexibly* and engaging in dialogue is essential for building a shared vision
- Being able to take *time* for the shared vision to unfold gradually
- Creative use of the Internet or intranet and social media to disseminate the vision and receive feedback
- Our very basic need to unfold in relationship to others and feel connected to others (Senge 2006, p. 192)

Resource Box 12.4: Putting the people-oriented agenda to work for creating a shared vision

The people-oriented agenda for creating a shared vision

Contact:

Getting in touch with your personal vision. What is it that really matters to YOU?
Actively seeking people and inviting them in for creating a truly shared vision.

Transparency of goals, vision, and participants:

Openness to own and others' feelings and thoughts
Increased self-experience and self-awareness
Sensing where we are (not)
Inquiring into others' visions
Voicing with clarity, match between feeling, thought, expression, and (inter) action
Expressiveness, engagement
Feeling motivated and even passionate for following the shared vision.

Respecting the other, oneself, and the environment:

Including the other
The other feels welcome and received in the context of sharing their vision
Difference is valued as much as similarity in the process of building a shared vision.

Trying to understand and to be understood comprehensively and thoroughly:

Being actively interested in what the other is sharing at multiple levels
Gaining clarity about what is essential via listening and dialogue
Attending to customer/end user and their experience
Trying to understand the motivation and perspective of each stakeholder
Facilitating the group/team to form the shared vision by including personal visions.

Collaboration and sharing:

Articulating one's personal vision and sharing thoughts and feelings that come up in the process
Showing interest and actively inquiring into other's thoughts and feelings
Taking an active effort in approaching a vision that integrates and expresses the personal visions as far as possible.

Intriguingly, creating and holding a shared vision illustrates the tight connection between acceptance and inclusion. To truly accept someone without letting them become part of ourselves, including them in some aspect of us would be a void, superficial kind of tolerance. Vice versa, including another's ideas, thought, or values in our vision—at least to some genuine degree—expresses acceptance of them and makes the vision richer, more encompassing, more interconnected with their origins, the people who hold them. In particular, people from different cultural, social, or scientific origins tend to hold completely complementary visions that may seem hard to embrace. If, however, inclusion is accomplished, the result may be much more than the sum of its parts.

Example from experience
Last year when the winter holidays were just about to start, the international staff of my (Renate's) department decided to have a small season's get-together. People were kindly asked to bring some dish with them that would be typical for their national/religious tradition. In a seminar room with lighted candles, we tried the various snacks, shared about our traditions, and sang songs. While learning about the colleague's background cultures, the feeling of community was amazing and unforgettable.

Personally, I (Renate) tend to be fascinated and enriched by cooperating with people from other cultures and disciplines. The major obstacle to putting a shared vision into practice for me is the issue of *synchronicity*. When both or all people are busy, it is really hard to coordinate activities and advance in putting a shared vision into practice. Often, then, one person takes the lead, necessarily with a focus on their contribution and talents, or the vision is never realized in practice. Nevertheless, from my experience with working in wonderful teams, I fully subscribe to Peter Senge, who wrote (2006, p. 205): "A group of people truly committed to a common vision is an awesome force." I'd add to this: "And, if this group furthermore has the capacity to honestly and deeply understand and accept each other, it is a true pleasure and ongoing enrichment to be part of that group!"

12.4 Negotiation

In light of the rapid changes we are facing, the agile management movement brought up the slogan: *stop negotiating, start collaborating* (Anderson 2008). The issue is to transfer a significant portion of time that traditionally went into negotiating into collaborating on early prototypes and gradually refine them to approximate the envisaged system or product. Clearly, requirements are likely to change as the system moves toward maturation and new aspects or technologies emerge. What may have been negotiated at one point in time can become obsolete fast and renegotiation would consume ever more resources at the cost of productive work concerning the product. In such a situation, transparent communication and a realistic amount of trust throughout the project are indispensable for success and the question comes up if, for effectiveness, they would not better substitute part of the effort that traditionally goes into negotiation? This sounds perfectly reasonable, in particular if the parties know and trust each other and have a chance to stay in touch intensively, such that upcoming questions can be resolved immediately. In all these cases, the people-oriented agenda and in particular its fifth item, collaboration and sharing, plays a central role and takes over much of the effort that otherwise goes in negotiating. The contract does not become obsolete, but what is more important is that the agile project delivers true value to the customer.

In other cases, business, strategic or political, etc., contract negotiation keeps its vital function and negotiation increasingly requires high levels of emotional intelligence (Ryback 1998). In a business or political setting, negotiation definitely involves preparation on many fronts. If the negotiation is between adversarial factions, then the process begins with a fair degree of fear, trepidation, defensiveness, and some degree of negativity, even hostility. So preparation begins with "knowing your enemy." What is your team going to face initially? Will there be threats or a sense of cooperation? Will the early demands and expectations be overly one-sided, so there is more room for compromise later on? Will the adversary begin by attacking our team's point of view? All these are unknowns.

There are legal and technical factors to consider if the negotiation is complex. What experts might be necessary to counter the adversary's position? Who are the personalities to be faced on the other side? What are their levels of competence, education, and negotiating experience? What emotions might they bring to the table?

Planning ahead, it is important to determine some plan on how compromise is to be achieved. What is our bottom line? What do we project the adversary's bottom line to be?

Having said all this on the objective plane, what are we to look at for the people-oriented aspect? Here, there is more focus on the feelings and openness of the process. My (David's) rules are as follows:

1. Begin by explaining your position honestly and forthrightly.
2. Include your feelings in your presentation.
3. Avoid tangential emotional issues.
4. Work for the future as well as the present.
5. State clearly what you want to take away from this negotiation.
6. Ask for and appreciate the other side's needs, and keep this in mind for the duration of the negotiation process.

One superb example of effective negotiation on an international political level is that by Richard Holbrooke in accomplishing the Dayton Agreement, putting an end to the 3 1/2-year-long Bosnian war between the Serbs and Croats. Characterized as a "construction of necessity" (Keane 2001) and as "the most impressive example of conflict resolution" (David 2001), this accord was the quintessence of person-centered negotiation. Here is why.

1. To begin with, Holbrooke was direct and forthright from the beginning with all involved parties. He was determined to find a peaceful resolution and was open about that. This honesty convinced all parties of his integrity and built trust.

2. Holbrooke was quite open about his feelings regarding his intentions. This emotional honesty also built trust, which would serve him well over the rough spots of such a challenging endeavor.
3. His focus was clear, and he would not be sidetracked by tangential issues, no matter how others may have tried to do so. No matter how persistent others may have tried to divert attention from the main target by focusing on details of their own perspectives, Holbrooke would not be deterred.
4. His ability to see the larger perspective which took into consideration how the accord would grow into the future of all countries concerned was paramount. He had the grand view of the outcome, regardless of the complexity of such a view. This took tremendous ability to see each perspective clearly from its own ethnic and historical beginnings. No one could be totally satisfied, and viewing each perspective with empathy took enormous effort to then put it all in a larger view that all could live with, even though not easily. The accord would not last without this long-term view and empathic concern. As is often said, you know you have a good outcome of negotiation when no one is happy. Unfortunately, this almost always turns out to be true. Neither side was happy. As a matter of fact, Alija Izetbegovic, the head of the Muslim Serbs, refused to sign the accord at first, but then realized that this was the only way out, even though he strongly felt that the accord did not do justice to the crimes committed by Slobodan Milosevic.
5. Holbrooke was crystal clear that he wanted an agreement with which no one was totally satisfied, yet was the best solution taking into consideration all possibilities. This was daunting, yet he persevered with much effort and energy and focus.
6. Holbrooke was determined to be as fair-minded as possible, taking into consideration the deepest needs and requirements of each signatory. He spent much time ensuring that he understood this from each of the respective parties involved. That took incredible energy to empathize with each view and then follow that up with some conclusion that still held integrity for the complexity of the resolution. He persevered in his nonpartisan approach, not yielding to any particular effort to gain points from either of the adversaries. Only openness and a commitment to seeing all views clearly as possible would work in the long run and result in triumph despite the daunting challenges. He was an advocate for all, an agent for none.

Looking at this in terms of person-centered attitudes, we can see the acceptance of the need to be emotionally open, to be empathic to all parties concerned and to avoid becoming victim to negative emotions which might shift the attention away from the most important quality of all, a sense of fairness. All of this characterized Holbrooke's efforts.

Resource Box 12.5 summarizes how the items of the people-oriented agenda can be expressed in the negotiation process.

Resource Box 12.5: Putting the people-oriented agenda to work in negotiation

The people-oriented agenda in negotiation

Contact:

Establishing contact with oneself: What is it that I want to achieve and don't want to give up at any price?
Establishing contact with the other(s) and the environment by trying to find out who they are and what mattes to them
Finding a place where one can fully focus on the negotiation without being distracted by everyday business
Establishing a connection through holding something in common by starting with issues on which you probably agree with the other.

Transparency of goals, vision, and participants:

Being open to what is most important at a given moment
Overcoming prejudices
Not obscuring matters by sidetracking
Listening to all of oneself, feeling, thoughts, meanings, knowledge, and trying to come up with a response in which all these are in accord.

Respecting the other, oneself, and the environment:

Respecting the other(s) as persons; thinking, how this respect could be expressed
Appreciating the time/energy that the other(s) are willing to invest in the negotiation Showing interest in the other person, his or her position, interest, goals, current situation, etc. (Fisher and Ury 1991).

Trying to understand and to be understood comprehensively and thoroughly:

Attentive, active listening, trying to understand customers, teammates
Trying to understand the other's position, interest, circumstances, options, constraints, etc.
Asking questions to clarify issues and interests
Seeing the situation from the other's perspective, mind-set, and culture

Collaboration and sharing:

Articulating your interest and feelings transparently such that others can understand them and are motivated to respond in the same transparent way
Endeavoring to reach results that both/all consider fair, acceptable, and a good start for the future.

This is quite opposite from what we see happening in current American government, for example, which is strongly partisan. And this is not conducive to successful negotiation. Instead, we have gridlock and the absence of cooperation. Duke University psychologists have done research, showing the connection between attitude entrenchment and a sense of superiority over the adversary. In other words, when Rogers' qualities of openness and genuineness are absent, there is more likelihood that the negotiators will refuse to budge from their strong positions and progress is very unlikely. "These findings help to explain why politicians with more extreme views can't reach across the aisle," said Kaitlin Toner (Toner et al. 2013), lead scientist in the study. "As more extreme candidates get elected to Congress, compromise becomes more difficult and deadlocks increase because those with more extreme views are more certain that they are right."

"The tendency for people with extreme views to be overly confident is not limited to politics," according to the researchers. This can happen in other spheres of negotiation as well. On the other hand, an openness to others' attitudes and feelings allows for the flexibility necessary for successful negotiations.

12.5 A Person-Centered Approach to Conflict

Since conflict is inevitable (Stillwell and Moormon 1997), much has been written about various kinds of conflict, such as conflict of interest, goal conflict, scheduling of limited resources, inner conflict, ideological conflict, and team conflict. To fit into this book on transforming communication at work, we are going to constrain our encounter with conflict to deal centrally with the questions:

What is an interpersonal conflict, how can it be induced by a conflict of interest, and with which attitudes can it be approached?
In which ways can the theories of the PCA contribute to deal constructively with conflict?

At the outset, let us ask: What is a conflict or in other words what phenomenon do we designate as a conflict? Is having a difference with our partner already a conflict? In accordance with Johnson and Johnson (1975/2006), we describe a conflict to be any situation in which at least one person has negative emotions.

When talking about conflict from a person-centered mind-set, it is helpful to know our attitude toward conflict: Do I prefer to manage a problem without going into conflict and try to avoid it as long as possible, or do I tend to feel free to go into conflict fast as a means to make my point and stand up for myself? Interestingly, people differ as to their readiness to go into conflict. While some are convinced that conflict is the (only) means to deal with problems and bring about change, others are equally convinced that conflict causes so much trouble, seeds negative emotions, and costs so much energy that this energy is better invested otherwise and conflict is only the ultimate choice if anything else fails. Now, let us ask: To which camp do you belong? Regardless of one's manifested attitude toward conflict, it may be helpful to know that other people may not share our attitude and hence behave differently. This may be perceived as inappropriate, suspicious, sneaky, etc., from our perspective. Vice versa, the other person is likely to reciprocate our negative emotions and express them overtly or covertly, setting in place a vicious cycle that we are all too familiar with from our own experience. So, is there a way to step out if this vicious cycle or not even start it?

Invitation to reflect:

Remember the last two to three conflicts you had (optimally not all with the same person).
Were you the one who tried to work toward resolve without going into conflict or was it you why actually went into a conflict?
Do you think the partner(s) in the conflicted situation wanted to go into conflict or tried to avoid it?
Was there anything you learned from these situations? How would you describe your learning and how do you feel about each of the situations now?

Once we are aware about our attitude toward conflict, let us identify what at all is essential for solving or transforming a conflict. The "or" in the previous sentence is essential since not every conflict can be resolved under given circumstances. In such a situation, in particular when the circumstances cannot be changed (fast enough), it is crucial to live with the conflict in such a way as to cause the least possible harm for each party. At the same time, all would stay alert to any opportunity that might change the circumstances or interests/positions of the conflicted subjects.

We authors frequently asked participants of person-centered communication workshops to share in small teams what they thought would be most crucial for a constructive approach to conflict resolution. Each team was asked to prepare three moderation cards with what seemed most vital to them. Subsequently, the teams, one after the other, pinned the cards on a board and explained their chosen features. Overlapping features which illustrated the high weight of some features were also captured in the form of partly overlapping cards. Once the feature mosaic was ready, participants were invited to interpret the result. While it came out similar each time, there were also slight differences that often reflected some focal themes or issues of the workshop. We find both the regularities and the differences amazing such that there is always something new to be learned from this exercise! Resource Box 12.6 lists features that had frequently been identified by participants.

Resource Box 12.6: What is essential for solving/transforming a conflict?
What is essential for solving/transforming a conflict?

What is the problem? Identifying the problem
Sensing one's feelings
Knowing what I (don't) want
Mutual interest in resolving the problem
Becoming aware of the power distribution between the parties. Am I in the position of power?
Is the other in the position of power?
Listening actively trying to understand the other side
Seeing the problem through the other's eyes
Respecting the other as well as oneself
Empathizing with the other taking the whole situation/environment into account
Letting oneself be touched by the problem
Communicating one's feelings and thoughts transparently yet respectfully
Considering the problem as something that needs to be attacked cooperatively
Perceiving the other as an ally toward resolving the problem
Being open-minded, allowing for criticism
Allowing time, not rushing into quick fixes
Willingness for compromise.

Invitation to reflect:

In your view, which of the items listed in Resource Box 12.6 did Holbrooke (referring to the example on negotiation) follow (even though he never saw this list)?

More formally, in the framework of his theory of interpersonal relationship, Carl Rogers specified the conditions for an improving relationship to be the following:

For communication to increase, and the relationship to improve, the following conditions are necessary:

1. A person, Y′, is willing to be in contact with person X′ and to receive communication from him.
2. Person X′ desires to communicate to and be in contact with Y′.
3. A high degree of congruence exists in X′ between the three following elements:
   (a) His experience of the subject of communication with Y′.
   (b) The symbolization of this experience in awareness in its relation to his self-concept.
   (c) His communicative expression of this experience (Rogers 1959, p. 239).

This formulation brings perhaps the most prominent feature into the foreground: the mutual willingness to be in contact and to receive communication. Once this willingness is mutual and is even felt as a "desire" by one person, this person being highly congruent in his or her experience (feelings), awareness of feelings and communicative expression is essential to initiate an improving relationship. In this process, a fascinating cyclic movement can be set in place (Rogers 1959, p. 239). In simplified terms, the following tends to happen:

The high level of congruence in the communication of one person is experienced by the other as a clear message. Hence, his/her response is more likely to express congruence in turn. Since the first person is congruent in the area related to his communication, he is able to perceive the response of the second person in an accurate manner, with empathy for his/her inner world. Feeling understood, the second person experiences some satisfaction of his need for positive regard and the first person feels good about having made a positive difference to the other person. Hence reciprocally, both persons feel positive regard for each other, the second person feels empathically understood by the first, and both feel increasingly congruent in the area of communication. Hence, communication in both directions becomes increasingly congruent, is increasingly accurately perceived, and contains more reciprocal positive regard—the best "ingredients" for joining efforts to resolve a conflict.

The situation is much harder, at times hopeless, if one party (or even both) does not want to resolve the problem and/or does not seek to communicate with each other. If the relationship is not important or can be sacrificed, one or both parties can simply flee from the relationship and not care in which state they are leaving the other behind. The hardest situation, however, occurs if the relationship is important and breaking it up would have disastrous effects.

In the following, let us go through 3 vignettes of conflict and consider which of the resources presented above might help to deal with the conflict and which conflict features are so unique that they need specific attention, empathy, and thought.

12.5.1 Classical Versus Agile Management

A frequent source of conflict is the mismatch between a project specification produced in the beginning of the project and the tasks and activities perceived as making most sense to be done at any particular phase of the project. While in traditional project management practice—that is prevailing in government-funded projects or international granting agencies—project success is measured in terms of meeting the specified targets, agile management is different. It calls to regularly re-evaluate the specification against the actually perceived targets and, if necessary, adapt the specification to meet the customer's needs as perceived at each iteration.

Recently, an international project consortium (of which Renate leads one of the partners) who worked toward meeting the specified goals became highly conflicted about an awkward decision. The specification said that existing training material would be integrated in a coherent online training module for users with special needs.

However, no really appropriate materials were found and those that existed would cost a lot to be adapted by external firms who owned the code. It appeared that the consortium would have to decide which of those inappropriate materials would be selected for adaptations and how partners would accommodate for the extra cost not calculated in the project. The alternative was to produce a small set of highly appropriate training materials, but this would delay the project and require a shift of finances to the partner who would produce the materials. The consortium desperately sought for a decision, and partners were split because they felt the nonsense of strictly following the plan but equally wanted to fulfill the project specification. Fortunately, during the next review meeting when the consortium had to justify why they didn't yet adapt the training materials, the partners expressed the dilemma to the reviewers. After a brief consultation, they made an official recommendation in favor of producing a small set of highly appropriate materials. While this resolved the dilemma, the consortium kept struggling between adapting to the changed situation and following the official plan. Some partners felt very uncomfortable due to constant changes and a lack of precise rules, while others felt comfortable with an agile process.

12.5.2 Breaking up a Relationship (Is Hard to Do)

A careful and quite skilled programmer from a foreign country was seeking employment. He was lucky and was offered a job in accordance with his skills in a small enterprise. Initially, he was happy about the employment and the midterm job security working as a key programmer on an important project. After a few weeks, something strange happened: His communication became avoiding and very unfriendly. Once he confronted his employer and told him that he felt cheated and underpaid, as he had found figures of salaries on the Internet that were higher than his salary. The employer gave him his arguments for the salary they had negotiated in the beginning and explained why it was indeed fair. A few days later, the employee asked for a compensation of 600 EUR for the previous month. Otherwise, he would leave by the end of the month. As he did not get it on the next day, he simply left for his home country one week before the end of the month, taking with him the salary of the whole month and terminating any further communication. The employer had to work hard to finish the project in time and concurrently seek for a new programmer. Fortunately, he found one soon who was happy with the salary and had a perfect understanding with the rest of the team.

Invitation to reflect:

Which of the conditions for an improving relationship were not met? In your view, did the employer have a chance at all to keep up the initially so positive relationship with the programmer?
Do you agree that for solving a problem one always depends on the other(s)?

12.5.3 *Conflict with Your Boss*

Imagine you have been working for an organization for several years and established your position. In general, you respect your boss as a capable leader with strong strategic skills. However, you and he or she are quite diverse, having different attitudes toward transparency and regarding how to deal with people such that on several occasions, you strongly disagree with how he/she acts from the base of his authority. For example, he/she hardly acknowledges your extra effort, hides important strategic issues from employees, and often acts strategically, basically ignoring people's feelings and even their diverse achievements. Positive regard is strictly conditional, based on the performance indicators set up by the organization. Matching a given model precedes a more holistic valuing. While you are aware that these resentments, if not expressed directly, keep undermining your basically respectful and collaborative stance to your boss, you tend to think more than twice to say something. It would not make any difference anyway and could even earn ironic responses, negative emotions, and negative consequences. The important question arises: Am I still being congruent in my work situation? Does compliance with the situation and relationship at hand automatically mean quiet agreement?

12.5.4 *Is Rogers "General Law of Interpersonal Relationships" also Valid in the Workplace?*

Above, we illustrated some of the complexities involved in conflict and indicated that an interpersonal conflict hardly ever can be attributed to one person but rather exists in the dynamics between them and external circumstances. In the following, let us investigate whether a fascinating lawfulness in interpersonal relationship that Carl Rogers discovered from his experience in thousands of counseling interviews is also valid for a wider range of work-related relationships and whether it needs to be adapted. Rogers himself emphasized that while the statement of his hypothesized "general law" was bold to capture the essence of his experience in concise form, his thinking about the relationship was quite tentative. The question we are going to pose below is in how far Rogers' "general law" quoted in Resource Box 12.7 has validity also for other contexts such as team leader or customer relationships.

Resource Box 12.7: Rogers' tentative statement of the general law of interpersonal relationships (Rogers 1961, pp. 344–345)

A tentative statement of a general law of interpersonal relationships

Assuming (a) a minimal willingness on the part of two people to be in contact; (b) an ability and minimal willingness on the part of each to receive communication from the other; and (c) assuming the contact to continue over a period of time; then, the following relationship is hypothesized to hold true:

> The greater the congruence of experience, awareness, and communication on the part of one individual, the more the ensuing relationship will involve a tendency toward reciprocal communication with a quality of increasing congruence; a tendency toward more mutually accurate understanding of the communications; improved psychological adjustment and functioning in both parties; mutual satisfaction in the relationship.
> Conversely, the greater the communicated incongruence of experience and awareness, the more the ensuing relationship will involve: further communication with the same quality; disintegration of accurate understanding, less adequate psychological adjustment and functioning in both parties; and mutual dissatisfaction in the relationship.

> The Existential Choice.
> "Do I dare to communicate the full degree of congruence which I feel? Do I dare match my experience, and my awareness of that experience, with my communication? Do I dare to communicate myself as I am or must my communication be somewhat less than or different from this?" The sharpness of this issue lies in the often vividly foreseen possibility of threat or rejection. To communicate one's full awareness of the relevant experience is a risk in interpersonal relationships. [..] In this moment by moment choice in a relationship may lie the answer as to whether the movement is in one direction [improvement] or the other [deterioration] in terms of this hypothesized law.

In order to elaborate whether Rogers' "general law of interpersonal relationship" is also valid in the business context and which adaptations we suggest, let us first of all attempt to "translate" the law into simper language: Essentially, it says that if I am able to sense into myself without distorting or ignoring my feelings and can openly and transparently yet also respectfully and understandingly be and express myself, then the ensuing relationship will lead to improved communication and understanding and mutual satisfaction. If, however, this is not the case, meaning that I need to hide or distort facets of my experience over a period of time, the relationship will deteriorate.

We know that openness bears a high risk such that in the work context, it needs to be weighed carefully. Is my criticism worth exposing myself as a critic and potentially even losing my job or job opportunity? Consequently, Rogers' "law" must not be interpreted in a way that promotes radical openness in any situation at any price, in the sense of giving up any protection and making oneself fully vulnerable. This is not what the "law" is about. Instead of looking for a silver bullet for improved relationships, each situation and relationship needs to be experienced afresh to determine one's degree of congruence in it. If it is constantly low, this would ring the alarm clock to change something. Perhaps a suitable situation can be found in which a large degree of respectful openness is appropriate without risking too much. Or it might be better to confront, leave, innovate, etc. In any case, Rogers "law" expresses very distinctly that if I can't be congruent, i.e., need to hide relevant aspects of my thinking or feeling, and need to disguise and act as if I was someone else, in the long run this would not be psychologically healthy and would be destined to lead to dissatisfaction and even disintegration—definitely no good perspective for work satisfaction and achievement. So our sense is that Rogers indeed captured something we dare to call a "natural social law" and a "barometer" for indicating the moment-to-moment quality of any interpersonal relationship.

From my experience (Renate), I'd like to add that if I *can* be congruent in a relationship, this not only improves the communication, but it also enormously adds to my *motivation*. I feel this as a confluence of motivational energy that invades interpersonal as well as work-related fields. I love to cooperate with people with whom there is appropriate openness such that we can move toward, for example, work-related goals and thereby learn meaningfully, mutually, and often also have fun at moving forward. Together with Godfrey Barrett-Lennard, we have come to refer to the underlying process as "co-actualization" (Motschnig-Pitrik and Barret-Lennard 2010). Note, in particular, that co-actualization does not exclude conflict. It would, however, be dealt with constructively.

12.5.5 The People-Oriented Agenda in Situations of Conflict

To summarize our investigation into conflict, readers interested in putting the people-oriented agenda to work in situations of conflict are referred to Resource Box 12.8.

Resource Box 12.8: Putting the people-oriented agenda to work in situations of conflict.

The people-oriented agenda in situations of conflict

Contact:

Being in contact with oneself, the other and identifying what it is that is conflicted in myself

Seeking contact and communication with the other, if the time feels right

Transparency of goals, vision, and participants:

Sensing what is going on in me

Openness if appropriate

Clear expression of what is the problem for me, paired with respect for the other person

Expression of feelings if appropriate (to increase transparency and improve understanding).

Respecting the other, oneself, and the environment:

Taking time
Eye contact (if appropriate for the culture)
Paying attention
Speaking a language that the others can understand
Accepting the other despite their probable negative emotions directed against us
Asking: What is there that can be positively acknowledged?
First accepting the other despite craving for acceptance by them

Trying to understand and to be understood comprehensively and thoroughly:

Active listening, trying to understand the other(s) and the whole situation in context
Trying to understand the other's negative feelings from their perspective, even if they are directed against us

Collaboration and sharing:

Is it possible to view the other as my partner in solving or transforming *our* conflict?
Can I ask the other to share what he/she would wish to happen in the conflicted situation?
Can I share with the other what I'd wish to happen to resolve or transform the conflict?
Could a third person help us to step out of some vicious circle?

Invitation to reflect:

Remember, once again, the last two to three conflicts you had.
Did you wish to feel more respected by your opponent? Reciprocally, did you feel respect for your opponent? Could the conflict be termed a silly misunderstanding or a mutual fight for acknowledgement?
Were you risking yourself by being open? How did that feel to you?
Which of Rogers' core attitudes were missing? Did you have a chance to restore it? Why? Why not?

12.6 Conclusion

In this chapter, we elaborated in more detail than in the introductory chapter how the people-oriented agenda of transforming communication can be put to work in reoccurring situations such as holding meetings, forming a shared vision, negotiating, and going through conflict. In all these situations, it was possible to specialize the people-oriented agenda by suggesting how its five items can be expressed in each of the key situations, given the responsible persons hold the respective attitudes. All examples were primarily intended to reflect on our—you as reader and we as authors—cognitive and organismic reactions and support us in shaping our personal, unique way of transforming communication in our work environment. If any of the resources shared in this chapter contributes to making your communication more meaningful, more rewarding, more effective, then this chapter will have fulfilled its purpose.

References

Anderson, D. J. (2008). Stop negotiating, start collaborating. http://www.djaa.com/stop-negotiating-start-collaborating (last retrieved on Jan 04, 2016.

David, C.-P. (2001). Alice in Wonderland meets Frankenstein: Constructivism, realism and peace building in Bosnia. *Contemporary Security Policy, 22*(1).

Fisher, R., Ury, W. (1991). Getting to YES negotiating agreement without giving. In B. Patton (Ed.), (2nd ed.). NY/USA: Penguin Books.

Johnson, D. W., Johnson, F. P. (1975/2006). *Joining together, group theory and group skills.* Boston, USA: Pearson Education, Inc.

Keane, R. (2001). *Reconstructing sovereignty: Post-Dayton Bosnia uncovered* (p. 61). London: Ashgate.

Motschnig-Pitrik, R., & Barrett-Lennard, G. T. (2010). Co-actualization: A new construct for understanding well-functioning relationships. *Journal of Humanistic Psychology* (*JHP*), *50*(3), 374–398.

Rogers, C. R. (1959). A theory of therapy, personality, and interpersonal relationships, as developed in the client-centered framework. In S. Koch (Ed.), *Psychology: A study of a science* (Vol. 3). New York, Toronto, London: McGraw-Hill Inc.

Rogers, C. R. (1961). *On becoming a person—A psychotherapists view of psychotherapy*. London, UK: Constable.

Ryback, D. (1998). *Putting emotional intelligence to work.* Boston: Butterworth-Heinemann.

Senge, P. M. (2006). *The fifth discipline, the art & practice of the learning organization.* USA: Currency Doubleday.

Stillwell, W., & Moormon, J. (1997). *Conflict is inevitable. War is optional.* La Jolla, CA: The Center for the Studies of the Person.

Toner, K., Leary, M. R., & Asher, M. (2013, October). Feeling superior is a bipartisan issue. *Psychological Science.*

Chapter 13
Integrating the Two Agendas in Agile Management

In my clients and in myself I find that when life is richest and most rewarding it is a flowing process. To experience this is both fascinating and a bit frightening. I find I'm at my best when I can let the flow of my experience carry me in a direction which appears to be forward....

Carl Rogers (1961, p. 27)

This chapter focuses on

- Transforming communication in agile management/leadership practice and training;
- Agile principles and values and their coherence with the value base of the Person-Centered Approach;
- The requirements that agile processes pose on human resources;
- Putting the people-oriented agenda to work in agile projects; and
- The crucial function of person-centered and collaborative attitudes in agile management.

13.1 Introduction

This chapter deals with transforming communication in the agile management. Since more than a decade, agile management methods have been entering the field and are increasingly challenging more rigorous, classical project management methods. In this chapter, we investigate in how far and under what conditions agile values and principles are consistent with those of transformative communication. Subsequently, we exemplify how individual features of the people-oriented agenda can be expressed in agile projects and which consequences accrue for agile management practice and training. Moreover, the role of digital media and its dynamics in becoming more agile will be addressed and reflected in light of an organization's success. The thoughtful inclusion of the people-oriented agenda is expected to lead

R. Motschnig and D. Ryback, *Transforming Communication in Leadership and Teamwork*, DOI 10.1007/978-3-319-45486-3_13

to new, valuable insight regarding the integration of the task-oriented and the people-oriented agendas in agile management.

13.2 Agile Management Needs Agile People

One of the core values of agile management is flexibility in reacting to the environment while at the same time staying true to some basic principles. Interestingly, the principles of agile management and those of transforming communication by following the people-oriented agenda turn out to be coherent. This is quite surprising in light of the totally different roots of agile approaches—namely software development—and transformative communication—namely psychotherapy. However, when viewing psychotherapy as a means of personal development, the acquaintance lies in the word "development," typically something quite complex in both the technical and human domains.

Before capturing some essentials of agile management, let us explicate why agile management urgently needs agile, flexible persons: If the software or any other product is to flexibly adapt to the real needs of its users, it requires, first of all, people who are open to the changing requirements and optimally can sense and appreciate the changes rather than resisting them (Motschnig-Pitrik 2015). They need to be empathic to customers' changing requirements and thus open non-judgmental to the customers' and their own experience. They need to appreciate that business-value concordant change is part and parcel of thriving in business. So, while at a first glance agile methods and transformative communication seem quite far apart, in effect they are close allies in meeting a core shared value: optimal adaptation to the complex, current environment while staying true to the core business and personal values, respectively.

With accelerating speed, scientific and technological advances are altering product development processes and those changes require us to rethink the management of processes. "Linear thinking, prescriptive processes, and standardized, unvarying practices are no match for today's volatile product development environment. So as product development processes swing from anticipatory to adaptive, project management must change also." (Highsmith 2004, p. 5). In fact, this is but one instance of a more general characteristic of our time. According to Verna Allee (1997, p. 5), in modern thinking, "Change is all there is"—as opposed to traditional thinking where change is described as "Something to worry about."

Naturally, adapting continuously to the changing environment and yet not giving up one's core is an advantage in business as it has been in the evolution of species and cultural and legal systems (Damasio 2012).

Invitation to reflect:

What are your foundational values for your organization that you want to advance despite the ubiquitous dynamic developments?
What kind of change are you currently confronted with? How does it feel? How do you deal with it?
Do you think/feel that your colleagues/employees are open enough to changing conditions and can deal with them appropriately?
Which change is most difficult for you?

In the last decades, very little has changed at universities to support students in acquiring competences to become mentally fit for increasing and ubiquitous change. Rather, ever more intellectual information, sophisticated modeling, documentation, and precise planning for research are required, emphasizing intellectual, anticipatory processes while disengaging experiential, mindfully adaptive ones. Recently, the CIO of a medium-sized company in the Brno region (Czech Republic) said during a workshop:

> "The fact is that when graduates start working in our company, they tend to need several months to actually *unlearn* what they have been taught at universities: Namely, to wait for specific orders or exercises, to be passive unless called upon, to stop thinking whether something makes sense or not but rather follow orders, etc., etc. This is absolutely *not* what we need here! So actually we have to re-educate young employees from schools until they [...] assimilate the company's culture which is based much on sharing of responsibility and power, and on self-initiative" (iCom Team 2014, p. 53).

13.3 Agile Values and Principles

In the last two decades, agile methods have come to be appreciated in a variety of fields (Highsmith 2004). One prominent example is software development. In that field, the authors of the "Manifesto for Agile Software Development" (Beck et al. 2001) could improve the ways of developing software by adopting the following value *preferences*. They value:

- Individuals and interactions over processes and tools;
- Working software over comprehensive documentation;
- Customer collaboration over contract negotiation; and
- Responding to change over following a plan.

Thus, even though the "traditional" values (right-hand side of the lines in the enumeration above) are not discarded, they lose their pivotal function giving way to the new guiding values on the left-hand side. Interestingly, these value preferences show a clear shift toward the collaborative and communicative relationship with fellow human beings—be it a teammate or a customer—and away from "rigid design constructs" such as contracts, plans, and documentations. This may be the response to traditional methods' overemphasis on the alienated artificial constructs as the only guiding principles "set in stone" and a missing connection to what is perceived as the "real issue" (Motschnig-Pitrik 2015).

Some preferences inherent in the agile "philosophy" are expressed still more distinctly in agile principles. Resource Box 13.1 lists 6 out of the 12 items from the principles behind the Agile Manifesto (Beck et al. 2001). These principles reveal the interpersonal and environmental qualities they demand for supporting agile management (italics added for emphasis). Intriguingly, all of them are coherent with the core values of the Person-Centered Approach that promotes the provision of proper environmental factors like being in contact, building trust, respecting the other, and listening for the self-organized unfolding of motivation and moving forward. Interestingly, the principles also call for an increase in communication and collaboration, valuing face-to-face contact!

Resource Box 13.1 Selected items from the Principles behind the Agile Manifesto (Beck et al. 2001).

- Welcome changing requirements, even late in development. Agile processes harness *change for* the *customer's* competitive *advantage.*
- Business people and developers must *work together daily* throughout the project.
- Build projects around *motivated individuals. Give them the environment and support they need and trust them* to get the job done.
- The most efficient and effective method of conveying information to and within a development team is *face-to-face conversation.*
- The best architectures, requirements, and designs emerge from *self-organizing teams.*
- At regular intervals, the team *reflects* on how to become more effective, then tunes and *adjusts* its behavior accordingly.

But how can the personal capacities to follow the principles and embrace agile values be developed? In the authors' view, a sustainable path enabling the unfolding of such values is to experience them in action. This could happen, for example, through participating in a well-functioning agile team or, in preparation for this, through participating in a workshop on person-centered communication (as described in Chap. 12 of this book). To illustrate the "learning" and movement in such a workshop, let us "listen" to some of the reactions participants reflected back:

> "I really liked the way the course is given, especially when we were sitting in the circle, not hiding behind the desk. Our facilitator and all the students were open to new ideas and trying to understand the others and this is what I really miss at other courses and generally in normal life. Maybe this could be a reason why the learning progress of this group is very unique."

"Sharing is simply a great way of thinking, speaking out gives the idea a somewhat new perspective."

"A remarkable point was our dialog exercise. I was surprised, that sometimes it's so hard to paraphrase what your partner said, and it's so extremely hard to explain your mind in simple understandable terms."

These excerpts illustrate that students perceive courses that offer experiential learning in communication as something special and worthwhile, since they offer a kind of learning that feels rare and desirable to them. It is this kind of experiential learning and direct communication that is the "daily bread" of agile teams. Yet, traditional education does not likely equip us sufficiently with the interpersonal capacities needed for agile management. Thus, creative paths need to be sought, and this chapter argues that transformative communication and the Person-Centered Approach can be viewed as conceptual allies to agile values and principles. Summarizing, Resource Box 13.2 explicates in which way each of the items of the people-oriented agenda can be helpful in supporting agile management at work.

Resource Box 13.2 Putting the people-oriented agenda to work in agile projects

Contact

Agile projects thrive on daily meetings and colocation of the project team
Short, frequent meetings help the team explicate the current contact with the task such as to discover deviations or problems early
Transparency of goals, vision, and participants
Sensing what is most important at a given moment
Transparent expression of what has been accomplished and what needs to be done
Transparency regarding any issue encountered
Transparency regarding any issue encountered
Clear expression of what is the problem for me
Achieving clarity about priorities
Coherence regarding business values, meaning that I'm personally OK with them
Respecting the other, oneself, and the environment
Respecting the other even if they change their mind
Appreciating a free, unhindered flow of information between teammates and with customer representatives
Showing interest in the other person, his or her ideas, interest, goals, current situation, etc.
Trying to understand and to be understood comprehensively and thoroughly
Attentive, active listening, trying to understand customers, teammates
Trying to understand the other's requirements, needs, and wants, even if they may lead to changes in the original specification, product, or plan

Empathic sensing into the whole situation in the team, the relationship with the customer and the market situation

Collaboration and sharing

The team chooses how to solve the task. Any problems are shared as they arise such that team members can collaborate on a resolution

The customer collaborates with the project team throughout the agile process such as to voice and prioritize their requirements at regular intervals

David, who was fortunate to have known Carl Rogers in person, imagined what would have been Rogers' response when being asked *today* how an organization or business could best become more agile, given the multiple communication channels we have at our disposition. The fictive response, made up from remembering several real dialogues with Rogers, is given in the case example from recollected ideas below.

Case example from recollected ideas based dialogues between Carl Rogers and David Ryback

If Rogers were alive today and asked about how an organization might become more agile in this modern, technological, media-focused culture, he might have respond as follows:

"Well, given how much so many people are burying their noses in these lit-up screens to get information and entertain themselves and connect with others, I would say that organizations—be they business, educational, or whatever—need to take that into consideration. Perhaps there is a need to practice a new kind of openness, one that could be communicated through these electronic machines. The challenge, I'm guessing, is that it's so easy to portray oneself in any old way, without much thought as to whether or not this is their true, authentic self, or just some arbitrary version. From what I read in these up-to-date newspapers and magazines, it seems there's a lot of lying and fabrication going on. That seems much easier than being thoughtful and taking the courage to be one's true self in this new medium."

"Even for an old codger like me, there's nothing like face-to-face contact, and I strongly doubt if anything will ever totally take its place. I have heard of such things as Skype and Go-to-Meeting that enable people to see one another in the moment as they communicate normally. So perhaps that allows for people to share their authentic selves, even though it's through electronic media. So, as long as people could see one another as they communicate in real time, then I believe my ideas about genuineness and empathy still mean what I hoped they'd mean when I first wrote them."

"The agility might involve an openness to changes that are real, authentic and relevant to people's needs and to keep agile about communicating these newly found changes on an ongoing basis. The most obvious thing, it seems

to me, is to convey their messages to many people, close and far away, using the technology, and I know that's happening already."
"The bigger question is, what is the place of my principles of openness and so on in business? I would like to think that the values I put forth would make for better business, but that would be more apparent in the long run, where greed and dishonesty might win out in the short run. I guess this would involve decisions to get fuel by mining the earth, and of course worsening the global pollution problem, which has really taken on an accelerating course, if the scientists are correct. So, I think the values I proposed long ago are more crucial not only to our long-term success but even to our survival in the not-too-distant future. So, yes, openness, respect and an extended form of empathy for the whole environment are more essential these days than ever before. If our culture fails to see this, then I really have failed. But I'm an optimistic old bird and I think we can still turn things around. That's my true feeling."

Let us end this chapter with a (real) quote by Carl Rogers:

> Perhaps the most basic of these essential attitudes is realness, or genuineness. When the facilitator is a real person, being what he or she is, entering into relationships with the learners without presenting a front or a facade, the facilitator is much more likely to be effective. This means, that the feelings the facilitator is experiencing are available to his or her awareness, that he or she is able to live these feelings, to be them, and able to communicate them if appropriate. (Rogers 1983, p. 121)

What Carl Rogers expressed so clearly about the appropriate communication of feelings, agile teams need to accomplish for the transparent communication of all those aspects of a project that are relevant for the next step of its completion. This "realness" needs to make sense at the task-oriented level as well as consider the team collaborating on task-accomplishment in a way to satisfy the customer and yet do not "burn out." So once again, balancing the task- and the people-oriented agendas in each agile cycle becomes a key issue for success!

13.4 Conclusion

In this chapter, we elaborated in more detail than in the introductory chapter how the people-oriented agenda of transforming communication can be put to work in agile projects. In particular, we analyzed basic agile principles and found them to be coherent with person-centered values and a collaborative attitude. As a consequence, we suggested how the five items the people-oriented agenda can be expressed in agile management under the condition that the responsible persons hold the respective attitudes. All examples were primarily intended to reflect on our—you as reader and us as authors—cognitive and organismic reactions and support us in shaping our personal, unique way of transforming communication in our increasingly agile and changing work environment. If any of the resources shared in this chapter contributes to making your communication more meaningful, more rewarding, and more effective, then this chapter will have fulfilled its purpose.

References

Allee, V. (1997). *The knowledge evolution: Expanding organizational intelligence*. Newton, USA: Butterworth-Heinemann.

Beck, K., et al. (2001). The agile manifesto, agile alliance. http://www.agilealliance.org/the-alliance/the-agile-manifesto/ (retrieved on February 05, 2016).

Damasio, A. R. (2012). *The self comes to mind*. London: Vintage.

Highsmith, J. (2004). *Agile project management: Creating innovative products*. Redwood City, CA, USA: Addison Wesley Longman Publishing Co.

iCom Team. (2014). *Constructive communication in international teams*. Münster, DE: Waxmann.

Motschnig-Pitrik, R. (2015). Developing personal flexibility as a key to agile management practice. In: Sushil & G. Chroust (Eds.), *Systemic flexibility and business agility* (pp. 131–142). *Flexible Systems Management Series*. India: Springer.

Rogers, C. R. (1961). *On becoming a person—A psychotherapists view of psychotherapy*. London, UK: Constable.

Rogers, C. R. (1983). *Freedom to learn for the 80's*. Columbus, OH: Charles E. Merrill Publishing Company, A Bell & Howell Company.

Chapter 14
Building and Developing Well-Functioning Teams—The Impact of Transformative Communication

Congruence or genuineness involves letting the other person know "where you are" emotionally. It may involve confrontation and the straightforward expression of personally owned feelings—both negative and positive. Thus congruence is a basis for living together in a climate of realness.

Carl Rogers (1980, p. 160)

This chapter focuses on the following:

- Characteristics of well-functioning teams;
- Resources for transforming communication in:
  - ob interviews;
  - Decision-making;
- Case examples and reflective dialogue;
- The function of self-organizing principles and effects of drawing on them;
- The people-oriented agenda in teamwork.

14.1 Introduction

In this chapter, the team as social and professional enabler for any collaborative task is in the foreground. First, the characteristics of well-functioning teams are investigated. Subsequently, we share insights on the hiring process as an essential step in building "healthy," happy, and productive teams. Another ubiquitous task in working with a team is decision-making. In order to help mastering this complex challenge, a few vignettes of decision-making situations with or in teams will be presented, observed, and reflected upon, aiming at facilitating experiential learning. Finally, we investigate how the people-oriented agenda can be put to work in teams that excel on the task- as well as people-oriented level.

R. Motschnig and D. Ryback, *Transforming Communication in Leadership and Teamwork*, DOI 10.1007/978-3-319-45486-3_14

14.2 Characteristics of Well-Functioning Teams

Earlier, we introduced the two-agenda approach to meetings and other key situations in management and leadership. In this chapter, we extend it to teams. These, too, can be considered to work at a task-specific level and a basic, people-oriented level. Both are interdependent and tightly intertwined (Johnson and Johnson 1975/2006). In this work, however, we chose to focus our attention on the people-oriented aspects and assume that the required task- or job-related skills are covered by the team members such that they are provided in the team as a whole and allow the team to competently handle the task at hand. This means that, for example, the crew of an aircraft would have members who can competently deal with the list of activities they are expected to handle, such as admitting passengers, flying and landing the aircraft, storing cabin luggage safely, serving refreshments, dealing with the technology on board, and making announcements. This task-oriented level is more apparent than the people-oriented one that often lies hidden but cannot be ignored if the team is to take on any responsibility. The people-oriented level or agenda in a team could be compared with the "energy system" in the team that delivers energy and impulses to the whole team and its members to stimulate one other and act in concert.

High-performing teams whose members enjoy their team confirm what Maureen O'Hara witnessed in person-centered encounter groups.

> When groups can provide the necessary conditions for each of their members to become fully present to themselves and each other, the group's capacity for self-organizing emerges, and when the individuals also begin to tune into and reflect on the workings of the whole, we consider that a form of consciousness. At this stage, the group may become capable of exquisitely creative, responsible, and wise collective action that goes well beyond that of any of the particular individual participants within the group. (O'Hara 2003, p. 74)

Apparently, in a work context, the phrase "to become fully present to themselves and each other" would need to be complemented by also becoming coherent with the organization's or project's goals such that there is a flow between the people as well each person's professional function and their personal striving.

Appreciating that well-functioning teams are a reality, indeed, it is tempting to ask: What is it that supports a group of people to function well together and achieve shared goals?

Based on the literature research and Renate's empirical research (Motschnig-Pitrik 2006, 2008, 2013) and experience in working in and with teams, as well as influenced by intensive conversations with Godfrey Barrett-Lennard and Ladislav Nykl, we suggest the following as a preliminary response to the question: How can we form a team in which mutual growth and unfolding of our team are prevalent while some task or project is being accomplished? Team members, including the leader, in particular:

- Are as open as appropriate to their experience as well the others' experience. They welcome experience as a source of growth and promote it appropriately → *openness to one's own and others' experience;*
- Feel an active, genuine interest in the project, the others, and the ensuing relationships. This is expressed in transparent sharing of ideas, meanings, feelings, goals, work, reactions, etc., whenever deemed appropriate → *sharing;*
- Aim to understand the messages of the others as thoroughly and completely as possible and express themselves in a way that makes it easy for the others to understand them → *encompassing understanding;*
- Tend to collaborate or "compete" in a friendly, playful fashion rather than feed destructive rivalry, distortion, or ignorance in their relationship → *cooperative attitude;*
- Dynamically balance their need for autonomy as well as relatedness and coherence with the project goals → *relatedness and coherence as well as autonomy;*
- Are mindfully aware of their own need to actualize themselves as well as the tendency of the relationship to form as a larger, more complex, dynamically ordered whole, the bond it creates, the influence it exerts on the partners and teammates, and the effects it receives and passes on through interacting with the environment → *organism as part of a larger whole, interdependence;*
- Appreciate that conflicting goals, directions, and opinions tend to create tension. If they manage to deal with problems cooperatively, that may even strengthen their relationship or lead to some transformation that helps both/all relationship partners to move forward → *acknowledgment of and dealing with tension;*
- Reduce negative stress and transform it into creative tension. This can happen by realizing autonomy and self-acceptance concurrently with respecting the others and the environment → *stress reduction and respect;*
- Promote the unfolding of the other as well as self and the relationship. This can happen by including the others and aiming to provide space and opportunities for them to be present, contributing, and facilitative or cooperative in their own ways. This will allow relationship partners to feel more accepted (by others and self) and to express acceptance → *inclusion/participation with acceptance.*

Viewed from a systemic perspective, the encompassing social environment interactively contributes to and benefits from the team. We tend to refer to the respective relationships as "*co-actualizing*" as an expression of the self-organizing principle in humans who actualize themselves *and* the whole team or relationship system through their constructive interaction (Motschnig-Pitrik and Barrett-Lennard 2010).

Whereas further research on the tendency toward co-actualization is urgently needed, there is an equally pressing need to "apply" the early findings in the practice of living and working together. So what does this mean in the practice of teamwork? Here are some incentives.

14.2.1 Genuine Interaction, Relatedness, and a High Degree of Autonomy Versus Imposing, Controlling, and Manipulating

As Rogers wrote in his famous article with Farson on active listening in *Communicating in Business Today* (1987), we tend not to want to be changed or manipulated by others, forced to defend our self-image. Each attempt at imposing something on us, be it meeting a deadline, documenting code, and speaking a particular language, will be met with initial resistance. The more push one person exerts on the other and the more control s/he takes over the other, the less that person's actualizing tendency will be able to unfold and the less both/all will be able to co-actualize.

Thus, if the situation allows both or all team members to genuinely share their feelings, meanings, and views, each can be a part of the solution (Ryback 1998). However, if partners differ significantly, considerable effort may be needed to reach consensus and tension would surface along the way. Therefore, advanced empathizing and moderation competencies, as well as personal maturity of all concerned, are needed in order to enable, initiate, and facilitate genuine interaction and to stop it at the right point in time without getting lost in the complexity of the interaction (iCom Team 2014). An example will follow shorty (see Sect. 14.5).

14.2.2 Considering Whether Collaborative Problem Solving and Collaboration Is an Option

When there is a problem, we are inclined to think that someone must have caused it and hence is to be blamed for the negative consequences. While this may hold in the mechanical world of parts, materials, and products, it is highly problematic in the complexity of interpersonal relationship in which cause and effect tend to interweave in complex patterns (Kriz 2013). Frequently, undesirable or annoying behavior of one person is very likely to come as a reaction to some frustrated need or experience. For example, a colleague's "misbehaving" may well be the consequence of this person's not receiving proper attention or being under-/over-challenged. In such cases, a shift in the perspective in which we look at problems may be helpful for all involved. Instead of labeling the colleague as "problematic" or asking who is the "bad guy," we could realize that "we have a problem" and see how we can join efforts to resolve it. Aiming for transformative communication and, in particular, co-actualization in that case would mean that "if I am to facilitate the personal growth of others in relation to me, then I must grow, and while this is often painful it is also enriching" (Rogers 1961, p. 51).

Summarizing, the process of transforming communication in a team can be significantly facilitated or hindered by external factors such those listed in Table 14.1.

Table 14.1 External factors supporting or hindering transformative communication and teamwork

Supportive	Hindering
Executive support	Top management is in opposition to the idea or project
Engagement in a shared goal	Following separate or antagonistic goals
Accounting for flexibility and managing change	Restrictive regulations forbidding or strongly restricting flexibility
Social sharing acknowledged as a "part of the deal"	Strict task orientation with no time for social sharing
Information flows naturally as appropriate	Information is hidden, distorted, or gets stuck
Devotion of adequate time to prepare when a decision is due	Lack of time making it impossible to prepare thoughtfully
Collaboration and friendly competition	Rivalry and tough competition
Adequate skills and/or competencies for the challenge at hand	Missing skills and/or competencies for the challenge at hand

Unfavorable contexts tend to impose heavy burdens on relationships, teams, and their leaders. Such circumstances need to be recognized to "free the path" for well-functioning teams and co-actualizing processes. If this seems not to be realistically possible, the question remains whether to engage in that context at all, or even to consciously give up on the particular context, or to try to change (or flee or fight) the circumstances. Part II of this book provides a variety of case examples how people in leadership positions put the people-oriented agenda to work and what consequences accrued for them and their teams or workgroups.

Invitation to reflect and complement Table 14.1:

Can you list other factors supporting or hindering transformative communication and teamwork based on your experience?
Can you distill yet further factors from the case examples given in Part II of this book?

14.3 Job Interviews

Undoubtedly, the most precious and constituting resource of any team is its members. Hence, getting the right people to work together is a crucially important task and is far too often underestimated in the rush of everyday obligations. Let me share my recent story in this context: I (Renate) was fortunate to win a large EU-wide project in which the University of Vienna was the lead partner. As project leads, we collaborated with the head of the postgraduate center of the University of Vienna who, by the way, also happens to be a systemic coach. I was amazed by the way we arranged the hiring process for new teammates who were supposed to collaborate with the already existing core-team. It felt exactly right to me and was what I'd call a prototypical example of transformative communication. My whole experience during the hiring process was so clearly positive and united that I feel an urge to share the process for potential reuse. Its structured parts are presented as Resource Box 14.1, and some annotations follow.

Resource Box 14.1: Transformative communication in job interviews

Preparation phase

Collaborate and co-think in putting together the job announcement. Share your proposal with colleagues who will interface with the new person and consider their inputs

Share the candidates' applications with those who are interested. If several people have applied, take the time to sort the applications regarding quality from your perspective, not to demand too much of your colleagues' time

Agree whom to invite in a first round and propose time and location for the interviews. Plan sufficient time (e.g., one hour between interviews) so that you can reflect upon each candidate right after the interview

During the interview

Meet the candidate at eye level of authenticity

Share relevant information transparently

Let the candidates ask questions about what they want to know

Listen actively and show your genuine interest in the candidate

Ask the relevant questions that are on your mind while always respecting the candidates' private sphere. Sometimes, it is helpful to prepare some questions based on the candidate's application or CV if something impressed or struck you in particular. As well, address the financial aspects, whether they are negotiable or fixed

At the end, you may want to ask the candidates how they felt about the interview and whether their interest in the job was still the same as before. Let the candidates know about the next steps from your perspective. If you feel thankful for the candidate's effort to come to the interview, you may want to share this feeling

Reflection

Leave some amount of time between the interviews to "digest" your impression and clear your mind before the next person comes

If you get the chance to reflect upon the interview with colleagues, take that opportunity. Voicing impressions and sharing feelings with trusted colleagues may be worth a lot in the complex situation of hiring future colleagues. We all come with mental models that contain mind shadings that we are hardly aware of and an open sharing with colleagues can compensate for our "blind spots" or biases

14.4 Case Example: The Hiring Process for Team Members for an EU Project

14.4.1 Job Announcement

The initiators of the project (3 dedicated people) sat together to share ideas and consult about an appropriate text for 3 job announcements. Each of us would primarily interface with one of the positions to be filled, but eventually, we all would form a team. This is why, from the beginning, we consulted each other regarding the respective job descriptions. Each of us contributed to the content as well as to a concise, understandable, and attractive wording of the job ad. What did each of us really expect from the candidate? What kind of previous experience would be most helpful? Which qualification would be indispensable? What could we offer? How would we describe the project and its/our vision?

We produced the first version of the job ad during the meeting and made it accessible to all three of us to edit it before publicizing the announcement. In fact, some of us revised the text slightly and, fortunately, we were all in favor of the minor changes, perhaps because we had a shared vision of the project and knew and accepted each other's interests. The job announcements got done in time and were published together.

14.4.2 Preparation for Job Interviews

The applications were presorted by a secretary, and each of the three project initiators got the applications for the three positions to look at them and suggest with whom they would like to talk in person. We agreed that, time permitting, all three of us would participate in the interviews. In the case of time constraints, at least the person who would primarily interface with the candidate would need to be present, and in case of doubt, there would be a second interview. This seemed reasonable and time-efficient to all, still utilizing as many of the core-team's perceptions as possible, without the stress to have to be present at each interview. Before actually inviting the candidates, we conversed by phone and mail to share our preferences and consult whom actually to invite in the first round. For me, these consultations were really helpful since they opened my eyes to issues I had not attended to at first sight but that were definitely relevant: Would that person be able to use computerized tools and social media fluently to allow for cross-border collaboration despite her advanced age?

14.4.3 *Job Interviews*

First of all, we went into the interviews with the attitude that we need a bright colleague for our team and thus were thankful to the applicants to respond to our call and take the time to come for the interview. This allowed us to meet the candidates at eye level, since they, too, needed something from us, namely the job. So no one party basically was in a position of power and the conversation was carried on with a high level of respect and sensitivity and, interestingly, also openness, once candidates started to feel safe in our environment.

We dynamically assigned one of us to lead the interview and introduce the candidate to our institution, the other participants, and the project at hand. Often, the first question to the candidates was how he or she found the announcement and what made them apply. No part of the interview was made up or designed in advance; rather, the conversation followed a natural flow of questions and answers. The questions asked most frequently showed a genuine interest in the candidate and his or her potential fit to the vacant position. Examples of such questions were as follows: What brings you here? What is it that you resonated to in the announcement? Is there anything in the announcement that you wish to understand better or that you are not sure you can handle properly? If so, what is it and what questions or doubts to you have along those lines?

Further frequent questions addressed the candidate's previous occupation. We were interested what the candidates liked and did not like in their previous job, what makes them want to change, and why they thought they would be the person to fill the vacant position. To each response, the interviewing team gave their responses in turn in order to reveal as much from the job profile and actual tasks to be accomplished as possible and allow the candidate to react.

Yet further questions probed into the candidates' plans for the future: Where they were heading to in their career? Whether they would be available for the position for the whole project period? And when they could start? Finally, we made clear that we had just very little space to adjust salaries because they were regulated by the project's grant. Nevertheless, we were interested what candidates had expected to earn and thus asked them. Based on their response and our impression from how the interview went so far, we tried to negotiate the expectations with some options and benefits we could offer. At the very end, we asked whether the candidate had further questions and said good-bye and when, approximately, the candidates would hear back from us. We also asked them kindly to let us know in case they were no longer interested.

14.4.4 *Reflection*

After each interview that lasted about 30 min, we took at least 20 min to share our impressions on how the interview went, how we liked the candidate, and how well they would fit with us, respectively, with the candidates already preselected. The reflection helped to open up new perspectives and to compare our often similar but at times also diverging perceptions and interpretations. I feel I learned a lot in particular through these reflections and could understand, for example, why my colleague valued the previous job experience of one of the colleagues so highly and that it indeed could be a particular bonus for administering our project.

In no case did I feel it necessary to trick out a candidate with a question or apply any technique to reveal something that they would prefer to hide. Intriguingly, some candidates were quite open regarding some criteria they did not fully meet. For example, a young lady with excellent language skills in three European languages admitted that her English was not quite so good but that she would definitely be willing to work at improving it. The thoughtful openness of some candidates made them appear honest, present, and sympathetic. It had the effect that the interviewing team reconsidered the importance of part of the job criteria and weighed the candidate's presented profile against what we thought would be most needed in their job and in our team.

Invitation to reflect:

What effect do you think did the collaborative job interviews have on the core-team (i.e., the project initiators)?
How, as a candidate, would you feel at a job interview in which three to four persons take part actively?
Do you think that the interview procedure described above is effective and efficient in finding the best candidate? Can you think of any improvement?

Retrospectively, the collaborative hiring process had the following effects:

- Deepening of project vision;
- Getting to know each other and learning about priorities, particular interests, skills, and oneself, leading to an increased transparency;
- Growing as a team and learning from each other;
- Clear responsibilities in the interview with an option but no urge to participate;
- Interviewees are dealt with at eye level, not as someone who wants something from us. Everybody is respected for who s/he is;
- New employees get the impression that they are accepted into a well-functioning team and, from the first moment, are inspired by the transformative communication that they can join in naturally.

14.5 Decision-Making in and with a Team—The Role of Transformative Communication

Decision-making is a crucial activity faced by every leader, manager, and in fact by every person on a daily basis. It means to choose which potentials to realize and which to discard and thus how to move on in the present and future. Because of the vital importance of decision-making for all areas of our life and even planet, innumerable research studies have been and are still being performed and published (for a very readable summary on the theme consult, e.g., Johnson and Johnson 1975/2006). This is why this section emphasizes on the dynamics of transformative communication in group decision-making. Moreover, focusing on experiential learning, we provide a few illustrative case examples in the first place and subsequently accompany readers in their making sense and deriving insight from the examples through reflection.

The assumption that communication plays a decisive role in the quality of a group's or team's decisions is confirmed, for example, by Johnson and Johnson (1975/2006, p. 291), who wrote that factors enhancing group decision-making include, among others, positive interdependence, face-to-face promotive interaction, and social skills. Another significant finding from research concerns the benefits of involving the group in decision-making. According to Johnson and Johnson (1975/2006), who draw on a rich base of original studies by Kurt Lewin, his group, and others, the following benefits accrue when involving group members in decisions concerning the group/team.

First, the quality of a decision can be enhanced by utilizing the resources of each member. In particular, members responsible for implementing the decision should be most knowledgeable about what the decision should be and that knowledge is best released through being involved in making the decision. In this respect, being able to voice information transparently, and in a way that others understand it, is an enormous benefit that transformative communication can contribute.

Second, and no less important, the members' commitment to implement the decision increases when being part of the process leading to a decision. The members' allegiance to the group/team tends to increase significantly when being involved in decision-making and so do their outcomes. This is not surprising since, in our terms, inclusion and involvement are expressions of respect, one of the core conditions of a promotive climate. Moreover, being able to co-determine the direction of the team rather than being imposed from the outside is more in line with each person's actualizing process and thus his or her intrinsic motivation, a most powerful source of motivational energy.

Another argument in favor of involving a team in making decisions is that, in groups, incorrect solutions are more likely to be recognized and rejected (Johnson and Johnson 1975/2006, p. 271). This is because the transactive memory of a group or team exceeds that of an individual member. Thereby, the *transactive memory* "is the knowledge of each individual member and the ways to exchange it through communication" (Wegner 1995), cited in (Johnson and Johnson 1975/2006,

p. 272). However, group discussion should last long enough to get beyond what everyone already knows (Larson et al. 1998).

So, generally, there exist good reasons for utilizing a team's resources for making important decisions rather than having one person make the decision. This does not mean, however, that collaborative decision-making is always effective or easy and smooth. This brings up another question: Can transformative communication also help to reduce some of the obstacles of effective decision-making in groups?

In our experience that is confirmed by the case examples in Part II, it can help to overcome some of the hindrances and creatively transform others. For example, if the composition of the group is unfavorable with too widely dispersed interests of members, insufficient knowledge or skills in relevant fields, or too little time available, transformative communication would reach its limits. With such massive hindrances standing in the way, it cannot directly unfold its full potential to contribute to high-quality decisions. It can, however, let the group experience and realize the problem at hand quickly and help transform the whole situation, potentially leading to a different constellation or a totally different course of action. In brief, under adverse circumstances, transformative communication would not directly contribute to an optimal decision by a given team but would help members and leaders to recognize that the constellation is inappropriate and ring the bell for a creative solution that would step out of the given frame and reframe the problem or setting. For example, if a team realizes that it does not have time for collaborative decision-making but nevertheless trusts its leader, the members might just share their views and delegate the decision to the leader or one or two knowledgeable persons whom they trust to find the optimum under the given circumstances.

After this brief theoretical reasoning, let us turn to real-life situations.

Case example *Including the group in a decision may not be enough*!

During a further education program for counselors, a 3-h workshop on the application of "focusing" for dealing with difficult situations was offered (Gendlin 1978). About 30 people attended the workshop that started with a brief introduction of the facilitator and the theme, a quick round on participants' reasons for attending the workshop, and a brief focusing exercise that was reflected in the plenum. For the remaining two hours, the facilitator gave us, the participants, the choice, whether we wanted to go into the theory in detail, or rather would prefer to practice and reflect upon focusing in the group. She made clear at the outset that a mix would not be possible since each part needed the whole time to be covered meaningfully. She asked those around to voice their preferences. Intriguingly, participants turned out to be distributed almost exactly half-half, with each camp having perfect arguments why either theory or practice would be preferable. Clearly, the group was split into two camps. Then, the facilitator tried to negotiate some solution, but it seemed that half of the group would be dissatisfied and somehow even feel cheated for not getting what they wanted. Interestingly, then, the facilitator shared that this was indeed a difficult situation. Then, she took the space to illustrate the application of her focusing technique in the situation at hand, hoping to find a solution while verbalizing her thoughts and feelings. However, in the already strained situation—none were actually getting what they wanted—the criticism became even louder. “This seems like manipulation! You’re trying to put something into our mouths that you want but that we didn’t ask for!”

The facilitator became somewhat defensive and admitted that the technique would help her in finding her personal solution strategy in the given context, but of course would not help to unite the split group. This openness resulted in participants’ becoming more accepting of the difficult group situation. At the same time, the participants’ genuine interest in the (theoretical) constraints and (practical) opportunities of the technique arose and an interesting dialogue evolved around the steps that the facilitator had taken in her search of a solution and the theoretical grounding for these steps. So voices of each camp paved the way for themselves to nurture their interests. Above all, however, we participants learned experientially and significantly about the sophistication of group decision-making: Including the group with best intentions may not be enough! Or may it have been enough?

Invitation to reflect:

What, in your view, was the problem in the case example above?
How would you have gone about the whole process, in retrospect?
What insight are you taking with you from the case example?
Do you agree that, in sum, the group directed the process of “delivering” to participants the best mix of learning possible in the given situation?
Do you feel you would like to have been a participant in that group or are you happy you didn’t have to go through that strained situation?

Case example *When to schedule follow-up meetings*?

A project team of 10 people met regularly face-to-face every two weeks for their jour fixe that lasted about 2 h. The major services were delivered to the customer as planned. For the last project month, the schedule was such that one little service was due to be installed in about two weeks’ time and a brief project reflection and closing session should take place at the end of the month. The team leader was not sure whether a short jour fixe before the delivery of the last service was necessary or whether the service delivery could proceed without a prior meeting and, just in case of complications, could be revised in the very final meeting along with the project reflection. She thought: Should we just continue the routine of jour fixes or would members appreciate to spend more time with installing the service at the customer's site and talking to them and then bring everything into the final reflection meeting? Why not ask the team? But: What to do if they have different opinions regarding the solution? Wouldn't the decision take too long and waste participants' time?

The team leader was really curious what team members would prefer and, as there were still 15 min left in the jour fixe, she decided to check with the team, but not let this become an endless discussion. She started voicing the question, clearly presenting the two alternatives, and letting the team know that, in case we do not find a decision quickly, she would make one, based on the team members' voices and her own preference. Astonishingly, all team members expressed their preference in having just one final, but potentially longer, jour fixe. For many of them, this would help to transfer valuable time to spend with the customer. The team leader ended the jour fixe with the words: "This was a very smooth process and clear sign of what you prefer. I had thought we might play it safe and meet in two weeks, but I'm happy with your decision." All went well and the "final" reflection session became one in which even a follow-up of the project was considered. All were fully present!

☕ Invitation to reflect:

Do you think/feel it was a good idea to include the team? Why do you think so?
Why, in your view, was the decision-making in the above case example successful?
How would you have gone about the whole process?
What insight are you taking with you from the case example?
Do you feel you would like to have been a member in that team?
Do you think that, as a team member, you can contribute to effective team decision-making? What are your potentials as a member and which limitations do you encounter?

Case example *Decide, whether to buy or build software*

Context: An international project team of 18 people from 7 partners is having its 3rd consortium meeting. It is becoming increasingly evident that some training software that is needed for an important project component cannot be reused as is, as was assumed in the project specification.

Coordinator: "You know that by now it is pretty clear that the software we wanted to integrate into our portal isn't available in the languages we need. A translation and system-adaptation would cost about 20,000 EUR and we can't rely on it to serve all our needs reliably and be finished in time so that integration testing can start as scheduled. I know that nobody had expected this complication and three partners already negotiated intensively with the company owning of the software. They will tell you more, if you want. I wish to thank you, Kate, Suzan, and Tony for all your effort to find out what we know now about that software!

My sense is that we need to come to a resolution during this meeting such that partners can move on. And we have more on our agenda for today, so let me suggest the following:

In my view, there are three options:

- Buy from owner,
- build our own, or
- apply for a change of the project specification.

As the last option comes with a high risk of rejection of the whole project by the commission, I am strongly suggesting refraining from that option. Any of the other two options will require a shift in all or some of the partners' budgets, because even if we don't buy the software, one of the partners will need resources to produce it. We should discuss that now. So let's see what each of you thinks and then go for lunch together. Hopefully we find a consensus by 3 p.m. today, because then we need to move to other issues that are at least as important as this one. (*Participants nod their heads.*) If we don't find a solution by this evening, I will make a decision based on my assessment of the situation. Is that o.k. or do you have another suggestion?" … [As there are no other suggestions, partners start sharing their views.]

Invitation to reflect:
How does the decision-making effort on "buy or build" resonate with you?
Do you consider the above an example of effective communication? Why?
Is there anything you object to? How would you have acted in the same situation?
How do you feel about the coordinator?

Summarizing, Resource Box 14.2 offers some inputs and considerations that the authors find helpful in transformative decision-making. While the first four points are derived from Johnson and Johnson (1975/2006), the others originate from the authors' experience.

Resource Box 14.2: Some resources regarding transformative decision-making in/with teams are as follows:.

What leaders and team members might want to know about decision-making in teams

- Involvement in decision-making increases members' commitment to implement the decision and facilitates the steps, activities, and adaptations needed to implement the decision (Johnson and Johnson 1975/2006, p. 273). This can be understood such that personal interests and directions are considered and aligned from the outset rather than unaligned regulations being imposed from the outside, often via formal authority and with little or no connection to the people concerned
- The more the persons involved in the decision-making, the longer it will tend to take to reach a decision
  - If the time needed for both making and implementing a decision is considered, however, the time factor becomes less clear. Often, the extra time taken to arrive at a consensual decision will greatly reduce the time needed to implement it (Johnson and Johnson 1975/2006, p. 290)
- In groups, incorrect solutions are more likely to be recognized and rejected (Johnson and Johnson 1975/2006, p. 271)
- On a meta-communication level, share your perceptions and given constraints regarding the decision process. Provide all useful information needed to make an informed decision. Be transparent regarding the process, time available, and your experience. On a meta-level, you may want to share your genuine hopes and doubts. Share why we need a decision and when we need it
- Sometimes, inviting participants to position themselves in a room along an axis with two extremes (such as buy a commercial tool versus adapt open source software) may help to reveal the team's current attitude toward an issue. Members can be asked to share why they stand at their chosen position. This increases transparency and brings dynamics more clearly into a session
- Use of social media. While face-to-face meetings tend to promote creativity and allow for rich social interaction, it may not always appropriate to call such a meeting. Social media, if utilized thoughtfully, can help to keep members connected and informed between regular sessions
- Tools such as skype or Skype for Business™ (a registered trademark of Microsoft) or mobile apps offer, for example, surveys that make it easy to share one's preference and see the team's position. This, for example, can help to orient oneself without consuming too much of the team's time

After having had a chance to witness—though only in a recorded, textual version that lacks several social clues—a few situations that challenged a team and their leader or manager, let us try to distill potential expressions of the items of the people-oriented agenda in those and similar situations. Before reading on, readers may want to produce their own resource box on these expressions and then compare their list with the exemplary features proposed by us authors in Resource Box 14.3.

Resource Box 14.3: Putting the people-oriented agenda to work in/with teams

Contact

The team leader and team members make themselves available to each other whenever appropriate

Frequent contact will facilitate the team's alignment and coherent direction

Collocation can significantly improve contact

Online communication can support contact but—due to the reduced social channel—cannot fully substitute face-to-face meetings

A proper blend between virtual and face-to-face meeting has the potential to combine the benefits and overcome the disadvantages of the two modes of communication (Motschnig-Pitrik and Nykl 2014)

Transparency of goals, vision, and participants

The objectives, preferences, constraints, and interests are transparent; optimally, there is no hidden agenda

Members (including the leader) express themselves as openly as appropriate, yet with respect

Instead of blaming, members make an effort to learn from mistakes and make sure not to repeat them

Members can sense their resonance or dissonance and express themselves clearly

Whenever appropriate, feelings, be they positive, negative, or ambiguous, are expressed and attended to in order to increase transparency and improve understanding

Respect for each other, oneself, and the environment

Members feel included in all aspects and decisions regarding the team. This does not necessarily mean that every member participates in every decision process; it does, however, mean that as few as possible issues are imposed on team members without giving them a chance to be heard

Members experience that their presence, attention, participation, and honesty are appreciated

Members' time resources and schedules are respected as far as possible

Making oneself accessible to others while also staying true to one's own needs and interests

Speaking a language that the others understand is most essential

Trying to understand and to be understood comprehensively and thoroughly

Making explicit effort to really hear others to understand them from their context and perspective
Sensing where the team is as a whole. For example, how do others engage or not engage while I'm in conversation with another person? Does it make sense to include others too?
Sensing the situation at hand. What are we up to? Can the path we're following right now lead to a solution or are we heading toward a dead end and wasting our time?
Online: Responding to mails comprehensively, attending to all important issues at least briefly

Collaboration and sharing

Problems that are shared sooner can start being resolved collaboratively sooner
Sharing should not be constrained to task-related issues only, some social sharing proves to support team cohesion and satisfaction, and people can be whole and connect on more channels than the often tight task dimension (Johnson and Johnson 1975/2006; Böhm et al. 2013, 2014; Motschnig-Pitrik and Nykl 2014)

14.6 Conclusion

This chapter bought up several examples of situations that we encountered in teams, emphasizing the processes of selecting and interviewing future team members and team decision-making. Drawing on the literature and our own research and experience, we suggested essential characteristics of well-functioning teams and the co-actualizing processes that tend to flow in such teams.

Invitation to reflect:

Peter Schmid (2005, p. 15–16) said that the therapist is nothing less than challenged to risk building—together with the client—a unique relationship through *co-experiencing, co-reflecting, co-constructing of alternatives, and hence "co-responding"* to the existential situation. Do you think the same holds true for the team leader or manager? Does it equally hold true for each person collaborating in a team and wanting to promote transformative communication?

We hope that some of our resources and case examples will prove useful for you as you navigate and reflect your own path through the exciting and challenging landscape of teamwork and team leadership.

References

Böhm, C., Motschnig-Pitrik, R., & Obiagwu, L. (2014). Constructive communication in teams that succeed. In *Proceedings of the Fifth International Conference on Social Communication in the Real and Virtual World (CMEP 2014), Wroclaw, Poland, November 25–27.*

Böhm, C., Motschnig-Pitrik, R., Obiagwu, L. (2013). Communication and media use in self-organized teams in a technology-enhanced project management course. In J. Herrington, et al. (Eds.), *Proceedings of World Conference on Educational Multimedia, Hypermedia and Telecommunications* (EDMEDIA) 2013 (pp. 966–975). Chesapeake, VA: ACCE.

Gendlin, E. (1978). *Focusing*. New York: Bentam Books.

iCom Team. (2014). *Constructive communication in international teams*. Münster: Waxmann.

Johnson D. W., & Johnson F. P. (1975/2006). *Joining together, group theory and group skills*. Boston, MA: Pearson Education, Inc.

Kriz, J. (2013) Person-Centred Approach and Systems Theory, In: Cornelius-White, J.H.D., Motschnig-Pitrik, R. and Lux, M. (eds) Interdisciplinary handbook of the person-centered approach: Research and theory. New York, USA: Springer.

Larson, J., Foster-Fishman, P., & Franz, T. (1998). Leadership style and the discussion of shared and unshared information in decision-making groups. *Personality and Social Psychology Bulletin, 24*, 482–495.

Motschnig-Pitrik, R. (2006). Two technology-enhanced courses aimed at developing interpersonal attitudes and soft skills in project management. In W. Neijdl, K. Tochtermann (Eds.), *Innovative approaches for learning and knowledge sharing. Proceedings of the 1st European Conference on Technology Enhanced Learning,* EC-TEL 2006, Crete, Greece, LNCS 4227 (pp. 331–346). Heidelberg: Springer.

Motschnig-Pitrik, R. (2008). Significant learning communities as environments for actualizing human potentials. *International Journal of Knowledge and Learning (IJKL), 4*(4), 383–397.

Motschnig-Pitrik, R. (2013). Person-centered communication—An experiential learning course for teacher candidates. *Ricercazione*, Edizioni Centro Studii Erickson, *5*(2), 217–232 (ISSN: 2036-5330).

Motschnig-Pitrik, R., & Barrett-Lennard, G. T. (2010). Co-actualization: A new construct for understanding well-functioning relationships. *Journal of Humanistic Psychology (JHP), 50*(3), 374–398.

Motschnig-Pitrik, R., & Nykl, L. (2014). *Person-centred communication: Theory, skills, and practice*. McGraw Hill, UK: Open University Press.

O'Hara, M. (2003). Cultivating consciousness Carl Rogers's person-centered group process as transformational andragogy. *Journal of Transformative Education, 1*(1), 64–79.

Rogers, C. R. (1961). *On becoming a person—A psychotherapists view of psychotherapy*. London, UK: Constable.

Rogers, C. R. (1980). *A way of being*. Boston: Houghton Mifflin.

Ryback, D. (1998). *Putting emotional intelligence to work* (p. 136). Woburn, MA: Butterworth-Heinemann.

Schmid, P. F. (2005). Kreatives Nicht-Wissen Zu Diagnose, störungsspezifischem Vorgehen und zum gesellschaftskritischen Anspruch des Personzentrierten Ansatzes. *Person*. Facultas, 1/2005.

Wegner, D. M. (1995). A computer network model of human transactive memory. *Social Cognition, 13*(3), 1–21.

Part IV
What Are the Facts?

Chapter 15
How Neuroscience Can Help to Understand the Working of Emotions and Empathy in Leadership

When the facilitator is a real person, ... the feelings the facilitator is experiencing are available to his or her awareness, ... he or she is able to live these feelings, to be them, and able to communicate them if appropriate.

Carl Rogers (1980, p. 271)

This chapter focuses on:

- Facilitating the understanding of the function of emotions, thinking, and empathy at the workplace;
- The process of collaboration between the "old" brain and the "new" brain and the impact of this collaboration on congruence and coherence, in particular in difficult situations;
- Panksepp's system of basic emotions and how it can support people with leadership responsibilities in communicating and collaborating more effectively;
- The process of transformative empathy and its relevance for improving understanding; and
- The relationship between the emission of oxytocin and the increase in confidence as well as mutual positive regard.

15.1 Introduction

The Person-Centered Approach to communication in general and leadership in particular involves an awareness of emotional dynamics between leader and associates, as well as among multiple individuals in teams, committees, boards, etc. In this chapter, we provide some of the information neuroscience has revealed about how emotions spark, energize, or block us and how we affect one another in the context of the workplace. This information is intended to help us to better understand how communication works at the affective level and how it can be transformed so as to become more effective on an interpersonal and task-related level. Central questions to be dealt with are as follows: How does the brain function to

R. Motschnig and D. Ryback, *Transforming Communication in Leadership and Teamwork*, DOI 10.1007/978-3-319-45486-3_15

acquire a greater likelihood of openness, not only intellectually but emotionally as well? What happens physiologically if we feel understood and respected and what happens if we are threatened? How can a neuroscientifically grounded understanding of the Person-Centered Approach (PCA) contribute to transforming communication at the workplace and in leadership functions?

In this chapter we will briefly explore the components of the brain and their primary functions in the process of communication, and how the "old" emotional inner brain differs so radically from the "new, intellectual" forebrain. We will look at how the "old" intuitive, faster brain is so quick to perceive and judge what we perceive and how the "new" slower, rational brain takes much more time, relatively speaking, to understand what we perceive.

Then we will switch gears and explore the origin of basic emotions from deep within the old brain, as studied by Jaak Panksepp and his colleagues—FEAR, RAGE, GRIEF, SEEKING, PLAY, LUST, and CARE, and how they contribute to the skills involved in empathy and effective leadership. This path leading to a greater understanding of empathy ranges from Dr. Carl Rogers' early work all the way to Dr. Daniel Goleman's formulation of the concept of emotional intelligence and how this plays such a vital role in leadership in the workplace. The effort to better understand our affective resources has an even longer tradition. On the way, psychoanalysis and the Jungian concept of Individuation (and many other approaches to personal growth) help to integrate the "old" and the "new" brain, and can result in mindfulness and an emotionally intelligent approach to person-to-person relationships and effective leadership. The same holds true for the Person-Centered Approach, except that the focus is different. Instead of emphasizing the control or managing of emotions, it attempts to increase the flow between the "old" and the "new" brain. This happens by loosening rigidly held constructs such as prejudices, conditions of self-worth, or preconceptions of one's value as seen by others. Those who are able to experience their "whole organism" can experience what is going on with less bias or distortion. This tends to lead to better, more accurate decision-making (Rogers 1961) and allows people who are more emotionally flexible to adapt to a changing environment (O'Hara and Leicester 2012; Rogers 1980). A relatively new model, Positive Psychology (Seligman 2011), takes off from Abraham Maslow's model of personal authenticity (Maslow 1954) and advocates pursuing meaningful life by focusing on the expression of positive emotions and creating organizations and institutions that foster that.

The essence of understanding the deeper emotions of others was definitely pioneered by Carl Rogers, who wrote so artfully about the necessary components of empathy:

- *Improvising* and *openness to experience*: the client is "free to choose any direction" (Rogers 1986, p. 197).
- Allowing openness to the other's way of thinking can lead to a sense of togetherness and trust: *empathic understanding* is a reliable guide on this path (Rogers 1980).

- Mutual *respect*, leading to something new: “a tendency to grow, to develop, to realize its full potential” (Rogers 1986, p. 197).
- Playing along a cohesive theme: “being sensitive, moment to moment, to the changing felt meanings which flow in this other person” (Rogers 1980, p. 142).

So, how can the Person-Centered Approach, so important to transforming communication in all walks of life, be better understood in terms of the neuroscience of our brains?

15.2 A Simple Model for the Anatomy of the Brain

When complexity challenges the limit of understanding, models come in handy to highlight certain perspectives. In this sense the Resource Box 15.1 summarizes the very essence of our brain’s anatomy to provide the underlying brain topology for the subsequent discussion.

Resource Box 15.1: A Simple model of the anatomy of the brain

To easily understand a simple model for the anatomy of brain, imagine putting your hand into a boxing glove. Now imagine the following:

The wrist = **cerebellum** (which primary function includes such reflexive behaviors as catching a ball thrown to you, walking gait) + brain stem (heartbeat, breathing)

Hand & fingers = emotional **limbic system**

Glove = **cerebral cortex** (perceiving, thinking, motor behavior)

Front of glove = **neocortex** (reasoning, planning, consciousness)

Inside lining of top of glove = **medial prefrontal cortex** (MFPC), containing the anterior cingulate cortex and orbitofrontal cortex (both important in decision-making) and **insular cortex** and subcortical striatum (self-relevant information)

On both sides of glove are the **amygdalae**, considered the sentry of threat, leading to the fight-or-flight response.

You may have heard of the term, “amygdala hijack” (Goleman 1999, p. 87), when a perceived threat is routed as information directly from limbic system to the central nervous system, bypassing the frontal cortex where awareness takes place, resulting in escape behavior, hijacking the route through the thinking cortex. In this case, a person might act out against another without even having the opportunity to think about it. The ordinary route of perceptual information from the senses to the thalamus to the frontal cortex is “hijacked” and the perceptual information goes directly to the motor centers and the individual acts out without any forethought.

Sometimes the perceived threat can be quite subtle. Imagine an ordinary day at work. You are doing your job, but somehow you end up feeling that your work is not appreciated or you feel ignored, or someone gets credit for work you've done. Such incidents can lead to mild or not-so-mild experiences of subtle amygdala hijack. You may not lash out immediately, but you just may feel like leaving your job or telling someone off for their rude behavior, or harbor thoughts of quitting.

Here is a list of what can put us into a state of wanting to fight or get out of Dodge (or wherever your office happens to be):

Condescension or lack of respect
A sense of being treated unfairly
Lack of appreciation
Not being listened to
Unrealistic deadlines
Your computer refusing to work properly when you really need it.

There are two ways of reacting to such perceived "threat": Allowing amygdala hijack to take place and reacting emotionally inappropriately, or allowing the thinking brain to process what is happening and place it in a more objective, less personalized, context. Using the thinking brain allows for a choice of two possibilities once again. The first is to get an emotional sense of the situation, using your gut feeling and inner sense of awareness. The second is to think through the situation and analyze the process with your intellect. Some say the first of these choices (emotional awareness) occurs in the limbic system and right brain, while the second (logical thinking) occurs in the left brain with a focus on the prefrontal cortex.

According to Daniel Kahneman, in his book, *Thinking, Fast and Slow* (2011), these two options are called:

- **System 1** (intuitive)—Quick: automatic and emotional (like Gladwell's (2007) concept of Blink)—through right brain interacting with limbic system
- **System 2** (rational)—Logical: slower, thinking, conscious deciding function—through left brain interacting with prefrontal cortex.

According to Kahneman, "System 1 operates automatically and quickly, with little or no effort and no sense of voluntary control. System 2 allocates attention to the effortful mental activities that demand it, including complex computations. The operations of System 2 are often associated with the subjective experience of agency, choice, and concentration … The automatic operations of System 1 generate surprisingly complex patterns of ideas, but only the slower System 2 can construct thoughts in an orderly series of steps" (pp. 20–21).

As we go into a bit more detail in the neuroscience of how the brain works, we go beneath the outer layer of the cerebral cortex down to a lower layer, where we find the insular cortex, the neural "home" of organismic valuing process (System 1), or making the final decision after taking all input together, both from the senses and from a combination of gut feeling and rational analysis (System 2). The insular cortex makes the best decision possible by taking (1) incoming perceptual data from eyes, ears, etc., (2) emotional awareness from the limbic system, and (3) intellectual problem-solving information from thinking frontal cortex. All this influx of information can create a sense of "right" decision—especially when aided by a sense of mindfulness to help interpret the data by combining the benefits of both Systems 1 and 2.

The neural pathways then travel from the insular cortex both to amygdala and motor areas, as well as the frontal cortex to execute the final decision. So what is happening is that both of Kahneman's System 1 and System 2 are now being integrated in the insular cortex to allow for the "right" decision, taking all available data into consideration from both systems.

As Kahneman puts it, "System 1 continuously generates suggestions for System 2: impressions, intuitions, intentions, and feelings. If endorsed by System 2, impressions and intuitions turn into beliefs, and impulses turn into voluntary actions" (p. 24).

At the moment of decision, we use the full benefit of awareness of emotional cues (System 1) as processed information travels from the insular cortex to the frontal cortex which integrates emotional sensations with the benefit of mindfulness. The thinking cortex takes over now, remembering past mistakes and the lessons of experience (System 2). *Mindfulness*, or mindful awareness, can be seen as the bridge that connects the emotional limbic system with the thinking neocortex to come up with "right" decisions.

An earlier phrase used by Rogers to describe mindful awareness was "to experience more fully in awareness," meaning to symbolize sensory or visceral impulses "in some accurate form at the conscious level" (Rogers 1959, p. 197), leading to an increased congruence (match) between the self-structure ("new brain") and experience ("old brain"). Note that in the first part of this book *congruence* was one of the preconditions of following the people-oriented agenda and its crucial role in leadership was expressed in several case-studies on transformative communication in leadership.

15.3 The Neuroscience of Transformational Empathy

In order to understand how someone feels, it is necessary to identify their emotions. Yet emotions are known to be extremely complex and diverse. However, science reduces such complexity to relatively few basic emotions. For example, Ekman (2009), known for his work on classification of emotions over many years, breaks them down into 6 basic emotions: happiness, sadness, anger, fear, disgust, and surprise.

For most of our needs, we can discard disgust and surprise, and even happiness, as this last emotion is hardly a problem, and we are left with 3 basic emotions to deal with: sadness, anger, and fear, all formed in the limbic system, and subsequently recognized and identified as such in the thinking frontal cortex.

Another scientist with a reputation for laboratory research on emotions, Jaak Panksepp, in his book, *The Archaeology of Mind* (2012), categorizes 7 what he calls semi-independent emotional command circuits, or neural "packages," operating independent of the thinking brain: four are positive—SEEKING, CARE, PLAY, and LUST, and three are negative—RAGE, FEAR, and GRIEF (very similar to Ekman's anger, fear and sadness, respectively).

So how do we best use this scientific information to better understand our associates? Well, according to another expert on emotions, Antonio Damasio (*The Feeling of What Happens*, 1999; *Self Comes to Mind*, 2012), we must first be able to sense our own emotions as we go through the vagaries of life's challenges. In other words, how can we be a better leader by connecting more effectively with our feelings and consequently also those of our associates? How can we get into the implicit aspect and communicate more deeply so that the rapport achieved can lead to more trust, loyalty, and devotion to the bottom line on the part of the associates with whom we can connect in this manner? By making a commitment to this process:

(a) We identify the other's emotion and choose some past memory to evoke a similar reaction in ourselves.
(b) We allow this evoked emotion ("acquired dispositional representation" Goleman (1999, p. 136) calls it) to deepen, in both our emotional and intellectual awareness.
(c) We allow our frontal cortex and limbic system to work in concert to create bodily sensations, affecting our facial and body language. The brain states of both ourselves and the other are now in shared state, what Goleman (1999) calls "limbic tango" (p. 87).

This would be the best precondition for our associate to feel understood, appreciated, and valued. This is most likely to translate into someone who feels more fulfilled and therefore more willing to devote her/his energies to the challenges at hand. In the following, let us illustrate how this may work and feel by two examples, a more detailed one from a strategic meeting and a short one from the virtual word.

Example from experience illustrating the emotional process leading to deeper understanding

Our patience will achieve more than our force.
—Edmund Burke (18th-century author and British statesman)

At the time of this writing, I (David) was consulting with an organization at which the CEO and one of the directors had a difference of opinion regarding the degree of independence that this director insisted on in the carrying out of her duties. When I talked with each one separately, I heard how each had no idea of how the other was really thinking, let alone feeling. Interestingly, each used the work "pathological" to describe the other's behavior when meeting with me, neither knowing of that dire judgment on the other's part. Laura, the director, quit, yet all the other leaders in the organization believed that she was really fired. They realized that the director's choice to stand up to her

CEO and not back down forced her to "quit," even though the CEO made a point of insisting in the morning meeting that she had indeed quit of her own volition. In fact, all the leaders in the organization respected Laura and believed she was doing an excellent job. This was clearly a personality clash between two strong-willed individuals. Neither was willing to understand the other in any emotional sense and just acted and communicated with their defenses at full tilt.

I already had met with the director and understood her perspective. In her mind, the CEO was intruding on her territory with an agenda that was contrary to hers. Even though he had delegated the necessary responsibilities to her, he was now encroaching on her territory and forcing her to yield to his ways or "quit." She would not back down, so she was forced to "quit."

It was now up to me to straighten out this conflict which would have put the organization in grave peril, without the excellent management skills of this top director, whom everyone loved. I spent over two hours talking with Don, the CEO. I avoided starting with the conflict between him and the director because I knew all I would get would be his defensive posture. So I started off limiting our conversation to differences in values, primarily the values of the Person-Centered Approach versus his ideal of task-oriented priorities. He was one of the strongest proponents of task focus, and seeing relationship focus not only as a waste of time for him, but also as injurious to the bottom line. So we debated these philosophies for over an hour. I was doing my best to understand where he was coming from, where he acquired such values and why they were so important to him.

I first of all attempted to identify his emotional landscape. There was anger—or RAGE in Panskepp's structure. There was also some concern about making the wrong decision—or FEAR. And a bit of sadness about having this conflict rise to the point of losing a valued associate—or GRIEF. So, as I talked with Don, I reflected on my own experiences of being angry when someone attacked my values and what I stood for; of concern about making a wrong decision, especially in light of some conflict with another; and of the sadness that inevitably comes when people disagree strongly. I allowed these emotions to deepen within me at different points as he explained his situation, and to express them as they flowed through my body, my face, and my voice, but putting them all in the context of the CEO's narrative. "So what you're feeling," I would say, "is that you …" and then finish each statement with my own emotional "dispositional representations," based on my own memories of my past, but in his framework. My emotional expressions "clicked" with those of Don and we entered into that state which Goleman refers to as the "limbic tango," where our emotional brains were in sync with one another. Don opened up about his history and the development of his task-oriented values.

Over time, I began to understand the CEO and the basis of his stance. He had built an excellent organization with splendid results in a very competitive environment. I now fully appreciated his perspective. Had he "converted" me? Yes, in the sense of fully understanding his perspective, but not in the sense of losing my own perspective that the two of them could and should continue to work together despite their differences.
By fully engaging his perspective, I won his trust. By winning his trust, I earned his ear. Now, he was listening with less defensiveness.
Finally, I brought up the conflict between the two of them. I did not take either side, but rather the side of the organization itself. I did not defend the director against the CEO but rather put myself in a position to help Don make the best decision for the organization. I made it clear I was not defending the director, preferring her people-oriented approach against his task-oriented approach, but rather inviting him to look at the big picture and put personal differences aside. He is not the type to take advice from others. However, slowly but surely, he was listening to another perspective—mine—and slow as he was to do so, his openness was increasing. I could feel it in my gut, even though there was no decision forthcoming at the moment.
A few times, as he reflected on our discussion, he uncharacteristically seemed to ask for help. "What should I do?" I heard him ask. This was very unusual for him to be indecisive. He always had a clear, decisive answer, no matter what the issue. But now he was reflecting in a way that was uncharacteristic of him. Somehow, in my Person-Centered Approach to the issue, understanding his perspective, getting him to see Laura as helpful to his organization rather than as an "enemy" to his values. But there was still no decision, so I invited him to another discussion the following day, as we both had time for that in our otherwise busy schedules, and the crisis had to be resolved one way or another.
The next day, more of the same: What would be best for the organization? I was able to put our joint perspective on the organization and not on the personal differences that were at the base of the conflict. Even after an hour of discussion, with more and more reflection on Don's part, there was no decision. And that is how we left our discussion on that second day. I had done my best and could do no more than that.
The next afternoon, when I arrived at the organization, I was surprised to hear that Don had taken Laura to lunch and that they had a powwow in which she had laid down her demands and, in some process of negotiation which only the two of them know, things worked out, there was an agreement to allow Laura to run things according to her conditions, and she was reinstated. Don then met privately with each of the other **associates** and engaged them in a discussion that was very different from what they had experienced with him in the past. For the first time, it seemed, Don was actually listening deeply as

well as talking decisively. It was hard for the **associates** to believe. I felt a surge of success.
What had I done? I had listened more than I talked. I had reframed my own memories of my similar experience into Don's perspective. He felt heard in a deep, personal sense. He began to allow his typical defensive posture to relax and to allow himself to reflect on more possibilities that did not exist in his mind previously. He saw the big picture more clearly. My listening closely—using Damasio's model—made him feel more understood, appreciated, and valued, not necessarily as the CEO but, more deeply, as a person. And then he was able to make the "right" decision. That's what it took.

In the next short example let us ask whether a "limbic tango" also be danced if the connection between the "dancers" is only virtual, mediated through written language? Common sense suggests that this would never be the full pleasure of dancing the tango. But since memories can be quite vivid, nothing would speak against a fair approximation. Indeed, recently I (Renate) got an email from David in which I felt completely understood, the match could not be better, and the response meant a perceivable relief from the tension I had felt. Let me share the situation.

Example from experience: Empathic understanding in email exchanges?

Situation: During a preChristmas weekend I (Renate) wanted to work intensively on one of the chapters of this book. However, the distractions and interrupts from colleagues and family were so numerous that I managed just a fragment of what I had wanted to do and send back to David.

Email exchange: In my mail to David, I had mentioned how hard it was "to find some quiet time for thinking and work, aside of all the other activities." David's response included the following:

Dear Renate,
… This is such a busy time of year. Everything piles up toward the end of the year. Good luck in getting everything done you need to get done.
David
(Quote from email correspondence, December, 6th, 2015.)

But if we are to understand and appreciate the feelings of our associates more effectively, it may help to know a bit more about the essence of such emotions. What are the basic, primary emotions and from where in the brain do they originate?

15.4 Primary Emotions—Awareness and Control for More Effective Leadership

Since Freud pioneered the path to analyzing our psyche on conscious and unconscious levels, psychotherapy aimed to help people resolve conflicts between unbridled emotion and our conscious self. According to Rogers, for example, the more overlap between the organismic, emotional self, and the conscious, self-aware self, the more mature and mentally healthy is the individual, and the closer she/he is to a "fully functioning person" or the ideal manager (Rogers 1978). Rogers saw the integrated, *congruent* self, one with a vast overlap between the conscious self and the organismic experience, as the ultimate goal of psychotherapy, personal growth, and leadership development.

But how can we see the inner, emotional world in a more differentiated way? Where do emotions come from? How do they affect us and what does that mean for people in leadership positions?

According to neuroscientist Panksepp and Biven (2012), all emotions come from only "seven basic affective systems: SEEKING (expectancy), FEAR (anxiety), RAGE (anger), LUST (sexual excitement), CARE (nurturance), PANIC/GRIEF (sadness), and PLAY (social joy)" (p. xi). They claim that there are 3 basic levels of emotional experience:

1. The primary process, where these emotions originate in the limbic system (old brain);
2. The secondary process, where emotional learning takes place (in certain components of the limbic system, such as the hippocampus);
3. The tertiary process, where thinking and decision-making takes place, in the prefrontal cortex (new brain). It is in this last tertiary process where the basic emotions become complicated, morphing into the human emotions such as pride, confidence, guilt, and dominance.

15.4.1 Stress, FEAR, and Relief

One of the challenges of leadership is dealing with the stress that comes with overarching responsibility. We understand that, at the top levels of leadership, decisions most often must be made in the absence of all the necessary information. Finding the right solution is easy when you have all the information. But that is not what real life brings to the table. So it is not surprising that leadership is often accompanied by a certain amount of stress. In Panskepp's system, the primary emotion of stress is the FEAR system, associated with the most common hormone of stress, cortisol. In animals, when the source of stress is removed, then the hypothalamus secretes a hormone that stops the secretion of cortisol and the animal relaxes. However, when the stress continues unabated, then the cortisol may continue to flow and this has a detrimental effect on the brain, mainly affecting memory and the ability to concentrate on abstract aspects of a challenge, sometimes leading to depression. In other words, our ability to think clearly about possible solutions becomes somewhat impaired. This negative process can be, according to the scientists, helped by being able to get relief from the challenges at hand and actually enjoy life enough to laugh and play.

15.4.2 Confidence and PLAY

Now, as we talk about the brain and its functions, some might ask, But what about the mind. Isn't that what really matters? And what about the character of leadership? How does that fit into neuroscience? Well, according to the scientists, one component of leadership is dominance, the ability to lead with confidence and charisma. They say that this has to do with the primary emotion of what Panksepp calls PLAY. PLAY allows for the learning of rules of social conduct, when to cooperate and when to compete, and how to let the other win without feeling the pain of defeat. (Recall how David encouraged the CEO to let his director "win" despite their differences.) Indeed, animals seem to have an innate sense of when to yield to the other's sense of failure by backing down at such times. Otherwise, the defeated animals will stop playing (when they lose about 70 % of the time).

15.4.3 Reciprocity and CARE

So, in order to keep playing, the winner learns to pull back and let the other "win" a little bit. According to Panksepp and Biven, they learn "the necessity of reciprocity and giving way on occasion" (p. xix). And, when it comes to effective leadership, it is clearly important to earn trust and respect of those being managed. "This implicit social contract," according to the scientists, "is built on the mutuality of the CARE system. They must give each other what *they* need to feel secure and to excel. Managers also know the importance of team cohesion." And this is done by "fostering a spirit of PLAY, whereby members of a large working group share the opportunity to interact in more intimate and relaxed environments. This kind of playful interaction cements social bonds that are important for the solidarity of the workforce" (p. xx). Careful readers will immediately realize that what is at stake in this process reflects Rogers' principle of the "reciprocity of unconditional positive regard" (Rogers 1959).

15.4.4 Trust and the Interplay of Emotions

The main dynamic between effective leaders and their associates is the level of trust. And it is fascinating that this one crucial dynamic is a result of the different primary emotions in the primary process of our brain: SEEKING to find out more about our work setting; FEAR when we must make decisions without having sufficient information to guarantee our success; RAGE when things do not work out as we hoped and expected; CARE about our fellow workers and the overall success they achieve; and PLAY, so we know about the give and take of reciprocity, so necessary in teamwork.

15.4.5 Do Leaders Need to Control Their Feelings?

Yes, they do. One of the keystone skills of effective leadership is to manage feelings rather than let them take over. Feelings or emotions are complex, hard to define at the moment, containing more information than we could possibly analyze in the moment. The way to master this is to become keenly aware of intentions and to know clearly the results that are aimed at.

As mentioned above, emotions begin in the primary process of the brain, specifically the 7 primary emotions. According to Wilson (2015), "We have paleolithic emotions," and these originate in the subcortical, deeper components of the brain. We learn to associate certain feelings to what we perceive in the secondary process, e.g., FEAR via the amygdala, SEEKING through the nucleus accumbens in the deepest part of the brain. The tertiary process takes place in the neocortex where we become aware of our actions through analysis and planning.

Example from experience: Attending to feelings while facilitating the interaction among executives

Anybody can become angry, that is easy, but to be angry with the right person, and to the right degree, and at the right time, and for the right purpose, and in the right way, that is not within everybody's power, that is not easy.

—Aristotle (320 B.C.)

One morning, while on a consulting trip for a large Federal organization, I (David) awoke with a disturbed feeling in my chest. It was one of those first-on-arising feelings that had no particular context to it. I rubbed my eyes and gathered whatever thoughts I could. I was in a hotel room, but in what city? What was I doing there?

Within a minute, I realized I was in Washington, DC, on a consulting trip with a Federal government agency. So how could I account for my uneasiness as I awoke? I had just delivered a highly successful talk. All the feedback was excellent. So, what was the problem?

As I thought over the past day, I recalled that I was asked to run a meeting that day, a meeting in which a conflict among a number of leaders was to be confronted and hopefully resolved. As the resident expert on transformative communication and leadership, I was the one being marked to come up with the solution to all this conflict. No wonder my heart was beating faster than normal. No wonder I felt an uneasy tension in my chest. Although some may have considered me the expert, I was also human.

Obviously, I was feeling anxious about having to confront the conflict among these strong personalities. I was experiencing FEAR, and this "paleolithic emotion" (Wilson 2015) was of a "primary process nature," according to Panksepp and Biven (2012), coming from "specific functional networks of evolutionarily very ancient regions of our brains" (p. xi). No wonder I felt it so keenly, even before my conscious brain could make sense of where I was. Once I could gather my thoughts—in "the tertiary process (emotional thoughts and deliberations that are so evident in human experience)" (p. xi) in the prefrontal cortex, according to the scientists, then I could begin to analyze the situation and plan an approach that would help me put my best foot forward. In other words, I was ready to take the primitive emotion of FEAR and use my noggin (technical term for prefrontal cortex) to come up with a plan worthy of my reputation as the guru of transformative communication.

So, what to do? I thought of what I could do to resolve the sense of FEAR that I was feeling and that other key members of the leadership team might be feeling as well. What could I do to control this process and bring about a more productive feeling? And what feeling might that be? Certainly, one of the positive ones, with at least a component of CARE. But, more to the point, what would help convert FEAR to something more positive?

Recalling Panksepp's research on PLAY, in which his subjects allowed their mates to win at times, even if they were the weaker of the pair, I chose this emotion. A sense of one's own power is important to self-esteem in the workplace, but there is also the crucial importance of feeling part of the team. "Managers also know the importance of team cohesion," write Panksepp and Bevin, "by fostering a spirit of PLAY, whereby members of a large working group share the opportunity to interact in more intimate and relaxed environments. This kind of playful interaction cements social bonds that are important for the solidarity of the workforce" (p. xx).

The main focus of the conflict among this group of executives was Kevin. He was one of those self-assured "my-way-or-the-highway" types, with little room for negotiation. I was not eager to confront this imposing character in front of a group of his peers who could not find the resources to control him without my help. So I decided on a combination of CARE and PLAY, beginning with an honest sharing of my genuine, authentic emotions.

"If I tried to convince you that I wasn't at least a bit apprehensive about today's meeting, I'd be lying to you," I began. "So can we put our swords back in their scabbards? And maybe put more energy into listening to one another?"

My voice was assuring and confident, as I felt comfortable sharing how I really felt as opposed to pretending otherwise. I then followed this up with some self-deprecating humor to dive into a sense of PLAY, followed by my concern for the success of the agency, and the success of each of the players at the table to bring them into the mode of CARE. This soon led to a new respect for one another's concerns and even Kevin could not resist this tide of positive attitudes toward success of the agency. After hearing others' genuine sense of concern for the issues surrounding the conflict, Kevin's demeanor changed dramatically. He allowed himself to become part of the team, rather than its challenger.

Possibly, in his mind (tertiary process), he was shifting from his anger at certain individuals with whom he disagreed (RAGE) and moving closer to a feeling of group endeavor once he felt the genuine concerns of others (CARE) and invited to allow them to "win" despite the differences (PLAY). The executives, including Kevin, were now seeing success of the agency as a common endeavor. As the discussion evolved, the participants could better understand one another, including Kevin. CARE, according to Panksepp and Biven, "surely figures heavily in the emergence of empathy," and PLAY involves the movement "to learn through eager friendly competition (with repeated, adequately balanced give-and-take—winning and losing, in a manner of speaking) … resulting in a sense of secure belonging within the social order" (p. 438).

So, that morning, we all moved from Kevin's RAGE and some of the others' FEAR, emerging from the primary level, to a sense of CARE and PLAY as I facilitated the interaction among the executives. This new, positive sense traveled from the deeper parts of the unconscious brain to the prefrontal cortex as plans began to emerge to follow up with the sense of camaraderie that was beginning to unfold with a new set of strategies.

That is what happens in the brains of high-powered executives when thoughtful analysis and planning along with experience and personal sensitivity can overcome the "Paleolithic" emotions that can block individuals from working together in harmony.

15.4.6 Effect of Emotions on Decision-Making

Here is a clear overview of how emotions affect the decision-making of a leader. At the hormonal level, adrenaline and serotonin are responsible for the arousal level, making the leader alert and aware. The 7 primary emotions originate in the primary system, called "affective circuits" by Panksepp, in the deepest levels of the brain. At the secondary level, where the amygdala and other basal ganglia reside, these primary emotions are converted to the more complex good feelings, such as empathy and trust, or the complex "bad" feelings, such as blame, shame, and guilt. At the neo-cortex, the tertiary process, the leader can finally identify those feelings, and choose to control the negative ones by naming them and containing them, possibly with the use of such skills as mindfulness. Each of the primary emotions has its own place in the leader's repertoire.

I. SEEKING encourages exploratory inquisitiveness, where the leader approaches and engages those around him. Here is where a sense of purpose has a chance to develop. SEEKING also encourages finding the best solutions regarding risk-taking. A strong SEEKING emotion helps to overcome caution and trepidation, due to the more cautious emotion of FEAR.

II. RAGE, when it is controlled so that it is not expressed in its full intensity, can act as a motivator to compete effectively and with great enthusiasm against competitors or to confront associates who need guidance in a form that is vividly expressed. One ongoing question is whether good leaders should allow themselves to express anger. Our answer is that they should, as long as they do so in a controlled and intentional manner, knowing fully the consequences of such communication. Anger, expressed in such a controlled and intentional manner, on special occasions, can have a positive outcome, especially if it has the sense of authenticity, conveying the leader's deeper values with intensity. There is something about such vivid communication that stays in memory, because of the emotion it generates in the audience—of one or many. Again, let us emphasize, that when RAGE is expressed without control or intent, it can be seen as very negative, as a loss of control by the leader, and that is never a desirable outcome.

III. FEAR, by its very nature, is not the most comfortable emotion. It naturally can lead to stress and to an interruption of normal concentration and successful decision-making. Its hidden benefit involves triggering the motivation for more SEEKING to find suitable alternatives to the conditions leading to FEAR.

IV. LUST is the one emotion that needs total control, lest it lead to indiscretions that result in public shame. How often we hear of affairs where a married leader allows himself to be seduced into an illicit relationship that eventually becomes public! In the past few years, we can easily recall politicians, military leaders, and other celebrity types "caught in the act." LUST is a powerful motive and needs constant surveillance in order to contain it. Leadership itself appears to be highly attractive to the opposite sex and so opportunities for seduction abound. As Henry Kissinger is purported to say, "Power is the ultimate aphrodisiac."

V. CARE is one of the more interesting motivations arising from the primary affective circuits. It is part of empathy, leading to trust and loyalty. It is an essential ingredient of effective teamwork. It reverberates with a deep-seated need for group dedication. According to Wilson (2015), there are "deep-rooted instincts for belonging … a primordial group instinct," and CARE is at the center of this deep-seated need to be part of a working team. Wilson adds that this deep need in our systems for a sense of "tribalism" helps us understand why we sometimes put others' needs before our own, what he calls "instinctive self-sacrifice." In the work setting, it makes mentoring a pleasurable task rather than just another activity on the to-do list. It also helps us understand the deep devotion we feel toward effective leaders and how grief-stricken we can become at their untimely demise, e.g., the assassination of President Kennedy.

Now that we are acquainted with the basic emotions, let us trace them in an emotionally intense scenario, like firing an employee who has become a friend, or being fired, as in David's example below.

Example from experience: Basic emotions in breaking up an interpersonal, work-based relationship

Some years ago, I (David) was invited to consult with an international conglomerate by a friend whom I had known for years. We were not the closest of friends but, when we did get together, there was an ease and comfort to our sharing. After I started working at this organization, our friendship flourished, as Jim was able to share with me the inside awareness of the political dynamics that were going on with the individuals with whom I worked. This was very helpful and I looked forward to our lunches whenever our schedules allowed, both to get the latest news on the company politics and, as well, to catch up on personal matters that we could share.

This was a wonderful arrangement as it was helpful in a professional sense and it also allowed for a growing friendship. But all good things must come to an end and at one point, when there was a low ebb in the financial situation for this company, there was a decision at a higher level, to terminate my services. It was friend Jim's duty to inform me of this.

It is not hard to imagine the awkwardness of the situation. Jim was not happy about this. However, he had no choice but to communicate the bad news to me.

When he was able to sit down with me and share this bad news, there was an obvious discomfort on both our parts. Our shared emotion of CARE for one

another was clear. But there was no choice about the matter. My reaction was to accept what was being shared with me and to appreciate that we had a wonderful situation while it lasted. There was some sadness, of course, but to refer to it as GRIEF does not sound accurate.
What made it easier to deal with was Jim's genuine statement of how unhappy he was about this decision and, of course, I concurred. He was being authentic and genuine, not distancing himself from the inevitable discomfort of the situation. This meant a lot to me and we decided to continue our friendship by committing to meet for lunch at least once every few months, despite our busy schedules. We were able to look forward to some degree of what Panksepp refers to as PLAY and SEEKING as we would dig into the mysteries of dealing with the challenges of life, enjoying the openness we had built over time.
I felt sad about losing my affiliation with the organization, as I had invested my emotions in my work there, as I typically do. I felt sad, as well, about losing the ongoing connection with my friend. But, making the best of the situation, my friend and I could now look forward to continuing the personal aspect of our relationship. And this also opened a time slot for a new connection I would make with another organization, so I was ready to enter the enjoyable mode of SEEKING a new affiliation which would surely come along fairly soon. "When one door closes, another opens," goes the saying. So the sadness of losing one client gave way to the anticipation of acquiring a different client with new challenges and new relationships. It all worked well in large part to my friend's choice to be genuine and authentic in how he delivered the "bad" news to me.

Invitation to reflect:

In the example above, David, in his reflection, named the emotions he had experienced. Have you ever tried to label your emotions while reflecting on some emotionally challenging experience? Do you find it helpful to be aware of your emotions?
Do you think that being aware of your inner world can help you to act more in accordance with your values? Does it reveal valuable information to you that aids you in making decisions?

15.5 Confidence in Leadership—The Oxytocin Factor

An effective leader is usually seen as confident. One hormone that leads to confidence is what we usually characterize as the love hormone—oxytocin. But this neurochemical has proven to be associated with confidence as well. In addition, it is associated with increased levels of trust (Meyer-Lindenberg 2008). As well, it affects the sense of victory or defeat in competition, increasing gloating in victors and a stronger sense of envy in losers (Shamay-Tsoory et al. 2009). Similarly, it enhances cooperation among teammates but ironically fosters defensive attitudes toward those not in the group (De Dreu et al. 2010).

So this is not a simple process. It appears that oxytocin may make individuals more cooperative and easier to get along with, but also more confident in competing with others. This would account for such paradoxical effects mentioned in the above paragraph. In one study (Riters and Panksepp 1997), this paradox was explained by pointing out that oxytocin may make you feel peaceful, yet also confident. Another paradox of oxytocin is that, although it enhances cooperative behavior, it can also encourage independent behavior apart from the group. How come? Because, according to Panksepp and Biven (2012), the increased confidence allows for more independent activity, possibly with less social anxiety (Guastella et al. 2009).

Oxytocin apparently does increase confidence. Afraid of public speaking? Then oxytocin can help. "If oxytocin increases confidence," say Panksepp and Biven, "then performance anxiety should decrease" (p. 42). It even allows us to become more empathic in the sense that we would have less fear of more intimate eye contact for better communication. "For instance," continue the scientists, "oxytocin should increase our tendency to explore the eyes of another person, to try to read their mind, because you are feeling more secure. And in fact, it does that" (p. 42). They go on to say that "oxytocin in the brain has now been shown to mediate trusting behaviors in economic decision-making and perhaps the capacity to read other minds more sensitively" (p. 466).

So a leader's ability to come across with confidence (Panksepp 2009) and to be able to communicate in a way that reflects the PCA or emotional intelligence is enhanced by the hormone oxytocin. Ironically, oxytocin comes from feeling nurtured by others, so this is a two-way street that helps enhance successful leadership. Thus, besides congruence, integrity, and confidence, Rogers' concept of unconditional positive regard for others as a general social principle is an excellent basis for successful leadership.

Trust is a basic component of effective leadership. "Without that trust," write Panksepp and Biven (2012), "the endogenous opioid mediated feeling of social support cannot take hold … Without genuine empathy … there will always be a residue of suspicion, a feeling of being manipulated, as opposed to the deep acceptance that opens the portals for positive change" (p. 463).

15.6 Conclusion

One of the key elements of the Person-Centered Approach is to create a sense of safety, or, as Panksepp and Biven (2012) put it, an "island of safety" (p. 473). Rogers had this incalculably important ability to make people feel safe enough to open up with their self-doubts and personal vulnerability (for a personal example, see Ryback 1998, pp. 29–30). Having done so, they were much more receptive to learning how to integrate these self-doubting feelings into their total personality, making them more transparent and consequently authentic, and hopefully transformative leaders.

We have come a long way in our understanding of emotions since Darwin's (1872) seminal research on emotions in animals and humans. In this chapter, we have attempted to understand from where transformative communication originates and how it is expressed in the brain. We have looked at psychological theories and the structures of the brain leading to basic emotions and transformational empathy.

In summary, we have seen that the effective leader's brain works in two directions: healthy pathways of affect from the depths and, in counterbalance, solid experience from years of learning from experience, stored in the hippocampus and frontal cortex. As Panksepp and Biven (2012) put it, "higher brain functions may 'listen' to the lower ones and add additional cognition-parsed affective coloring to experience" leading to "a fundamental sense of *owning* their affective experiences" (p. 400). This resonates strongly with the self-management aspects of emotional intelligence and with Rogers' (1980) concepts of authenticity and personal integrity. The successful executive can have the best of lower brain and higher brain functions at his/her disposal. It is not just cognitive versus emotional functions, but rather a dynamic interplay between the two, at least for the most effective leaders, or, to put it another way, "a coherence of self and consciousness" (p. 410).

As well, the effective leader has the responsibility of engendering a basis of trust throughout the organization, beginning at the top and filtering down through the various levels. This begins at the top with authenticity, genuineness and a sense of openness to others. People need to feel part of the group, accepted and, above all, understood and appreciated. "This view was advanced by Carl Rogers," write Panksepp and Biven, "through his concept of unconditional positive regard" (p. 463).

At the end of the day, it appears that the brain acts as a complex organ, integrating all its components into the decision-making and action-oriented outcomes that we hope are correct and appropriate for any set of given circumstances. Although there are convergence points for conscious decision-making, there is no single center or structure that does it alone (Sukhotinsky et al. 2007). Yet neuroscientists are able to map certain areas that are more important than others for such activities (Mobbs et al. 2009). "Living brains, along with their minds—the invisible manifestation of their network-level neurobiological functions," write Panksepp and Biven (2012), "reflect a delicate balance … among vastly interacting neural circuits that work in and for living bodies and that respond to the challenges of the world by creating desired circumstances and avoiding those that are harmful" (p. 500).

Knowing how the brain responds to the challenge of leadership, and how that leads to desirable outcomes is what the neuroscience of leadership is all about.

References

Damasio, A. R. (1999). *The feeling of what happens*. NY: Harcourt Brace.

Damasio, A. R. (2012). *Self comes to mind*. NY: Vintage.

Darwin, C. (1872). *The expression of the emotions in man and animals*. London, UK: John Murray.

De Dreu, C. K., Greer, L. L., Handgraaf, M. J., Shalvi, S., Van Kleef, G. A., Baas, M., et al. (2010). The neuropeptide oxytocin regulates parochial altruism in intergroup conflict among humans. *Science, 328*, 1408–1411.

Ekman, P. (2009). *Telling lies*. NY: W.W. Norton.

Gladwell, M. (2007). *Blink*. NY: Black Bay Books.

Goleman, D. (1999). *Working with emotional intelligence*. NY: Bantam Books.

Guastella, A. J., Howard, A. L., Dadds, M. R., Mitchell, P., & Carson, D. S. (2009). A randomized controlled trial of intranasal oxytocin as an adjunct to exposure therapy for social anxiety disorder. *Psychoneuroendocrinology, 34*, 917–923.

Kahneman, D. (2011). *Thinking, fast and slow*. New York: Farrar, Strauss & Giroux.

Meyer-Lindenberg, A. (2008). Impact of prosocial neuropeptides on human brain function. *Progress in Brain Research, 170*, 463–470.

Maslow, A. (1954). *Motivation and personality* (p. 236). New York, NY: Harper.

Mobbs, D., Marchant, J. L., Hassabis, D., Seymour, B., Tan, G., Gray, M., et al. (2009). From threat to fear: The neural organization of defense fear systems in humans. *Journal of Neuroscience, 29*, 12236–12243.

O'Hara, M., & Leicester, G. (2012). *Dancing at the edge competence, culture and organization in the 21st century*. Devon, UK: Triarchy Press.

Panksepp, J. (2009). Primary process affects and brain oxytocin. *Biological Psychiatry, 65*, 725–727.

Panksepp, J., & Biven, L. (2012). *The archaeology of mind*. NY: W.W. Norton.

Riters, L. V., & Panksepp, J. (1997). Effects of vasotocin on aggressive behavior in male Japanese quail. *Annals of the New York Academy of Sciences, 807*, 478–480.

Rogers, C. R. (1959). A theory of therapy, personality, and interpersonal relationships, as developed in the client-centered framework. In S. Koch (Ed.), *Psychology: A study of a science* (Vol. 3). New York, Toronto, London: McGraw-Hill Inc.

Rogers, C. R. (1961). *On becoming a person—A psychotherapists view of psychotherapy*. London, UK: Constable.

Rogers, C. R. (1978). *On personal power*. London, UK: Constable.

Rogers, C. R. (1980). *A way of being*. Boston: Houghton Mifflin Co.

Rogers, C. R. (1986). A client-centered/person-centered approach to therapy. In I. Kutash & A. Wolfe (Eds.), *Psychotherapists' casebook* (pp. 197–208). San Francisco: Jossey-Bass.

Ryback, D. (1998). *Putting emotional intelligence to work*. Boston: Butterworth-Heinemann.

Seligman, M. E. P. (2011). *Flourish: A visionary new understanding of happiness and well-being*. New York: Free Press.

Shamay-Tsoory, S. G., Fischer, M., Dvash, J., Harari, H., Perach-Bloom, N., & Levkovitz, Y. (2009). Intranasal administration of oxytocin increases envy and schadenfreude (gloating). *Biological Psychiatry, 66*, 864–870.

Sukhotinsky, I., Zalkind, V., Lu, J., Hopkins, D. A., Saper, C. B., & Devor, M. (2007). Neural pathways associated with loss of consciousness caused by intracerebral microinjection of $GABA_A$-active anesthetics. *European Journal of Neuroscience, 25*, 1417–1436.
Wilson, E. O. (2015). *Of Ants and Men*. Sept: PBS broadcast 30.

Chapter 16
Tasks and People: What Neuroscience Reveals About Managing Both Effectively

When we are able to free the individual from defensiveness, so that he is open to the wide range of his own needs, as well as the wide range of environmental and social demands, his reactions may be trusted to be positive, forward-moving, constructive.

Carl Rogers (1961, p. 194)

This chapter focuses on:

- The neuroscientific foundations of the task- and people-oriented leadership styles and implications for effectively accommodating both styles.
- Two brain modalities or neural networks, termed the TPN (Task-Positive Network), and the DMN (Default-Mode Network).
- Characterizing the two brain networks by their primary functions and antagonistic relationship to each other.
- Implications for people with leadership responsibilities, and hints on how to improve using both networks effectively.
- The two-agenda approach as a practical means of calling each of the two networks to action such that task-accomplishment is integrated with people's needs and actualization demands.

16.1 Introduction

A central theme in this book is the two-agenda approach, referring to the task-oriented problem-solving process connected with the more relationship-aware, people-oriented process. This allows for richer communication and a climate in which people feel respected and can work together much more effectively. The chapter's objective is to uncover what neuroscientists have discovered about the neural support when we focus on accomplishing specific tasks on the one hand and when being more socially engaged or letting our mind wander on the other hand.

R. Motschnig and D. Ryback, *Transforming Communication in Leadership and Teamwork*, DOI 10.1007/978-3-319-45486-3_16

How can these two distinct modes be combined such that both "agendas" are accomplished effectively?

Intriguingly, neuroscientists have discovered that there are two brain modalities or networks, describing a surprising pattern of brain function involving the more focused, task-oriented thinking, and a resting "default-mode" pattern that hypothetically leads to a more people-oriented and relationship-centered mode of engagement. They are referred to as the task-positive network (TPN) and the default-mode network (DMN). These two appear to validate our own conception of the two agendas at work that are assumed to take turns in which one figures in the foreground while the other rests in the background, much like the dynamic between the TPN and DMN. The exciting news from the neurosciences is that the two neural networks are antagonistic, competing for activation. So can we employ both in order to be able to manage the two agendas and, if so, how? This chapter explores the "playground" of this ongoing competitive "game" and reveals promising paths that allow us to follow both agendas as effectively as possible.

16.2 This Is Your Brain at Rest—The Default-Mode Network

Thinking about practical issues and feelings of social-emotional issues compete for the activation of neural pathways. In the highly active resting state of the aware mind, one can reflect on oneself, undisturbed by external stimuli (for the most part).

This resting state or default-mode network (DMN–for further facts, please see the Resource Box TP), as some refer to it (Damoiseaux et al. 2006; Fox and Raichle 2007), is how we maintain our self-awareness as a consistent entity over time, despite the variety of experiences in our ongoing life stream. You are one and the same person despite the variety of emotions you experience, not to mention concepts you think of, over time. This constancy of self is due to the ongoing self-reflection in the face of all this change, both within and from without. Or, to modify Descartes' "I think, therefore I am," we might say, "I think *and* feel, therefore I am." This self-related focus, no doubt a component of the neuroscientifically described personality, may be a chief component of successful leadership. It allows for decisions based on the principles that an individual adheres to over time. What looks to the outside world like authenticity and integrity is basically an offshoot of constancy of self and the unchanging values that go with that.

The default-mode network is active when there is no apparent goal-oriented work for the brain to perform (Horn et al. 2013; Raichle 2015), except for daydreaming, lazily thinking of the past or the future, or thinking about others' perspectives (at least some component of empathy) (Buckner et al. 2008). It can be characterized as stream of consciousness, or processing recent experience to consolidate it by making sense of it all. Personal and social consolidation is the result, unless hindering circumstances stand in the way.

It was mentioned earlier that oxytocin can increase a sense of confidence (Riters and Panksepp 1997). It turns out that oxytocin also up-regulates the DMN (Bethlehem et al. 2013), implying that oxytocin encourages relationship-oriented leadership. Since oxytocin is naturally generated through nurturing relationships, it appears that there is an organic dynamic in any organization that allows for an upward spiral of DMN relationship orientation when all are authentically supportive of one another in the best of team tradition.

In fact, the upward spiral generated through nurturing relationships was formulated by Carl Rogers as early as 1951. He wrote that

> "the person (or persons or groups) who accepts himself thoroughly, will necessarily improve his relationship with those with whom he has personal contact, because of his greater understanding and acceptance of them.... Thus we have, in effect, a psychological 'chain reaction' which appears to have tremendous potentialities for the handling of problems of social relationships." (Rogers 1951, p. 522)

So what part does the default-mode network (DMN) play in successful leadership roles? Well, as far back as the 1950s, there has been interest in the need for social and emotional skills in leadership (Bales 1958), even dividing leadership skills into two areas: task-oriented and relationship-oriented. Only now, in the past decade or two, have we been able to correlate this with brain function and find scientific evidence for what has been known from practice for a long time: Not allowing time for the DMN with its personal and social functions would reduce leaders/managers to cold dictators with all the ramifications known to be insufficient for the vast majority of cases. But aside from providing an explanation for why leaders need the DMN to be active—while not focusing on tasks—does neuroscience also provide information on how to integrate DMN-facilitated, people-oriented processes while working on tasks? In other words, does it provide possibilities on how to integrate the two agendas at work effectively? Before dealing with this question, let us first examine the second (at work, so often the first) "player" in the competition, the TPN. Its key facts are summarized in Resource Box 16.1.

Resource Box 16.1: Anatomy, hypothesized functions, and relationship between the task-positive neural network (TPN) and the default-mode neural network (DMN).

The Task-Positive Network (TPN)

Anatomy: The neural pathways of the task-positive network (TPN) involve dorsal, parietal, and lateral sections of the prefrontal cortex (Jack et al. 2012).

Function: The TPN is employed for getting things accomplished (Andrews-Hanna 2012), such as problem solving and "mechanical" thinking. The TPN's job is to focus attention and assume control of problem-solving.

Thus, it supports focusing on well-defined tasks that require analytical, critical reasoning and are non-social in nature (Boyatzis et al. 2014).

The **Default-mode Network (DMN)**

Anatomy: The neural pathways of the DMN involve various areas of the cortex such as the medial parietal/posterior cingulate cortex, the medial prefrontal cortex, the lateral inferior parietal cortex, and the superior temporal cortex (Jack et al. 2012). Note that the nodes of the DMN are more dispersed than those of the TPN, with sections occupying a topologically central region of the cortex and being characterized by a high connectivity with long-range connections to other brain regions (Hagmann et al. 2008). This suggests integrating functions.

Function: In the DMN, *two primary circuits* can be distinguished (Boyatzis et al. 2014). The dorsal parts of the midline structures and the right temporo-parietal junction support us in thinking about our own and other's mental states. The more ventral parts of the midline structures support functions such as self-related processing, autobiographical memory, the cognitive representation of emotions, the self-regulation of emotion, and autonomic processing.

Overall, the DMN's function is emotional self-awareness, recognizing social stimuli, ethical decision-making, openness, and creating new ideas (Boyatzis et al. 2014). It is also typically involved in social cognition, a component of empathy (Mars et al. 2012).

Relationship between the TPN and DMN

The two neural networks are *physiologically antagonistic* (temporally anti-correlated) in the resting state and during task-performance (Jack et al. 2012). Activation of one deactivates the other. On tasks that are both analytic and social, however, the networks can cooperate to some degree.

The reciprocal inhibition appears to be purely physiological. According to (Jack et al. 2012) anatomical studies indicate that there are no *direct inhibitory links* between the DMN and the TPN.

Interestingly, a meta-analysis (Beissner et al. 2013) points to a close association of the TPN with the more active sympathetic nervous system and of the DMN with the more restful parasympathetic nervous system. This suggests a pervasive, "*whole-person*" *impact* of each of the neural network's activations.

16.3 The Task-Positive Network Gets the Job Done

The difference between the two leadership-skill styles has become a focal point for a number of studies, characterizing the task-oriented brain process as task-positive network (TPN) for getting things accomplished (Andrews-Hanna 2012), such as problem solving and "mechanical" thinking (see also Resource Box 16.1). The TPN significantly diminishes the activity of the DMN, the brain's more relaxed state. In other words, only one of these two systems can function fully at any one particular time (Jack et al. 2013b). And the DMN has, in part, the function of social cognition, a component of empathy (Mars et al. 2012) so necessary in effective leadership according to the proponents of the PCA and emotional intelligence.

Writing about social cognitive neuroscience in his book, *Social*, Matthew Lieberman (2013) compares two types of leadership based on these two brain networks. The TPN's role is more obvious. Less obvious is the role of the DMN in effective leadership. Some report that the DMN has the function of recognizing the cognitive and emotional states of others (Schilbach et al. 2008), or empathy, as well as reading the nonverbal signals of others (Nasr et al. 2015). Jack et al. (2012) have reported that the reverse correlation between the TPN and DMN "reflects a powerful human tendency to differentiate between conscious persons and inanimate objects in both our attitudes and modes of interaction" (p. 396). In other words, according to Jack et al. (2013a), the TPN is more likely to involve the creation of emotional distance between people, reducing the prospects of empathy and teamwork effectiveness.

So what we have here is a deeper understanding of two work cultures—one in which the focus on accomplishing tasks dominates people such that they are treated as objects with little concern for their emotions or mental states (the TPN taking control most of the time) and one which allows for personal connection based on social awareness and empathy (the DMN taking the lead). Practically, leaders are more likely to engage one or the other of the two leadership styles based on their personalities and the situation at hand (Blake and Mouton 1985; Ryback 1998, pp. 151–163).

Evidently, since the advent of increasing awareness of the PCA and of emotional intelligence, there is a vast literature on the superiority of emotional awareness and support in the workplace. So there is hope that gone are the days of the industrial age when bosses looked at the bottom line with no concern for the line workers. So much of this brunt work has been taken over by automation. Now we have a work force that is more involved in interpersonal management, relying on the importance of customer relations, mentoring, and motivational skills. The prospect of a business world connected electronically with the possibilities of instant communication across the globe make person-to-person awareness paramount. In the twenty-first century, using the TPN alone appears to be quite outmoded (O'Hara and Leicester 2012; Senge 2006).

16.4 Different Strokes (TPN/DMN) for Different Folks (Task-Oriented and People-Oriented)

At one time in the development of leadership theory, there was the prospect of two different styles, the task-oriented and the relationship-oriented leader. As discussed in the first part of this book, the first had to do with focus on production, bottom-line results, and accomplishing tasks with little regard for others' emotions, social contact, team satisfaction, etc. The second type was more concerned about fellow workers, of course, and focused on emotions and the welfare of others. As if it needed proof, by the turn of the century, it became quite clear that the more open, personal style of leadership led to increased job satisfaction and lower turnover (Yukl 2006, 2008).

But what about the prospect of a leader having both sets of skills—task-oriented at some times and relationship-oriented at others? This seems to be a natural consideration. Why limit ourselves to one or the other? This is exactly what Yukl (2008) considered, but found that "efforts to improve one performance determinant may have an adverse effect on another performance determinant … when leaders are preoccupied with responding to external threats (task), there is less time for people-oriented concerns such as being supportive and developing member skills" (pp. 711–714). So perhaps it is not so easy to embrace both styles within the same individual. Or, from another perspective, perhaps different jobs require different types of leaders (Jack et al. 2012), just as different types of students require different types of teachers (Ryback and Sanders 1980). Both the nature of the task as well as the value base of the workers—affecting their expectations—may have important qualities inviting one or the other types of leadership.

But how can a single leader be agile enough to have both skills in her/his repertoire. Just as it is said that one sign of intelligence is the ability to harbor two opposing thoughts at the same time, perhaps the mark of an effective leader is to have the flexibility to switch from the TPN to the DMN and back again as required by the specifics of a situation. Interestingly, Jack et al. (2012) found that most leaders have a disposition to one or the other of the two modes.

Much earlier, Carl Rogers experienced and described the separation, almost exclusion, between intellectual and emotional expression that appears to exemplify the antagonism between the TPN and the DMN. Let us turn to his words to share the phenomenon and its dynamics (Rogers 1980, p. 251):

Case example by Carl Rogers:

"I have conducted courses in which the whole group, including myself, have agreed that our feelings are as important a part of our curriculum as our ideas. Yet, if a member starts exploring some highly emotionalized experience into which he is beginning to gain understanding, other members hesitate to bring up anything but feeling reactions. And if one person starts a class meeting excitedly propounding the ideas involved in a budding theory he is just beginning to develop, that session tends to be intellectual in focus. Only occasionally has a group been able to be whole persons in the experience. Yet, when they have achieved this, the results have been unforgettable."

From experiences such as the above, Rogers concluded: "Most of us consist of two separated parts, trying desperately to bring them together into an integrated soma, where the distinctions between mind and body, feeling and intellect, would be obliterated." (Rogers 1980, p. 252)

Invitation to reflect:

Do you occasionally or frequently observe a similar effect that Rogers described at your workplace?
Does it ever happen, in your experience, that task-related issues are seen in the context of how people feel about them? How do you feel about the situation?
Do you think there is a chance that you can succeed in bringing up people- or task-related issues whenever the time is right, even though there is a focus on the antagonistic alternative? If not, what is it that hinders you? Can you think of a work-around?

What needs to be considered besides the leader's inclination is the interaction between leader and followers. What is the group norm of expectations of the followers? Do they expect to get tasks to accomplish without being asked for their inputs or is it the norm that they are included in decision-making? In sum, there is a very complex dynamic among the leaders, the followers, the job at hand, and the expectations involved. So can knowledge about our neuronal apparatus support us in leading and following more effectively? Please read on to form your view.

16.5 Becoming Figure and Ground, but not at the Same Time

Perhaps the best solution is a leader who has the flexibility to adapt to a situation as it calls for one or the other approach to leadership. French and Jack (2014) conclude that it is not only the ability to do either, but also the perceptual ability to scan the situation to decide which is appropriate at any given time. No doubt, this overarching skill develops with practice, possibly with mentoring, and coaching as well, from one who has mastered it. This flexibility is clearly preferable to one or the other mode held rigidly.

One must keep in mind, though, that there is still a distinction between the brain patterns in employing either type of leadership. It is not a combination, but rather a series of "transitions" as to which is more appropriate at any given situation. The leader, neuroscience tells us, tends to be either in the TPN mode or the DMN mode, not a combination, since the networks are negatively correlated and thus antagonistic. This is important to accept as there is the temptation to think that we can do both equally well at the same time and this assumption would be a mistake most of the time. Exceptions will be discussed later.

This leads to the question of whether the natural inclination of the leader, to either of the two modes, determines her/his likelihood of success in being "bi-modal." We can only guess that the leader with more intellect would naturally fare better with the TPN mode and the one with higher emotional intelligence would fare better with the DMN mode, even though both could make their way through either of the less-preferred modes, should they choose to be flexible. And this is what Graham et al. (2010) found, even when the task was identical for both types of leaders. Of course, the more experience the leaders have in this flexibility style, the more effective they would be expected to perform in this manner. Also, we might expect that those more relationship-centered leaders might tend to "choose" the DMN mode more frequently, just as the task-oriented would "choose" the TPN more frequently. This would be a natural bias, given the orientation of each.

Concerning the "effort" on neurological resources, Boyatzis et al. (2014, p. 9) suggest that "The opposing domains hypothesis should be framed as presenting a form of 'trade-off' between adopting roles favoring task-related leadership activities and therefore activating the TPN and suppressing the DMN and adopting roles favoring relationship building activities and therefore activating the DMN and suppressing the TPN." Thus, minimizing the activation of one network would also help to increase the highest potential activation of neurological resources of the antagonistic network.

For example, a person high in emotional intelligence or person-centered attitudes could access the DMN easily, not spending much effort in that area, and hence "save" neurological resources to be invested in focusing on the task at hand while, overall, the relational as well as the task dimension would be managed to the best possible extent. We conjecture that excellence or ease or experience in one area actually can free resources for the other area, thus helping to bridge the originally antagonistic relationship and achieving a kind of "symbiosis" or "cooperation" of the neurological resources, even though the DMN and TMN compete for activation. In our interpretation, the person-centered approach, considering the "whole person" is directed toward a friendly competition, in which all aspects of a leader's personality would get their voice when the time is right.

A practical consideration is that feedback be consistent with the mode. In other words, feedback on a task should be given in the TPN mode while it is in process and, similarly, with the DMN. The employee will be more receptive to like-minded feedback, whatever the mode. It would just be confusing to give feedback on personal issues when the focus is on task, as to give task-oriented feedback in a discussion of personal issues.

Example from experience: Feedback perceived as confusing versus fitting.

Context: In Renate's course on project management, small teams of students are asked to present project milestones from projects they are implementing. They can choose to get feedback from their peers and the instructor. Initially,

any feedback was welcome and content-related aspects were addressed amidst of aspects concerning the presentation style such as eye-contact, body language, and speed of presenting. In a subsequent reflection a student wrote: "In general, I appreciate feedback but last time I found the feedback confusing. There were too many aspects mentioned at once and that confused me, therefore I'd suggest setting the focus of the feedback on the content of the presentation only rather than criticizing the look and feel and how we were presenting. Every person has a subjective taste and hence it is not possible to choose the right style for everybody. For me, feedback makes sense only if I can learn something from it, such as how to improve the content of the milestone."
Based on a similar observation, the instructor moderated the feedback rounds in such a way that content-related feedback was sought first and only following this was feedback regarding the team's presentation style welcome. In a subsequent reflection a student wrote:
"The feedback rounds were well arranged. More precisely, I mean the separation between content-related issues and the way students presented. This methodology makes the mental 'arrangement' of the individual issues a lot easier."

Comment: Apparently, students had mainly focused on the milestone's tasks (i.e. content) and hence had expected feedback on this. At least some of them found it difficult to switch between modes. They clearly preferred the subsequent separation of feedback into "objective" and "subjective" people-related aspects.

16.6 Learning to Master the Two Domains

So what is the training necessary for success in this kind of flexibility? For one, those strong in either mode need to become familiarized with its "antagonistic" mode, and this is a challenge in itself. In our schools and academic systems, there tends to be an emphasis on learning to get tasks done, so many will have gone through such training from the proverbial Day One. The larger challenge is the strengthening of the socio-emotional mode unless you are a psychotherapist, counselor, coach, or something similar. One line of training has been popular for decades now yet still has a demand in the workplace: emotional intelligence.

Too many such programs consist of a lecture or even a weekend retreat, but it actually requires substantially more. That more has to do with ongoing experience and feedback from experts over months, as those strong in analytic skills only cannot easily be changed without ongoing feedback and support. The administration of such tests as the popular self-report, EQ-I (Bar-On 2006), with feedback is interesting but not transformative. It takes a greater commitment both on the part of the individual as well as the organization to make the changes necessary in people's value systems as they pertain to emotional openness. Such changes do not occur easily. To be genuine, they need to be assimilated into the deepest levels of our personality.

Another line of "training" is person-centered encounter group that was among the most potent social inventions of the twentieth century (Rogers 1970; Wood 2008). As discussed in an earlier chapter, such intensive workshops offer a powerful means to expand one's horizon regarding social and emotional intelligence. In general, they do not specifically aim at developing leadership skills or mastering the transition between TPN and DMN. However, it is not uncommon in such groups that situations occur that require exactly these skills. In that case, such skills can be tried out in advance, but this doesn't happen systematically.

We conjecture that the challenge of shifting to a personal mode when there is great concern and heated discussion over a task not being done well, or letting a highly intense personal interaction calm down, so that attention can revert back to the task at hand and can be completed on a timely basis. This takes a new kind of intelligence (bimodal intelligence?) that combines the skills of both realms. While training that focuses on the shifting between modes is being developed, the following might provide some inspiration on how to improve one's shifting capacity and hence facilitate the adoption of the 2agendas@work.

Case example on how to manage shifting between modes:

Underlying the following practices is the conviction that task-accomplishment *and* people issues are inextricably connected, like two sides of one coin, or two agendas: Considering each may add value to any situation

Recently on a hiring committee, I (Renate) experienced a process that to me felt very appropriate. Let me share: When hiring a new employee, the head of the hiring committee considered the candidate's qualification as well as his or her fitting into the team. He led the conversation such that we first considered the candidates' job qualification based on their CV's and credentials. In the next step, he asked us: "Well, these were the qualifications on paper. Now, for each candidate, imagine that this person would become your colleague, how would that feel? Do you think we could cooperate with him/her well?"

This was not at all an easy question but it felt exactly right to be asked because otherwise the people issues would likely stay in the background and, in any case, find some masked expression, making the decision-making process unnecessarily opaque and tricky. On a personal level, I personally felt accepting this question, as it reflected interest in my subjective opinion about the cooperation and not just the items on paper. All of me could contribute, not just my intellect—and one aspect came after the other, increasing the sense of wholeness, even though the decision was complex.

Comment: Reflecting on the situation, the following proved helpful:

- In line with the organizational culture, one agenda, in our case the task-related one, was chosen to be primary.
- Those who wanted to express their views had a chance to do so. Only then was the shift to the people-oriented agenda attempted.
- The shift was clearly indicated and introduced by a direct question. This may have helped to suspend the first agenda, at least for some time, and clear the space for the other.

For some time now, we have consciously observed situations at the workplace regarding the "voice" of each of the agendas or modes and the conditions under which switches have a chance to succeed or are destined to fail. We can warmly recommend this to sharpen one's personal instinct for shifting between the two agendas.

16.7 Agility for a Combined Solution

What the research clearly reveals, above all else, is that there are two distinct types of leadership, each characterized by a brain modality that is antagonistic to the other. So leadership, at its core, is bimodal, either social-emotionally based or, in its antagonistic state, focused on the task at hand. Yet, the highly evolved leader, either through experience or training, could seamlessly shift from one to the other as needed and thus give the impression that the two are acting in concert, as indeed they are, at least in effective outcome. Only the precise moments are discrete in terms of brain process, if not perceptually, to the objective onlooker. As a matter of fact, Jack et al. (2013a) suggest that it is possible—for tasks requiring collaboration between the two networks, such as answering concrete questions about social observations—that they can work in tandem and "co-create" a "combined" solution, creating more flow between the modes.

We suggest that the best leaders are capable of such interaction between the two networks, and that such skills can be learned. It is a matter of becoming adept at both modes, acquiring the ability to discern when each is appropriate and, in addition, to flow smoothly between the two as necessary. The brand new driver, for example, needs to concentrate on that skill and not be distracted by conversation. Most of us, however, having driven for years, can easily engage in conversation while driving. So with sufficient experience, and perhaps some training for good measure, the evolved leader will be able to manifest a cooperative interaction between the two modes as necessitated by his/her personal way of dealing with the challenges at hand.

For example, if you are now wondering if this is possible, and referencing your own experience, it is highly likely that you are at one moment, thinking of the logic of such a possibility (of "combining" the two modes) and, in the next discrete moment, getting a gut sense if it feels right for you in your own emotional awareness. So in the first moment you are engaging your TPN and, in the next, your DMN. Each mode takes its own time, as much as is needed. But the shift between them may be quick and this is where the seamless quality comes into being.

16.8 Conclusion

So we have the relationship-oriented and the task-oriented styles of leadership. The literature clearly reveals that, increasingly in our modern workplace, relationship-oriented leadership, or emotional intelligence, is key to success in business (for examples, see Ryback 2010, pp. 26–28). Of course, the tasks have to be completed as well, but we are at the stage of business development now that interpersonal skills and attitudes such as those cherished by the PCA are essential at all levels of management (see Ryback and Motschnig-Pitrik 2013, pp. 162–164) and for teamwork (iCom Team 2014; Motschnig-Pitrik and Standl 2013). Leaders as well as team members need these person-centered skills as well as focus on task completion. And the need to be sufficiently agile to embrace both task-oriented and people-oriented communication skills has never been greater than in increasingly complex activities involving electronic and other innovations at an accelerating rate.

In the final analysis, neuroscience has shed light on the "nature" of leadership styles, aided by the concepts of two mutually inhibiting brain patterns—the task-positive network (TPN) and the default-mode network (DMN), which some characterize as the two overarching roles in leadership (Boyatzis et al. 2014). The TPN is more affected by external stimuli and can be characterized as the "business brain," and the DMN, more of an introspective mode, as the "social brain." Indeed, the Person-Centered Approach emphasizes the value of looking at the whole person, and that would include such bimodal components as the TPN and DMN.

However, the ultimate goal that the research has explored is the possibility of avoiding being "stuck in set" (Boyatzis et al. 2014, p. 10). After all is said and done, there is a strong interest in the capacity of integrating the two modes by skillfully transforming the competitive aspects into cooperative resources. Transformative leaders have both modalities available, consider both "agendas," and can switch between the two, performing better than those held in captive by one or the other, even under stressful conditions.

References

Andrews-Hanna, J. R. (2012). The brain's default network and its adaptive role in internal mentation. *Neuroscientist, 18*, 251–270.

Bales R. F. (1958). Task roles and social roles in problem-solving groups. In E. Maccoby, T. Newcomb, E. Hartley (Eds.), *Readings in social psychology* (pp. 437–444). New York, NY: Rinehart & Winston.

Bar-On, R. (2006). The Bar-On model of emotional-social intelligence (ESI). *Psicothema, 18* (supl.), 13–25.

Beissner, F., Meissner, K., Bar, K., & Napadow, V. (2013). The autonomic brain: An activation likelihood estimation meta-analysis for central processing of autonomic function. *Journal of Neuroscience, 33*, 10503–10511.

Bethlehem, R. A., van Honk, J., Auyeung, B., & Baron-Cohen, S. (2013). Oxytocin, brain physiology, and functional connectivity: A review of intranasal oxytocin fMRI studies. *Psychoneuroendocrinology 38*, 962–974.

Blake, R., & Mouton, J. (1985). *The managerial grid III: The key to leadership excellence.* Houston: Gulf Publishing Co.

Boyatzis, R. E., Rochford, K., & Jack, A. I. (2014). Antagonistic neural networks underlying differentiated leadership roles. *Frontiers in Human Neuroscience, 8*(114).

Buckner, R. L., Andrews-Hanna, J. R., & Schacter, D. L. (2008). The brain's default network: Anatomy, function, and relevance to disease. *Annals of the New York Academy of Sciences, 1124*(1), 1–38.

Damoiseaux, J. S., et al. (2006). Consistent resting state networks across healthy subjects. *Proceedings of the National Academy of Sciences United States of America, 103*, 13848–13853.

Fox, M. D., & Raichle, M. E. (2007). Spontaneous fluctuations in brain activity observed with functional resonance imaging. *Nature Reviews Neuroscience, 8*, 700–711.

French S. E., & Jack A. I. (2014). Dehumanizing the enemy: The intersection of neuroethics and military ethics. In: D. Whetham, (Ed.), *The responsibility to protect: Alternative perspectives.* Martinus Nijhoff.

Graham, S., Jiang, J., Manning, V., Nejad, A. B., Zhisheng, K., Salleh, S. R., et al. (2010). IQ-related fMRI differences during cognitive set shifting. *Cerebral Cortex, 20,* 641–649.

Hagmann, P., Cammoun, L., Gigandet, X., Meuli, R., Honey, C. J., Wedeen, V. J., et al. (2008). Mapping the structural core of the human cerebral cortex. *PLoS Biology, 6*, e159. doi:10.1371/journal.pbio.0060159

Horn, A., Ostwald D., Reisert, M., & Blankenburg, F. (2013). The structural-functional connectome and the default mode network of the human brain. *NeuroImage, 13*, 1053–1119.

iCom Team (2014). Constructive communication in international teams an experience-based guide. DE: Waxmann (Co-authored in the iCom team with 12 authors).

Jack, A. I., Dawson, A., Begany, K., Leckie, R. L., Barry, K., Ciccia A., et al. (2012). fMRI reveals reciprocal inhibition between social and physical cognitive domains. *Neuroimage, 66C,* 385–401.

Jack, A. I., Dawson, A. J., & Norr, M. (2013a). Seeing human: Distinct and overlapping neural signatures associated with two forms of dehumanization. *Neuroimage, 79*, 313–328.

Jack, A. I., Robbins, P. A., Friedman, J. P., & Meyers C. D. (2013b). More than a feeling: Counterintuitive effects of compassion on moral judgment. In J. Sytsma, (Ed.), *Advances in experimental philosophy of mind.* Continuum.

Lieberman, M. D. (2013). *Social: Why our brains are wired to connect.* New York, NY: Crown Publishers.

Mars, R. B., Neubert, F. X., Noonan, M. P., Sallet, J., Toni, I., & Rushworth, M. F. (2012). On the relationship between the "default mode network" and the "social brain." *Frontiers in Human Neuroscience, 6*(189).

Motschnig-Pirtik, R., & Standl, B. (2013). Person-centered technology enhanced learning: Dimensions of added value. *Computers in Human Behavior, 29*(2), 401–409.

Nasr, S., Stemmann, H., Vanduffel, W., & Tootell, R. B. H. (2015). Increased visual stimulation systematically decreases activity in lateral intermediate cortex. *Cerebral Cortex, 25*(10), 4009–4028.

O'Hara, M., & Leicester, G. (2012). *Dancing at the edge competence, culture and organization in the 21st century*. Devon, UK: Triarchy Press.

Raichle, M. E. (2015). The brain's default mode network. *Annual Review of Neuroscience, 38*, 433–447.

Riters, L. V., & Panksepp, J. (1997). Effects of vasotocin on aggressive behavior in male Japanese quail. *Annals of the New York Academy of Sciences, 807*, 478–480.

Rogers, C. R. (1951/1995). *Client-centered therapy.* London, UK: Constable.

Rogers, C. R. (1961). *On becoming a person. A therapist's view of psychotherapy*. London: Constable.

Rogers, C. R. (1970). *Carl Rogers on encounter groups.* New York, USA: Harper and Row.

Rogers, C. R. (1980). *A way of being.* Boston: Houghton Mifflin.

Ryback, D. (1998). *Putting emotional intelligence to work.* Boston: Butterworth-Heinemann.

Ryback, D. (2010). *ConnectAbility*. New York: McGraw-Hill.

Ryback, D., & Motschnig-Pitrik, R. (2013). Successful management with the Person-Centered Approach. In J. H. D. Cornelius-White, R. Motschnig-Pitrik, & M. Lux, (Eds.), *Interdisciplinary applications of the Person-Centered Approach.* New York: Springer.

Ryback, D., & Sanders, J. J. (1980). Humanistic versus traditional teaching styles and student satisfaction. *Journal of Humanistic Psychology, 20*(1), 87–90.

Senge, P. M. (2006). *The fifth discipline. The art & practice of the learning organization*. New York: Doubleday.

Schilbach, L., Eickhoff, B., Rotarska-Jagiela, A., Fink, G. R., & Vogeley, K. (2008). Minds at rest? Social cognition as the default mode of cognizing and its putative relationship to the "default system" of the brain. *Consciousness Cognition, 17*, 457–467.

Wood, K. (2008). *Carl Rogers' Person-Centered Approach toward an understanding of its implications*. Ross on Wye/UK: PCCS Books.

Yukl, G. (2006). *Leadership in organizations* (6th ed.). Upper Saddle River, NJ: Prentice-Hall.

Yukl, G. (2008). How leaders influence organizational effectiveness. *Leadership Quarterly, 19*, 708–722.

Chapter 17
Study on Personal Perceptions of Communication in Organizations

I have wanted to understand, as profoundly as possible, the communication of the other, be he a client or friend or family member. I have wanted to be understood. I have tried to facilitate clarity of communication between individuals of the most diverse points of view.

Carl Rogers (1980, p. 64–65)

This chapter focuses on the following:

- How current human resources representatives estimate the importance of various aspects of communication?
- The function of listening side by side with other aspects of communication at work.
- The quality of listening as perceived by human resources representatives in their professional environment.
- Practical, immediately applicable ideas for improving communication.

17.1 Introduction

This chapter deals with the question whether and how active listening is practiced in todays' organizations. Moreover, it explores what human resources representatives think about communication in their organization. The chapter reports facts derived by asking 16 human resources representatives 5 questions about their view on the importance and quality of communication in their organization in general and the practice of good listening in particular. The results of the study indicate a vast potential for improvement in listening at the workplace in all but one area, namely when listening to customers is seen as part of the business. As a practical consequence of the insights revealed by the study, we offer immediately applicable ideas for improving communication.

R. Motschnig and D. Ryback, *Transforming Communication in Leadership and Teamwork*, DOI 10.1007/978-3-319-45486-3_17

17.2 Data Collection and Demographic Data

In order to find out how human resources personnel perceive various aspects of communication in their organization, a brief questionnaire consisting of 5 questions was designed. This structured questionnaire was applied at a recruiting fair called "success," organized by the Postgraduate Center of the University of Vienna. From about 27 profit-based organizations represented at the recruiting fare, 16 persons from 14 different organizations volunteered to spend 5–10 min to respond to the 5 questions. Fifteen persons responded orally, while 1 person preferred to be given the questionnaire to write down the responses and turn in the questionnaire after about 1 h. The respondents were picked on the basis of available time slots in which a representative was free and thus could be kindly asked whether he or she was willing to answer, from a personal perspective, the 5 questions. Each respondent was assured beforehand that no reference would be made as to which company the person represented and that the interviewer's interest was purely to do research in order to improve academic "training" regarding communication.

17.3 Questions, Results, and Discussion

In the following, for each of the 5 questions we present the results and share some observation based on the face-to-face interviews.

1. *What position does communication have in your company from your perspective?*

The range for responses went from "very important" to "not important" on a Likert 5-point scale. As a result, all 16 persons responded that it was very important. We observed 14 of the responses to come immediately, without any deliberation. Two persons (from 2 different companies) asked whether "internal" or "external" communication was meant. After the response: "They are both included, would it make a difference for you to differentiate between them?" One respondent said: "No, both are very important but we differentiate between them." The other respondent answered: "There is an absolute difference: Internal communication is very important, external communication is not!" Overall, this result speaks for itself: The importance of communication is clearly appreciated.

2. What, in your opinion, makes for good communication?"

Here is the detailed list of responses with the more frequent ones listed first. The interviewer observed that respondents tended to think for a while before responding. Some commented that it was hard to respond since the question was so general. Below, a tag cloud in Fig. 17.1 summarizes the results graphically.

Fig. 17.1 Tag cloud on features that make up good communication

- Openness, clarity, transparency (7×):
  - Open information policy,
  - Clear and distinct messages,
  - Clear structures and lines, how to pass on information,
  - Frequent sharing between individuals,
  - Getting to the point quickly,
  - Transparency (2×), e.g., an intranet, everybody knows where to find information, and
  - Information is accessible to everybody;
- Direct communication (3×):
  - The direct path,
  - The more distancing, the worse, and
  - Personal communication, personal contact;
- Recency (3×):
  - Crossing departmental borders, once information arrives, it should be distributed,
  - Associates are informed and are being informed about new things, and
  - To get information on time;
- Good listening (2×); Listening and responding to each other effectively
- Appearance (2×); If this is bad, you lose the project;
- Speaking skills;
- The cover, presentation;
- Amount of information that is transferred;
- As much as is necessary, not too much and as personal and personalized as possible;
- Approaching each other;
- To know the target group and how you can best approach it;
- Few mistakes caused through bad communication;
- The appropriate climate.

The responses to this question can be seen as to conform the items of the people-oriented agenda, with the most prominent aspect being openness, clarity, and transparency. This is fully in accord with Rogers' theories as, for example, expressed in the opening citation to this chapter.

3. *In your estimate, what share (in percent) does good listening have in good communication?*

The person who estimated a share of 100 % to good listening (see Fig. 17.2) commented: "I need to understand what the customer wants!" One person had not named "listening" in his or her response to "what makes up good communication." After responding to question 3, this person said that, of course, listening, too, was important for good communication. Interestingly, some individuals, if asked about communication, did not consciously think about listening, although, when asked explicitly, realized the significant importance of listening, as portrayed in Fig. 17.2.

4. *Are there many really good listeners in your work environment (i.e., if you want to share something, do you feel you are well heard)?*

Of the 16 respondents, 3 gave clearly positive responses. One of them said that there were about 60 % good listeners, and another responded that there were many and yet another said: "Yes, this is due to our business!" For 13 persons, the responses tended to take a little more time, as if they needed to go through a process of conscious checking and approval before being put into words and expressed in a low voice.

Respondents tended to become very thoughtful. This question, in several cases, evoked a true encounter with the interviewer. People started either to directly look into my eyes or to avoid this look, looking onto the ground or to the side into the "nowhere." As the interviewer, I realized that some kind of interpersonal bond started to build while sharing the response to this question. But this did not happen in all three cases where the response had been positive.

The person who had responded, "Not always, partly," shared an interesting perspective, indicating the mutual influence and even responsibility of being

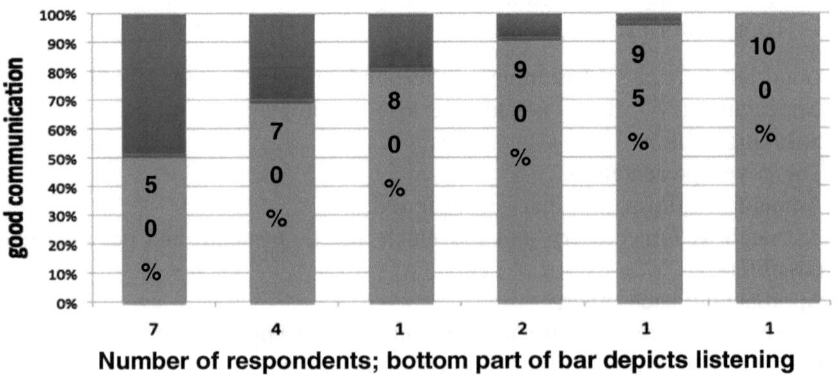

Fig. 17.2 Estimated share of good listening in good communication

listened to. She said: “In real appointments, my boss listens attentively to me. On other occasions, there is not much good listening, but I can take care myself to be listened to!”

The distribution of the responses is sketched in Fig. 17.3 and illustrates clearly that there is a gap between the quality of listening and the appreciation of communication as being very important.

Invitation to reflect:
Do you consider yourself a good listener at work? Are there situations in which you listen well and others in which you tend not to listen?
Are there people to whom you listen well and others to whom you tend not to listen? If so, what is it that causes the difference?
What value do you attribute to listening?
Are there many really good listeners in your work environment?
Do you think that your listening capacities make, or could make, a change in your team, department or organization?
What, in your view, is the biggest challenge to achieving good communication at work?

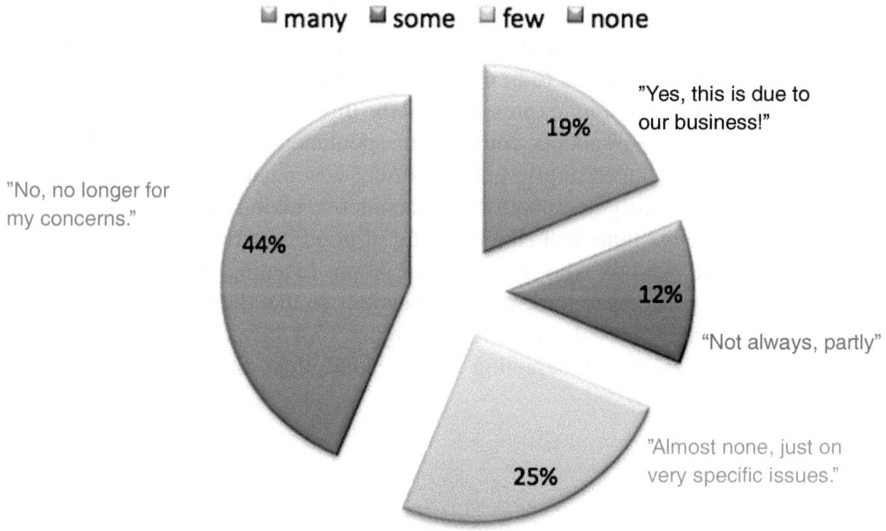

Fig. 17.3 Distribution of responses to the question: Are there many really good listeners in your work environment? (many: 19 %; some: 12 %; few: 25 %; none: 44 %)

5. *What is, in your view, the biggest challenge to reach good communication?*

As with the question regarding the characteristics of good communication, the responses were highly diverse. They included the following statements:

- Statements related to listening and empathy (7×):
  - learning to listen well (2×), providing free space for those who want to tell what to whom,
  - empathy (2×),
  - I feel it is to put oneself into the other's position and to do this again and again,
  - sender and recipient have the same understanding, and
  - listening well *is the* challenge;
- Talent for good comprehension (2×);
- Creating an open climate (2×), showing openness, getting rid of "wall thinking," communication should be directed to the collective, not only to individual persons;
- There are several factors (2×), asking oneself: What do I want to communicate? The environment, one's will …
- Overcoming rigid hierarchies, good communication fails due to old structures;
- Taking time for personal communication and to do this well;
- Finding the right persons to talk to;
- Continuous self-reflection;
- Creating an equal basis between partners in communication.

Some respondents were slightly stunned at this question. It seemed to be too big or too general to be responded to in a few words or sentences. As can be seen from the responses, some persons expressed exactly this impression with their words. Nevertheless, many respondents could quite spontaneously name something that came to their minds. Interestingly, good listening was recalled more often (3 times plus three times implicitly in empathy and perspective taking) in this question in the context of a challenge than as a characteristic of good communication. One reason may be that some persons who did not think about listening first remembered the importance of listening from the previous questions **so** that they recalled listening in the first place and expressed this thought. Figure 17.4 gives an impression of the frequency of responses by depicting a tag cloud that was produced from the respondents' responses.

Fig. 17.4 Tag cloud from the responses to the question regarding the biggest challenge to reach good communication

17.4 Ideas for Transformative Communication for Leaders, Managers, and Team Members

Based on this study:

1. Make it clear to others, whatever your position, that you put a high priority on *clear communication.* As a leader or manager, you can state this occasionally at group meetings or post it on a board or your entrance door in some imaginative fashion, e.g., "the weather for communication should be clear, not cloudy." Or "Clarity is my priority."
2. Make important information *accessible* to all relevant parties as soon as possible, whether at meetings or electronically. Don't expect the informal chain of communication to do the job.
3. For critical messages, *personal contact* is best when possible, whether in person or electronically.
4. Never permit the "silo effect" (where some departments are left out of the loop for important, relevant information because the sender focuses only on particular groups more familiar to him/her) to keep information from getting to relevant parties.
5. If news is important to one individual or some, consider that making that information *available to all concerned* might be advantageous. Unless there is a need to keep information private, why not share it with the largest number of associates who might be affected?
6. Since *listening skills* are so important in the workplace, raise the awareness of this fact by making it explicit. For example, this can happen by including it in the mission statement and/or in job announcements. To live up to your mission, consider ways of how to enhance these skills in accord with your organization's

culture. A series of seminars or workshops, coaching interventions, or a mentoring system are just a few examples of how to enhance communication skills. Though it is challenging to get leaders to take the time and effort to attend such workshops, it is most important at this level.

7. Similarly for *workshops focusing on group dynamics*, as this topic is of great importance for enhanced communication, a positive "side effect" of intensive workshops (Rogers 1961), if well facilitated, is the community building among participants who get to know each other a lot better than during the daily routine at work.
8. Organizations can foster better communication within by encouraging individuals to take the time to invite another to lunch or coffee for a "*listening session*" in which an important but complex or uncomfortable topic can be explored. If there is space, a special "conversation room" can be identified for this particular purpose and the session might include more colleagues (see the "open case" setting in Part III of this book). This would give a special priority to such important sharings rather than delaying them or ignoring them.

17.5 Conclusion

In sum, the study confirmed the expectation that even though knowledge about communication and its importance seem to be widespread among (human resources) management, the actual practice of careful listening seems to be falling behind. An exception to those cases is when listening is clearly perceived as directly contributing to the business goals. From this, we conjecture that business executives tend to be able to acquire listening competences and to apply them primarily if convinced about their necessity and consequent benefits. Hence, it appears to make sense to build sustainable awareness, skills, and knowledge about the transformations that indeed are possible if people communicate effectively. Apparently, transformative communication not only improves interpersonal relationships and trust, but also makes the work clearer and more meaningful—eventually paving the way for greater business success.

References

Rogers, C. R. (1961). *On becoming a person—A psychotherapists view of psychotherapy*. London, UK: Constable.

Rogers, C.R. (1980) *A Way of Being*. Boston: Houghton Mifflin Co.

Chapter 18
Transforming Communication in Multicultural Contexts

To understand another person's thoughts and feelings thoroughly, with the meanings they have for him, and to be thoroughly understood by this person in return—this is one of the most rewarding of human experiences, and all too rare.
Carl Rogers (1961 p. 323)

This chapter focuses on:

- The validity of the principles of transformative communication across cultures;
- Transforming communication in multicultural projects
  - Special opportunities, special effort—making multicultural teams a success factor;
  - Managers' perspectives on respect and empathic understanding in multicultural teams;
- Transformative communication as providing a "meta-culture" for intercultural contexts that transcends individual national cultures while being empathically and unconditionally attuned to them.

18.1 Introduction

The present workplace is often characterized by people of different origins, bringing with them diverse cultural and religious habits. The first part of the chapter deals with the question whether the conditions we set up for transforming communication are valid across cultures or whether they are culturally biased and restricted to their origin, namely Western culture. The second part addresses characteristics of multicultural teams, gives a glimpse on how today's managers think about dealing with cultural differences, and provides resources for transforming communication in teams whose members stem from different cultures. Finally, we suggest transformative communication as the basis and expression of a common meta-culture in multicultural settings living side by side with national cultures.

R. Motschnig and D. Ryback, *Transforming Communication in Leadership and Teamwork*, DOI 10.1007/978-3-319-45486-3_18

18.2 Intercultural Validity

In order to investigate the validity of the conditions for transformative communication across cultures, let us recall these conditions. They are grounded in the Person-Centered Approach by Carl Rogers and adapted for management, leadership, and teamwork. In essence, these conditions are centered in the principle of self-organization and Rogers' three core conditions of congruence, acceptance, and empathic understanding with an eye on the work of managers, where they have been expressed as the items of the people-oriented agenda (see Chap. 2). In this context, in particular, empathic understanding is extended to an encompassing, complex understanding of other persons and their overall context.

One essential question remains: Are the conditions for transformative communication valid across cultures? Since, to the best of our knowledge, no single study exists that would directly address the question, we are going to assemble studies and arguments that deal with the components of the question and support our hypothesis that, indeed, the conditions for transformative communication have intercultural validity.

18.2.1 Historical Perspective

Carl Rogers and his team acted as pioneers and provosts of cross-cultural communication and international peace-work. As a student, Rogers was selected as the US representative of the World Christian Student Federation to undertake an extensive trip to East Asia in 1922. During this formative time, he shaped his views about cultural diversity and communicating constructively across religions and cultures (Rogers 1980; Cornelius-White and Rogers 2012). Later on, Rogers became engaged in cross-cultural communication workshops, forms of which "survive" to date. Moreover, he facilitated peace-work with rival groups in Northern Ireland, in conflict zones like South Africa or South America, and even brought the encounter group movement to Russia. Toward the end of his life, Rogers was nominated for the Nobel Peace Prize but died prematurely in 1987. All these historical facts support the assumption that the principles for transformative communication transcend Western societies and have broad validity.

18.2.2 Presence and Application Across Continents

Practically as well as scientifically, the Person-Centered Approach is known on all continents. These days, cross-cultural, person-centered workshops are taking place all over the world (Rogers 1980; Lago and McMillan 1999; Wood 2008; Motschnig-Pitrik et al. 2013). Besides the workshop setting, the Person-Centered

Approach entered multicultural coaching, as exemplified by a recent coaching model for use in multicultural environments that has been developed in South Africa on the basis of positive psychology and the person-centered approach (Van Zyl and Stander 2013; Van Zyl et al. 2016).

Turning to the scientific basis, currently there exist various sources and arguments that speak in favor of the intercultural validity of the principles of transformative communication. These supportive sources include the following:

18.2.3 Backing by Cognitive Neuroscience

One of the roots of transformative communication is Rogers' *Theory of Personality and Behavior* (1951). Interestingly, it seems void of culture-specific statements. All parts of the theory for which a relationship to neuroscience was established were found to be consistent with neuroscientific findings such as those by Damasio (2000, 2003, 2012) and others (Motschnig-Pitrik and Lux 2008). Fascinating evidence on the support of basic principles of transformative communication by cognitive neuroscience was recently elaborated by Lux (2013), Ryback (2013), and Silani et al. 2013) and can be found in the *Interdisciplinary Handbook of the Person-Centered Approach* (Cornelius-White et al. 2013).

For the core conditions of congruence, acceptance, and empathic understanding, Motschnig-Pitrik and Nykl (2003, 2013) put forth and refined an associative model that maps the core conditions to cognitive-emotional processes. These support, for example, experiential learning, recognition, understanding, integration of feeling and meaning, and thus better decision-making and problem solving. Since such cognitive-emotional processes are part of the cognitive neuroscientific realm, they are deemed to basically apply to the whole human race (see also Chaps. 15 and 16).

18.2.4 Empirical Study on Being Yourself in Different Cultures

In a recent article, Lynch et al. (2009) aimed to find out whether deviations between ideal and actual self-concept—in other words, a measure of a person's lack of congruence—would be negatively associated with well-being and whether this association would hold across different cultures. Furthermore, the authors wanted to test their prediction that the deviations between ideal and actual self-concept would be smaller—meaning that people would be more congruent—when being with partners who support their autonomy, in other words are not imposing or controlling but rather accepting and even supporting one's autonomy. Again, the question was whether the assumed relationship between autonomy support—a feature of acceptance—and congruence would hold across cultures. Intriguingly, both hypotheses could be confirmed on a student population of 642 college students drawn from China, Russia, and the USA. Even though there was some moderation by country membership, associations were in the same direction for all countries.

This means that the condition that has been identified as perhaps most essential for transformative communication at work, congruence, is an indicator of well-being across cultures. This is absolutely in tune with our own study on communication presented in Chap. 17. Furthermore, the acceptance and even support for people's autonomy, meaning to respect the self-organizing principles inherent in each of us and consequently, for example, including team members in the process of building visions and decision-making, appear to be cross-culturally valid core principles of transformative communication. Numerous cases that illustrate these principles—both through their presence and when they were lacking—can be found in iCom Team (2014), an experience-based guide on constructive communication in international teams.

In summary, there is much evidence from history, practice, scientific studies, etc., that the person-centered core conditions which are key to transformative communication apply across cultures. They open up a path toward a "we" that has the capacity for being enriched by, and enriching, others while collaborating within or across cultures.

This, however, does not mean that cultural differences can be ignored. On the contrary, when working across cultures, congruence, empathy, and acceptance need to be sensitively "stretched" and transformed to encompass a broader range of mental models, settings, expressions, and behaviors. The rest of this chapter will provide more on this ambitious goal.

> Invitation to reflect:
> You may want to think of a friend or colleague having a cultural background different from yours:
> Can you be yourself in his/her presence or is some adjustment needed from on your part? How does it feel? Do you like it or does it rather put a burden on you?
> Does the other person in some way adjust to your expectations or needs? How does that feel to you?
> What would it mean for you to accept or support this person's autonomy?
> What would it mean to you if this person accepted or supported your autonomy?
> Is there anything you can learn from this person about yourself and your culture? What is it that the two of you share in common?

18.3 Transforming Communication in Multicultural Projects: Special Opportunities, Special Effort

A question often posed is: Does cultural diversity have a positive or negative effect on teams and the outcome of projects? The responses from reviews and meta-studies to this question are largely mixed (Avery 2011), some studies reporting quite positive and others negative effects. Even though diversity, teams, and projects are highly complex phenomena and details need to be distinguished and taken into account, strongly simplified the following can be concluded. Whether diversity in project teams is rather a benefit or an obstacle depends on a number of mediating issues besides the mere level of diversity in a team or workgroup. In particular, it has been hypothesized to depend, among others, on the surrounding organizational climate and the attitudes and competences of people working in/with culturally diverse teams (Avery 2011). In other words, since the quality of communication is a key factor reflecting the organizational climate, it is not difficult to appreciate that it would also be a pivotal factor in determining whether diversity—cultural or other—can be developed into a benefit or take the opposite direction. Hence, there is little doubt that the quality of communication constitutes a key factor in determining whether diversity in teams will contribute to work-related success or to failure (Böhm and Motschnig-Pitrik 2015). Consequently, the task for us remains to investigate whether transformative communication—by its very characteristics—has a diversity—supporting influence and, if this is the case, under what circumstances it would optimally support diversity.

In the first part of this chapter, we argue that transformative communication is applicable across nations, meaning that its principles transcend cultures and facilitate constructive communication regardless of one's cultural background. But does the cross-culturally positive influence of transformative communication also extend to a workplace exhibiting cultural diversity? In the authors' view, there are solid arguments that point to the beneficial effect of transformative communication on a diverse workplace.

First, let us recall that transformative communication builds upon and fosters the following principles (see also Chap. 2 on the two-agenda approach):

- Contact
- Transparency of goals, vision, and participants;
- Respect toward the other, oneself, and the environment;
- Trying to understand and to be understood comprehensively and thoroughly; and
- Collaboration and sharing.

Each of these seems essential and in fact indispensable for aligning different (re)sources to meet common goals. Taking an opposite perspective and looking at things from the other side, it is not difficult to imagine that avoiding contact, hiding goals and agendas, ignoring others, not tolerating their way, not caring what they mean to communicate, and acting as rivals would not tend to contribute to meeting shared goals. So, theoretically, the core principles of transformative communication are diversity endorsing and thus would be a beneficial moderator of positive outcome (not only) in a diverse workplace.

Second, on an experiential level, participants' reactions from communication workshops with international attendance illustrate intriguing trends and developments in such groups. They also shed some light on what is perceived as more difficult (and at the same time more exciting) in diverse groups than in more homogenous ones. Here are some examples:

18.3.1 Active Listening and Self-expression Are Harder to Achieve but Experienced as Essential

A young woman from South African needed a couple of tries to say in her own words what a Czech student had shared beforehand, until the Czech student felt sufficiently understood. The South African woman shared in her reaction:

> I was surprised that sometimes it is so hard to paraphrase what your partner said, and it's so extremely hard to explain your mind in simple, understandable words. (Motschnig and Nykl 2014, p. 205)

18.3.2 Understanding Needs Active Effort

A student from Egypt summarized his learning as follows:

> Finally, what I take with me from the whole experience is that better communication is always a key to understanding the full picture of a situation. What we need to achieve is to seamlessly interact with people in all of the situations in our daily lives. [...] I am actively trying to apply all of the newly learned terms and skills in my daily life. It is having a very positive impact, and making it a lot easier for me to express my feelings and thoughts which help in reaching the places I want to in my career. It has been an amazing experiment.

In general, using a language that is not one's native tongue makes it harder to express and understand the nuances of meaning that may be so important in any given situation. Part of the difficulty is that words carry with them connotations that may be different across languages such that the same word may come across as a different message. For example, the simple word "problem" in English can be understood as a synonym of "task," whereas in other languages, the same word might tend to carry a negative connotation such as something that is out of order. This is why an open mind and trust are needed to "come to terms" when using a non-native language.

18.3.3 Contact—Different Expectations and Habits

A student from Argentina shared that he wanted to finish his studies as soon as possible and then return to his country, because he was missing so much the closer contact with people so dear to him in his culture. He observed that when he approached colleagues to talk to them, they tended to take a step back, and when he wanted to greet them with a hug, they remained stiff and did not reciprocate. He was worried about being rejected and thought there was something wrong with him, until gradually he realized that Austrians tended to greet colleagues by shaking hands, and hugging was customary only between close friends. At the next break, students of southern origin gathered closely around him and gave him—and each other—a series of sympathetic hugs.

18.3.4 Loosening of National or Cultural Constructs

The following situation may indicate how participants start exploring different habits and typical behaviors rather than defending them and sticking to the old, familiar ones. An African student opened up about the unpleasant reactions he was receiving when starting to talk to people in a supermarket. Instead of joining the conversation, the addressees typically cast a dark and bothered look upon him which made him feel miserable. A Czech student noted in his reaction:

> I like our international mix. I think that this group is unique for discovering ideas, or maybe even making myself (and the others) think about my (their) patterns of behavior and responses. This is a condition for possible improvement. (Motschnig and Nykl 2014, p. 206)

What had happened in the session was that from the ongoing conversation he had sparked, the African student learned that, in large Czech cities, talking to foreigners while shopping was not customary. The behavior of not approaching other shoppers was just the "norm." The group then imagined how different public life might be if people were more outgoing. They suggested starting an experiment about becoming friendlier and to begin this immediately at the university.

Another glimpse on the loosening of cultural patterns comes from a student from Vietnam. He noted in his reaction sheet:

> I really like it when people started talking about different cultures. It seems every country has its own special things which are sometimes considered as strange and weird. However, when you listen to and understand people from that country, you know they have their own reason. Sometimes you will be surprised because the things behind why people do this or do that are reasonable and interesting, "Why Muslim people don't eat pork" or have "Ramadan" event for example. In conclusion, everything has its own reasons. In particular, we should respect people's routine in different countries. One of Vietnamese locutions is "Nước vua thua lệ làng", that means: King's rules lose village's (town's) rules.

18.3.5 *Learning Through Experiencing Transformative Communication in a Group*

Learning takes on versatile colorful forms. Let us take a glimpse by following a few examples:

A student from Macedonia reflected in his final reaction sheet:

> We were learning a lot of new stuff on this course and when we reach the end now I can see how much different this course is from other courses. I needed a couple minutes to think but then I realized that I as a person started to change. In my private life I had a little problem with acceptance but when I was in the group I didn't have a problem with it. Thus I will try to stay a more accepting person in my private life.

A Vietnamese student reflected after the final block:

> I found that it is good to know who is more or less similar or different to me. The reason is we can see the diversity of thinking, ideas or action from different people. And the most important thing is that from these points of view we can learn from each other. For instance, from our activities such as open case or giving feedback, we may know who is more accepting, congruent or suspending… so that we can keep some values that we think may be suitable for us. For me, I realize that too much suspending is not good and I should learn from people who are more active in sharing in class.

After the second block of the workshop at the Masaryk University in Brno, Czech Republic, a Czech student noted:

> I really like that we are not only Czech people in this group so we have to speak English all the time – also at lunch. This way our soft skills are improving the whole day. I also consider it great that we can listen to the different ideas and experiences from participants from different countries – this way we can learn something new about our own nationality, how others see and perceive us. (Motschnig and Nykl 2014, p. 206)

The concluding words of a student from Morocco express the increasing psychological safety and comfort experienced by this participant whose level of presence was awesome:

> As we got further together in the course, our society grew up and expanded, the "rules" of a person-centered class were assimilated, all necessities provided, and all anxieties tranquillized.

The following two excerpts (from a different workshop) show what impressed a student from Russia:

> Actually, I feel this approach strongly supports creativity. New ideas are not judged. Fear is not necessary. People cooperatively develop and learn.

> I now remember how we developed an acceptance of silence. At least I personally had a feeling that I enjoy some time for digestion of so many inputs after intensive sharing and was not feeling awkward in any way, as [it was the case during silence] in the first unit.

The same course evoked the following statement by a female South African student:

When I left this session I felt that the people who shared in depth on their experiences felt lighter and in turn I felt lighter. I believe that the level of respect keeps growing as we continue to learn so much about each other on a personal level. I really appreciated it.

Resource Box 18.1 attempts to capture, in a concise form, some features that, in our experience, contribute to beneficial transformations in multicultural settings.

Resource Box 18.1: Transformative communication in multicultural groups: Consequences for managers, leaders, and team members

- **More time** needs to be allowed for all the processes and tasks that involve people who are diverse. For example, building a shared vision with teams whose members are diverse will tend to take more time but create more ideas than with a homogenous team
- It turns out to be helpful to practice **active listening** as a habit to make sure that what you received is indeed what the speaker expressed. In a multicultural team, in particular, understanding cannot be taken for granted unless it is confirmed
- **Creating opportunities where people can socialize** tends to facilitate understanding of the complexities arising in collaboration across cultures. Sharing about areas beyond the tasks at hand tends to build a foundation for better understanding. At a minimum, proper breaks during meetings or workshops can be a first step in this direction
- Providing the team and customers with an **atmosphere** in which everybody feels safe to share their situation tends to free creativity and, in open-minded, experimental projects, can contribute to superior, above-standard solutions
- International participants may put off a burden once they arrive at **understanding** that some "strange" behavior of the national majority is due to a cultural habit rather than a rebuke of them as a person of different origins
- **Not judging** the other but taking them with a positively attuned, constructive mind-set in case of doubt or misunderstanding can help to put all on a constructive track again
- **Mediation** by a third party ("cultural translator") in case of difficulties between individuals can help to minimize misunderstandings that are caused by different conceptions of terms, phrases, behaviors, patterns, etc.
- **Flexibility** and loosening of constructs are key assets for meeting unexpected challenges

In multicultural groups, participants actually are confronted with real "stories" from people of different cultures and thus can assemble valuable knowledge about cultures. This knowledge, besides the skills and attitudes, can support them in better understanding aspects of the respective cultures and thus reduce misunderstanding during cooperation. Taken together, the transformations happening through transforming communication in multicultural groups would indicate a higher degree of respect, understanding, flexibility, and less rigidity (Rogers 1959; Senge 2006) so urgently needed in our multinational society.

18.4 Managers' Perspectives on Respect and Empathic Understanding in Multicultural Teams

In a recent study in the course of her PhD thesis, Güver (2016) interviewed 18 managers from international projects about features of a communication culture in multicultural teams. Here are some responses that illustrate their thinking and are intended to inspire or provoke your reactions and thoughts on the challenge of respect, and encompassing and empathic understanding in the context of business.

18.4.1 Question on Respect

What do you think about the effect of "an approach that attends to each individual person and tries to respect their culture-specific attitudes and behavior"?

Please indicate whether it contributes

significantly moderately somewhat just a little not at all

to the success of the multicultural team.

Interestingly, managers either chose "moderately" or "significantly." Those who selected "*moderately*" wrote:

- There is an obvious effect on that, but the key point is it needs to be mutual. If cross approach cannot be maintained, the moderate effect will decrease to "not at all."
- [This is] important, because we should remember that every individual is a "human," and if you concentrate only on methodology, tasks and workflows, in case of any problem, you may not be able to energise the team immediately. But [it] should not be significant, because in a professional life, each member should be aware of the general principles.
- Moderately: This can have a value. However, […] getting the job done should be paramount, and dealing with the person's sensitivity regarding nationality or culture should become part of their overall professionalism.

Managers who chose "*significantly*" remarked:

- When evaluating culturally specific practices, project success should also be taken into account. When privileges are given to someone, in response, he/she should give special care for both the leader and the team members.
- If people feel respected, they tend to respect others and will feel better. This would motivate them to put their whole energy into the project rather than in excuses, coping, and proving.
- It is the silver bullet to work together.

18.4.2 Question on Understanding

What do you think about the effect of "an approach that aims at deep understanding of individual's feelings, meanings, and thoughts"?

Please indicate whether it contributes

significantly moderately somewhat just a little not at all

to the success of the multicultural team.

Here, the respondents made use of all the response options except "not at all":

- *Just a little:* Project management is about getting the goals of the project completed on time and within budget. Focusing too much on a deep understanding of individual feelings is a distraction from that purpose, because it drains needed time and energy away from the core reason that the project team exists. If project team members require a lot of special attention from the project manager and the other team members, then they should be replaced immediately with more professional teammates who do not require the additional time and attention to be productive.
- *Somewhat*: Very few leaders have this. It depends on the purpose and leadership style.
- *Moderately*: It does improve the success of the team but takes a long time if you manage a large team. Not always practical
- *Moderately*: It is not virtually possible to attend [to] each individual's feelings, meanings, and thoughts. Anyhow, if it is possible, it should be done for increased motivation.
- *Significantly*: Because, the visible part of people is just like an iceberg/the tip of [the] iceberg. The main part of the iceberg, maybe five-sixths of it underneath, consists of their feelings, thoughts, values, concepts, and coding. I need to go to that level and approach them accordingly. The leader/manager who understands people's worlds of emotions will be 100 % successful.
- *Significantly*: This is the most difficult one to achieve, because it takes a lot of time and effort, not to mention a significant amount of managerial skill. Individuals will get more motivated as they see their inputs are being valued at its deepest level and a feedback loop will result that will increase the efficiency of the output multiple-fold.
- *Significantly*: Project managers should pay attention of contributors' feelings, meanings, and thought. Otherwise, it is impossible to become a team and run in the same direction and target all together
- *Significantly*: It is needed to maintain at the beginning of the business operation as a project team culture. If it cannot be developed at the early stages, there will be significant effect on business.

18.4.3 Question on Empathic Understanding

Can you describe what "empathic understanding" means for you? Do you think that a manager should try to empathically understand her/his employees? What would that mean, in your view, and what could be the benefits or risks?

- Emphatic understanding means to try to understand the people by taking into account their world. It is something a manager definitely needs to do. If you perceive somebody with his/her background and try to look at events as he/she would, as well as if you protect the interests of him/her, then you have already established a successful communication.
- Yes, this is very important. A manager has to have an appreciation for what is important to others. Without it, there will be a frequent and widening communication disconnect. I believe an empathic understanding will automatically follow from the behaviors explained in [the previous] questions and is mostly about listening, showing an interest and displaying that your understanding is based on understanding the individual as a whole. And yes, a manager should certainly use these tools and display these values. The benefits are numerous again as explained above, and I cannot think of any risks.
- Empathy is an important component of effective relationships. A manager should try to empathically understand her/his employees. It always helps the project manager to understand the situation better. I don't see any risk since the project manager still can use her own judgment in the process of making intelligent decisions.
- Yes, of course, a manager should try this. This will help the team member to possess the project and also will make him/her feel that he is not a "slave" which should do whatever requested from him/her. On the other hand, too much empathy should not create an environment where decisions cannot be taken due to "oversensitivity."
- Balancing getting the job done and empathic understanding of the members of the team is what makes a good manager.

In summary, this research shows that managers of multicultural teams are pretty well aware of the core principles of transformative communication. The majority of them seem to be attuned to a realistic balance with business goals. We conjecture that this is a very welcome "healthy" step in the right direction, even though actual practice still may require maturation of attitudes and skills.

18.5 Transformative Communication as Providing a "Meta-Culture" for Multicultural Groups and Teams

So far, we have presented evidence that the very basic principles of transformative communication apply regardless of any particular cultural background. Furthermore, they were shown to facilitate communication in teams whose members are of diverse cultural origin. This is due to the person-centered mind-set underlying transformative communication that acknowledges self-organizing principles of people and systems and requires interpersonal attitudes and skills based on meeting the other at eye level of personhood (Rogers 1959; Kriz 2008; Motschnig-Pitrik et al. 2013). These traits are optimally complemented with a good command of a shared language and knowledge about diverse cultural habits, patterns, and preferences.

In order to conceptualize and delineate the function that transformative communication carries in an organization or a project, let us resort to a simple yet smart model of the typology of diversity support in organizations according to Avery (2011) (see Fig. 18.1). To characterize diversity support, Avery distinguishes two dimensions: endorsement and activism. While endorsement captures the attitude toward diversity which can be either supportive or opposing, activism serves to characterize the level of activity devoted to either supporting or opposing diversity. This typology allows one to distinguish four quadrants, ranging from active opposition over silent opposition and silent endorsement to active support or championing of diversity.

So where are we going to position transformative communication in that structured typology? Whereas a communication style or practice such as

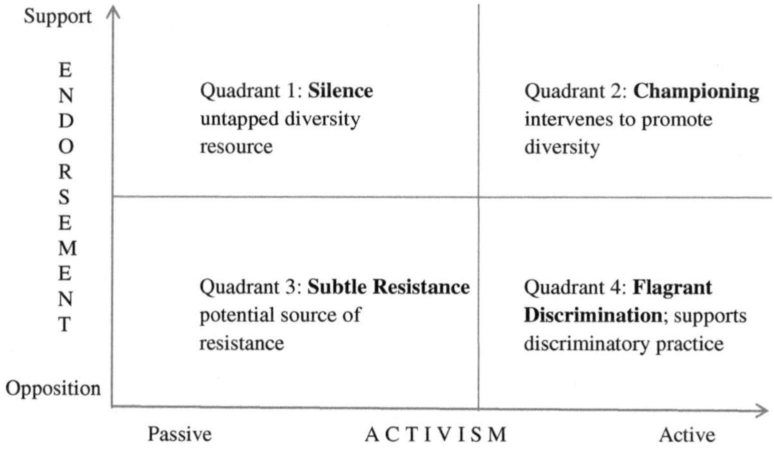

Fig. 18.1 The typology of diversity support in organizations (shortened from Avery (2011, p. 242)

transformative communication per se does not determine an organization's or project's strategy toward diversity, intriguingly, the values propelled by transformative communication rule out the quadrants that encompass opposition and allow us to position transformative communication in the upper two quadrants: silent or active support. The level of activism, indeed, would depend on individual project characteristics such as its duration, complexity, the level of diversity in the team, and the leadership style, in resonance with several of the project managers' statements above.

Invitation to reflect:
Do you consider the typology helpful for localizing your projects' or organization's position in the area spanned by the axis of diversity endorsement and activism? Can you give reasons why you like or dislike the representation?
Which level of diversity endorsement and activism do you aim at in your projects? Is there a difference across projects? What are the features that you consider as indicative for the placement in the typology?
What are visible signs of a healthy communication culture? To what degree are they present in your work environment?

When trying to distill the features of transformative communication that most contribute to its diversity-endorsing character, the fact that it embraces both respect and facilitative openness would be pivotal. Taken together, these two features counter prejudice and rigid preconceptions while furthering the loosening of constructs based on the moment-to-moment encounter and dialogue with colleagues and super-/subordinates.

Transformative communication is often a nonlinear, experiential, and mindful process toward the often extremely challenging goal of mutual understanding. When reached, we tend to be rewarded with a feeling of pleasure, indicating the "proper" direction of moving forward on the agendas we are following more or less consciously.

In a nutshell, the investigations undertaken lead us to propose transformative communication as an unfolding interactional "meta-culture" of interpersonal relating (Lago 2011; Motschnig-Pitrik et al. 2013). This level exists beyond, or side by side with, "traditional" cultures and business goals and needs that all must be respected while none can be ignored. It emerges when people manage business objectives with a sufficient space for self-organization, congruence, respect, inclusion, and encompassing understanding of each other in their work environment. Leaders and managers who wish to actively build communication skills in their multinational teams will find a small activity in Resource Box 18.2.

Resource Box 18.2: An exercise aimed at improving intercultural understanding, adapted from (Motschnig and Nykl 2014)

- A step toward better intercultural understanding can be achieved through an exercise on active listening in triads:
- Students of different nationalities form triads. One person who volunteers to be the speaker shares how he or she perceives his/her own nationality and what he or she thinks about the peculiarities of their nationality. The active listener accompanies the speaker, while the observer observes how the conversation develops and how well the listener accompanies the speaker. Then, the roles are exchanged so that every participant takes on each role.

Invitation to reflect:
Colin Lago (2013, p. 211), a pioneer of transcultural counseling and group-work, characterizes the capacities needed for enhancing communication as: "The capacity of being real and fully present, of fully accepting the other, of striving for a respectful understanding-seeking stance towards the other without giving up on one's own ideas and values", and, moreover, "not only being fully open to others but also being open to the possibility of being changed by the encounter."
What, in your view, is essential for enhancing communication in your work context?
What, in your view, is pivotal for virtual multicultural communication?

18.6 Conclusion

Despite their origin in Western culture, the principles of transformative communication are not restricted to Western nations. This is supported by ample historical evidence, applications, and contemporary research. However, for transforming communication across cultural needs, in particular, contact with people from different cultures, patience and time, special efforts in active listening, flexibility, and the loosening of national and cultural constructs are vital. With these conditions in place, transformative communication would qualify as perhaps the best candidate for leading multicultural groups and teams to success. This meta-culture would live with respect for the individual national cultures that acknowledge congruence, acceptance, and understanding and form a bridge between them without ever giving up their perspective and its own underlying principles (Motschnig-Pitrik et al. 2013).

References

Avery, D. R. (2011). Support for diversity in organizations: A theoretical exploration of its origins and offshoots. *Organizational Psychology Review, 1*(3), 239–256.

Böhm, C., & Motschnig-Pitrik, R. (2015). New research perspective on managing diversity in International ICT Project Teams. In G. Chroust & Sushil (Eds.), *Systemic flexibility and business agility* (pp. 21–31). India: Springer.

Cornelius-White, J. H. D., & Rogers, C. R. (2012). *Carl Rogers: The China diary*. Ross-on-Wye, UK: PCCS Books.

Cornelius-White, J. H. D., Motschnig-Pitrik, R., & Lux, M. (2013). *Interdisciplinary handbook of the person-centered approach: Research and Theory*. New York, USA: Springer.

Damasio, A. R. (2000). *The feeling of what happens: Body and emotion in the making of consciousness*. London, UK: Vintage.

Damasio, A. R. (2003). *Looking for Spinoza: Joy, sorrow and the feeling brain*. Orlando, FL: Harcourt.

Damasio, A. R. (2012). *The self comes to mind*. London, UK: Vintage.

Güver, S. (2016). *Communication in multicultural project Teams: Developing a communication model*. PhD thesis concept, submitted to the Faculty of Management, University of Vienna.

iCom Team. (2014). *Constructive communication in international teams: An experience-based guide*. DE: Waxmann.

Kriz, J. (2008). Self-actualization: Person-centred approach and systems theory. Ross-on-Wye, UK: PCCS-books. ISBN 978-1-906254-03-2

Lago, C. and McMillan, M. (1999) *Experiences in Relatedness: Groupwork in the Person Centered Approach*. Llangarron, Ross-on-Wye, UK: PCCS Books.

Lago, C. (2011). *The handbook of transcultural counselling and psychotherapy*. UK: McGraw Hill.

Lago, C. (2013). The Person-Centered Approach and its capacity to enhance constructive international communication. In J. H. D. Cornelius-White, R. Motschnig-Pitrik, & M. Lux (Eds.), *Interdisciplinary applications of the person-centered approach*. New York, USA: Springer.

Lux, M. (2013). The circle of contact: A neuroscience view on the formation of relationships. In J. H. D. Cornelius-White, R. Motschnig-Pitrik, & M. Lux (Eds.), *Interdisciplinary handbook of the person-centered approach: Research and theory*. New York, USA: Springer.

Lynch, M., La Guardia, J. G., & Ryan, R. M. (2009). On being yourself in different cultures: Ideal and actual self-concept, autonomy support, and well-being in China, Russia, and the United States. *The Journal of Positive Psychology, 4*(4), 290–304.

Motschnig-Pitrik, R., & Lux, M. (2008). The Person-Centered Approach meets neuroscience: Mutual support for C. R. Rogers's and A. Damasio's theories. *Journal of Humanistic Psychology, 48*, 287–319.

Motschnig-Pitrik, R., Lux, M., & Cornelius-White, J. H. D. (2013). The Person-Centered Approach: An emergent paradigm. In J. H. D. Cornelius-White, R. Motschnig-Pitrik, & M. Lux (Eds.), *Interdisciplinary applications of the person-centered approach*. New York, USA: Springer.

Motschnig-Pitrik, R., & Nykl, L. (2003). Towards a cognitive-emotional model of Rogers' Person-Centered Approach. *Journal of Humanistic Psychology, 43*(4), 8–45.

Motschnig-Pitrik, R., & Nykl, L. (2013). An interactive cognitive-emotional model of the Person-Centered Approach. In J. H. D. Cornelius-White, R. Motschnig-Pitrik, & M. Lux (Eds.), *Interdisciplinary handbook of the person-centered approach: Research and theory*. New York, USA: Springer.

Motschnig, R., & Nykl, L. (2014). *Person-Centred communication: Theory, skills, and practice*. McGraw Hill, UK: Open University Press.

Rogers, C.R. (1980) *A Way of Being*. Boston: Houghton Mifflin Co.

Ryback, D. (2013). Mindfulness, authentic connection, and making "right" decisions: Using neuroscience to build a bridge with the Person-Centered Approach. In J. H. D. Cornelius-White, R. Motschnig-Pitrik, & M. Lux (Eds.), *Interdisciplinary handbook of the person-centered approach: Research and theory*. New York, USA: Springer.

Senge, P.M. (2006) *The Fifth Discipline, The Art & Practice of the Learning Organization*. USA: Currency Doubleday.

Silani, G., Zucconi, A., & Lamm, C. (2013). Carl Rogers meets the neurosciences: Insights from social neuroscience for client-centered therapy. In J. H. D. Cornelius-White, R. Motschnig-Pitrik, & M. Lux (Eds.), *Interdisciplinary handbook of the person-centered approach: Research and theory*. New York, USA: Springer.

Van Zyl, L., & Stander, M. (2013). A strengths-based approach towards coaching in a multicultural environment. In J. H. D. Cornelius-White, R. Motschnig-Pitrik, & M. Lux (Eds.), *Interdisciplinary handbook of the person-centered approach: Research and theory*. New York, USA: Springer.

Van Zyl, L. E., Motschnig-Pitrik, R., & Stander, M. W. (2016). Exploring positive psychology and person-centred psychology in multi-cultural coaching. In L. E. Van Zyl, M. W. Stander, & A. Odendaal (Eds.), *Coaching psychology: Meta-theoretical perspectives and applications in multicultural contexts* (pp. 315–356). Springer International Publishing Switzerland.

Wood, J., K. (2008) *Carl Rogers' person-centered approach: Toward an understanding of its implications*. Ross-on-Wye, UK: PCCS-books.

Part V
Conclusions

Chapter 19
The Social and Value Ramification: Well-Functioning Teams, Collaboration, and Co-actualization

They [very large experiential groups] *could develop a sense of community in which respect for others and cooperation rather than competition were keynotes.*

Carl Rogers (1980, p. 335).

This chapter focuses on:

- The core questions and tasks of this book
- Revisiting and "upgrading" Rogers' approach to the valuing process
- Valuing directions at work in the era of globalization and rapid change
- The goal: Well-functioning teams, partnerships, and departments.

19.1 Introduction

Currently, wars, feuds, and destructive competition signal that the human being has a capacity for the destructive—he/she can be radicalized and manipulated. Rogers, however, devoted his life work to exploring the climate in which human beings can become the best they can. Why not make use of the findings in the context of the occupation in which people usually spend most time with—their work?

Intriguingly, for unfolding in a constructive direction, people need significant others, at least one, who provide them with the proper socio-environmental conditions. So, naturally, we cannot accomplish our (self-)actualization on our own but need others. At work, these are peers, partners, superiors, or subordinates, etc., who co-form the work climate and co-influence actualization processes.

Initially, we had planned to frame separate chapters for managers/leaders and team members. However, in the process of writing, we found that there were so many overlaps and issues being relevant for both—members and leaders—that we gave up on the structural, and in fact hierarchical, division. This signals that every person can be a leader in some respect while taking on the complementary function of being a follower, learner, subordinate in another respect. Addressing both

R. Motschnig and D. Ryback, *Transforming Communication in Leadership and Teamwork*, DOI 10.1007/978-3-319-45486-3_19

audiences together shall, however, not mean to disregard the special competencies and skills required by leaders and managers who tend to have the final responsibility for decisions.

So, for leaders, managers, and team members all together, the core questions and tasks this book has been aiming to address are as follows:

- What are the features of a work-atmosphere in which we *and* the business or project or department, etc., can blossom? How can we offer each other such an atmosphere?
- What are the challenges that the current and future workplace, with its rapid change, modern technology, and multiculturalism, typically brings along? Which socio-environmental conditions need to be in place and which capacities do we need to meet such challenges?
- To what extent can the theories, insights, and each person's precognitive resources that the emerging person-centered paradigm acknowledges, provide a base to turn to (not to say to hold on to, since this gives the wrong illusion of something static), in a world in which everything is changing?

19.2 Mapping Global Developments to the Items of the People-Oriented Agenda

In the following, we reflect on how recent developments relate to five aspects proposed to be basic to forming the people-oriented "agenda" of transformative communication at work:

19.2.1 Contact

Intriguingly, modern Internet technology thrives on providing exactly this feature. When used as a supplement rather than substitution for face-to-face contact, it appears to facilitate interpersonal connection vastly, even across the globe.

19.2.2 Transparency and Openness

Transparency and openness are broadly supported by social media and web-technology, in general, leveraging self-presentation and interaction and, at the same time, making the hiding of information ever more difficult and expensive. This wide and influential open-source movement can be seen as another indicator of our appreciation of transparency and open access to resources—world-wide.

19.2.3 Respect and Inclusion

Respect, kindness, a caring attitude, agape or whatever term one wants to use, has always been *the* virtue unequivocally demanded by any religion and spiritual tradition. We consider inclusion an immediate consequence of respect and observe its increasing importance in our daily lives. Accessibility, inclusive education, multicultural teams, mindfulness, participatory design, shared vision, acknowledgment of self-organization, and limits of exerting power over all are different expressions of this core principle that is moving humankind. There could be more awareness and manifestation of this attitude, virtue, and practice, though.

19.2.4 Understanding

Learning of languages, investments into translation technology, multilingual governments and Web pages, active listening, sensing, increased acknowledgement of the necessity to aim for understanding others empathically and comprehensively all are signs that to understand another and to be understood is a deep human need and indispensable for collaboration as well as personal growth.

19.2.5 Collaboration and Interdependence

World organizations and associations, globalization, international conferences and summits, chambers of commerce, team efforts, communities of practice, interdisciplinary research teams, awareness of self-organization principles, systems thinking, flattening of hierarchies, etc., all illustrate this evolutionary facet that tends to become ever more important as individuals become tiny particles of the ever more complex working of the whole.

Invitation to reflect:

Can you think of other features that you'd like to add to the basic agenda? If so, what are they, how would you describe them? Do they concur with developments or trends of the twenty-first century?

All these movements confirm the direction of the person-centered approach, even though these are general trends that are very rarely declared as off-springs of the PCA. And it may very well be that the self-organization principles or "zeitgeist," or whatever you believe in, would bring them about anyway, without Rogers' wise grasping and foreshadowing of these developments that were gradually assimilated into the mainstream. In any case, calling the respective attitudes, values, and directions of unfolding to mind, and deliberately exploring what they mean for our working lives, seem worth the investment, if we want to be on the front rather than the backside of evolution and innovation, pioneers rather than those lagging behind.

19.3 Forming Values: The Mature Person Once and Now

Naturally, the way we communicate and behave espouses our values. So how would we acquire or form values that would be helpful in meeting the challenges of a twenty-first-century workplace? In order to approach a solution, we turn to Rogers' theory of the valuing process and see whether it is still valid and what we can learn from it.

Rogers' theory of the valuing process is an experiential one, being derived from Rogers' extensive experience of working with clients. In a nutshell, he realized huge differences in how values were formed in small children, adults, and mature people. He observed that infants rely almost exclusively on their inner organismic sensations to assign values to experiences like hunger, fatigue, play, smiling, and to react according to the criteria whether such experiences are perceived as actualizing or not. In the adolescent and adult person, this capacity to include the organism into the valuing process tends to get lost. We often take over values or evaluations from others like parents, the school system, bosses, to gain or keep their regard or love. Such values are introjected and "ready-made" or fixed. They come from outside and hence miss the experiential basis that would allow them to be revised or adapted based on new experience and thus held flexibly, open to change.

Those people who get a chance to mature—through life experiences, coaching, psychotherapy, etc.—succeed in restoring or never losing their contact with (organismic) experience and at the same time manage to draw on the rich sources of outside evidence. They form their values flexibly but these are far more differentiated than those of youngsters since mature people can draw on rich sources of experience and external information. We quote Rogers to retain as much meaning as possible for describing the complex valuing process in the mature person:

> There is also involved in this valuing process a letting oneself down into the immediacy of what one is experiencing, endeavoring to sense and to clarify all its complex meanings. […] In the mature person, […] there is involved in the present moment of experiencing the memory traces of all the relevant learning from the past. This moment has not only its immediate sensory impact, but it has meaning growing out of similar experiences in the past. It has both the new and the old in it. So when I experience a painting or a person, my experiencing contains within it the learning I have accumulated from past meetings with paintings or persons, as well as the new impact of this particular encounter. Likewise the moment of experience contains, for the mature adult, hypotheses about consequences. "I feel now that I would enjoy a third drink, but past learnings indicate that I may regret it in the morning." "It is not pleasant to express forthrightly my negative feelings to this person,

but past experience indicates that in a continuing relationship it will be helpful in the long run." Past and future are both in this moment and enter into the valuing.

The criterion of the valuing process is the degree to which the object of the experience actualizes the individual himself. Does it make him a richer, more complete, more fully developed person? This may sound as though it were a selfish or unsocial criterion, but it does not prove to be so, since deep and helpful relationships with others are experienced as actualizing. (Rogers 1964, pp. 164–165)

Interestingly, people around the globe tend to prefer the *same* value directions in a climate of respect and freedom (Rogers 1964). Even though mature people would not have a stable system of conceived values, the valuing process within them would lead to emerging value directions being constant across cultures. The resulting values would be re-formed on the basis of organismic experience taking a complex vector of immediate and past, inner and external experience into account along with an estimate of the future. People "would tend to value those objects, experiences, and goals which make for their own survival, growth, and development, and for the survival and development of others" (Rogers 1964 p. 166).

As a consequence, people with a fluid valuing process are assumed to become more readily adaptive to new challenges and situations. They must be accurate in their appreciation of ever changing "reality," able to select that which is valuable even in complex, unfamiliar situations.

Thus, specified but unspecific *value directions* appear to be *universal*! Intriguingly, they are not imposed by some external source or authority but emerge from the experiencing of people, being directed toward their and their peers' survival and development. Rogers' idea is that

though modern man no longer trusts religion or science or philosophy nor any system of beliefs to give him his values, he may find an organismic valuing base within himself which, if he can learn again to be in touch with it, will prove to be an organized, adaptive and social approach to the perplexing value issues which face all of us (Rogers 1964, p. 166).

So what can we deduce from this for peoples' communication at the modern workplace? Astonishingly, not too much seems to have changed regarding the nature of the challenges of "modern man" from 1964 to the one of now, half a century later. What has changed is the speed and scope of communication and the increase of complexity, information, technological opportunities and thus the scope of choices and interdependencies among us and the technological services we depend on. Hence, we conjecture that what Rogers experienced and theorized to be needed for the mature person of his days is even more extensively and urgently needed in our time. And it is needed not only for decision-makers, leaders, and managers but increasingly for all employees who participate in a project or department and who are co-responsible for its success.

Drawing on Rogers' work (1964) let us characterize those directions of personal growth that appear to be most relevant for the work context. People moving toward maturity:

- Tend to move away from facades. Pretense, defensiveness, and putting up a front, all tend to be negatively valued. Being real is positively valued. Mature people at work tend to move toward being themselves, expressing their real feelings, being what they are and putting their unique strengths to practice. This seems to be a very significant preference.
- Come to value openness to all of their inner and outer experience. To be open and sensitive to their own inner reactions and feelings, the reactions and feelings of others and the realities of the objective world becomes a most valued resource.
- Value self-direction positively. An increasing confidence and satisfaction in making one's own choices and guiding one's own course of action is discovered. One's reactions are considered as being relevant and worthwhile.
- Sense being a process as something valuable rather than troubling. From desiring some fixed goal, people come to prefer the excitement about a process of potentialities being manifested.
- Value sensitivity to others and acceptance of others positively. Peers come to appreciate others for who they are, just as they have come to respect themselves for who they are.
- Long for deep, genuine, and mutually supporting relationships with others. To achieve a close, real, fully communicative relationship with another colleague, unit, institution, etc., seems to meet a deep need and is very highly valued.

19.3.1 An Adaptation

The range of people needing a differentiated and flexible valuing process to allow them to move in the directions described, and deal with ever faster changes, is rapidly increasing, Indeed, today's tasks are typically so complex such that they easily exceed the capacity, creativity, and potentialities of a single person and hinge on good collaborative relationships with peers (iCom Team 2014; Cornelius-White et al. 2013). This calls for one essential adaptation of the valuing process: The locus of evaluation needs to shift to include, besides one's own organism, more prominently the interwoven, valued, undistorted "messages" of one's peers, regardless of their position in an organizational hierarchy. All of the case examples in this book unequivocally communicated that message.

So, *in addition to* the criterion of the valuing process being the degree to which the object of the experience *actualizes the individual* himself, there would be another criterion to complement the original one: The degree to which the object of the experience *reciprocally co-actualizes the relationship system*, be it partners, a team, a department or a community. Does it make the relationship partners both or all move forward (in the longer run), do members experience their relationships as mutually supportive rather than constraining them unnecessarily, is the team viable?

Let us spell out some of the additional directions for this adapted valuing process supporting *co-actualization*. People in teams, (business-)partnerships, departments moving to a better co-functioning need, in particular:

19.3.2 Contact

- They tend to connect, keep in touch, and consult each other whenever they feel they can be more effective, happy, confident, safe, etc., together than on their own.
- They express genuine interest rather than attempting to control the other. They respect and dynamically balance their needs both for autonomy and relatedness.

19.3.3 Transparency and Openness

- They nurture the transparent flow of information with an expressiveness and clarity of meaning in both formal and informal communicative interchanges (Barrett-Lennard 1998).
- They are as open as possible to their and the others' experience. These people welcome such sharing as a source of expansion and promote it appropriately.
- They achieve the goals agreed on by engaging each member of the team in a manner that invites openness, both emotional and intellectual, whenever appropriate.
- They allow to admit personal weakness as well as to present personal power.

19.3.4 Respect and Inclusion

- They foster a sense of mutual respect and support for one another, even in times of crisis.
- People promote the unfolding of the other as well as self and the work relationship. This can happen by including the other(s) and aiming to provide space and opportunities for them to be present, contributing, and facilitative or cooperative in their own, unique ways. This will allow relationship partners to feel accepted (by others and self) and to express acceptance.
- They reduce negative stress and transform it into creative tension. This can happen by realizing autonomy and self-acceptance concurrently with respecting the other(s) and the work environment.

19.3.5 Encompassing Understanding

- They aim to understand the messages of the other(s) as thoroughly and completely as possible, and express themselves in a way that makes it easy for the other(s) to understand them.
- They appreciate that conflicting goals, directions, and opinions tend to create tension. They can live with ambiguity when being confronted with—and open to—conflicting data.
- They acknowledge that if they manage to deal with problems cooperatively, that may even strengthen their relationship or lead to some transformation that helps both/all relationship partners to move forward.

19.3.6 Collaboration and Interdependence

- People feel an active, genuine interest in the other and the relationship. This is expressed in transparent sharing of ideas, meanings, feelings, goals, work, reactions, etc., whenever deemed appropriate. It is further expressed in the peers' making way for each other as an expression of mutual interest and their experience or expectation of their "we" as having resources in addition to those of each single person. Each peer finds meaning in his/her own experience (self-trust), looks for it in what the other expresses, and draws on both jointly and separately discovered meanings (Barrett-Lennard 1998, p. 182).
- They approach relationships with a cooperative attitude. They tend to collaborate or "compete" in a friendly, playful fashion rather than feed destructive rivalry, distortion or ignorance in their relationship.
- They are mindfully aware of their own need to actualize themselves as well as the tendency of the relationship to form as a larger, more complex, dynamically ordered whole. This awareness extends to the bond a relationship may create, the influence it exerts on the partners, and the effects it receives and passes on through interacting within the team or organization and with the environment.
- They create a pervasive sense of togetherness that strengthens the team or group because of the caring that each has for the others.
- They are aware that genuine communication is an engine for change.

19.4 Conclusion and Final Call to Action

Yes, transformative communication is contagious by nature—you cannot hold on to it on your own but need to share it with others. To us, it is transformative in two ways. One the one hand, it transforms rigid, ingrained communication patterns to flexible, task- and people-oriented practices. On the other hand, it transforms the cutting-edge values and competencies from Rogers' Person-Centered Approach to a timely as well as deeply natural approach to healthy, honest, and effective communication in the workplace. If you have had the experience that this transformative wave has reached some aspect in your own awareness, then we consider the purpose of our book as fulfilled.

References

Barrett-Lennard, G. T. (1998). *Carl Rogers' helping system: Journey and substance*. London, UK: SAGE Publications.

Cornelius-White, J. H. D., Motschnig-Pitrik, R., & Lux, M. (2013). *Interdisciplinary applications of the person-centered approach*. New York, USA: Springer.

iCom Team. (2014). *Constructive communication in international teams an experience based guide*. Münster, DE: Waxmann.

Rogers, C. R. (1964). Toward a modern approach to values: The valuing process in the mature person. *Journal of Abnormal and Social Psychology, 68*(2), 160–167.

Index

Note: Page numbers followed by *b*, *f*, and *t* indicate boxes, figures, and tables, respectively.

R. Motschnig and D. Ryback, *Transforming Communication in Leadership and Teamwork*, DOI 10.1007/978-3-319-45486-3

MIX
Papier aus verantwortungsvollen Quellen
Paper from responsible sources
FSC® C105338

If you have any concerns about our products,
you can contact us on
ProductSafety@springernature.com

In case Publisher is established outside the EU,
the EU authorized representative is:
Springer Nature Customer Service Center GmbH
Europaplatz 3, 69115 Heidelberg, Germany

Printed by Libri Plureos GmbH
in Hamburg, Germany